D1475562

THE COURAGE TO LEARN

THE COURAGE TO LEARN

Honoring the Complexity of Learning for
Educators and Students

Marcia Eames-Sheavly, Paul Michalec, and
Catherine Wehlburg

Foreword by Laura I. Rendón

Afterword by Estrus Tucker

Copublished in association with

CENTER *for*
COURAGE *&*
RENEWAL

Routledge
Taylor & Francis Group

NEW YORK AND LONDON

First published in 2023 by Stylus Publishing, LLC.

Published in 2023 by Routledge
605 Third Avenue, New York, NY 10017
4 Park Square, Milton Park, Abingdon, Oxon OX14 4RN

Routledge is an imprint of the Taylor & Francis Group, an informa business.

Library of Congress Cataloging-in-Publication-Data
Names. Eames-Sheavly, Marcia, author. | Michalec, Paul, author. | Wehlburg, Catherine, author.
Title: The courage to learn : honoring the complexity of learning for
   educators and students / Marcia Eames-Sheavly, Paul Michalec, Catherine
   Wehlburg ; Foreword by Laura I. Rendón ; Afterword by Estrus Tucker.
Description: First edition. | Sterling, Virginia : Stylus Publishing, LLC,
   2023 | Includes bibliographical references and index.
Identifiers: LCCN 2023010714
ISBN 9781620369067 (cloth) | ISBN 9781620369074 (paperback)
Subjects: LCSH: Learning, Psychology of. | Teaching--Psychological aspects.
   | Teachers. | Education--Philosophy.
Classification: LCC LB1060 .E24 2023
   DDC 370.15/23--dc23/eng/20230415
LC record available at https://lccn.loc.gov/2023010714

ISBN: 978-1-62036-906-7 (hbk)
ISBN: 978-1-62036-907-4 (pbk)
ISBN: 978-1-00344-772-6 (ebk)

DOI: 10.4324/9781003447726

To Parker J. Palmer
Teacher, mentor, inspiration, friend

To our families
With gratitude

To the learners
*Who broke our hearts, shared their wisdom, and
taught us how to see learning anew*

CONTENTS

FOREWORD   ix
Laura I. Rendón

PREFACE   xiii

ACKNOWLEDGMENTS   xxv

1 CENTERING LEARNING   1

2 THE JOURNEY OF THE LEARNER   23

3 AN INTRODUCTION TO THE *WHAT*, *HOW*, *WHY*, AND
   WHO OF LEARNING   39

4 THE *WHAT* OF LEARNING   51

5 THE *HOW* OF LEARNING   72

6 THE *WHY* OF LEARNING   96

7 THE *WHO* OF LEARNING   112

8 FROM REFLECTION TO ACTION
   Expanding the Conversation   134

   AFTERWORD
   What's Next? A Wise Glance Ahead to the Next Steps Toward a
   More Inclusive and Equitable "Courageous Learning"   149
   Estrus Tucker

   REFERENCES   155

   ABOUT THE AUTHORS   161

   INDEX   163

FOREWORD

Teachers open the door, but you must enter by yourself.

—Zen proverb

I n the late 1990s, a book came my way that was to transform my views about teaching. *The Courage to Teach: Exploring the Inner Landscape of a Teacher's Life* was written by someone I respectfully consider to be a true maestro/wisdom teacher, Parker J. Palmer. In his revolutionary text, Palmer (1998) had the courage to challenge entrenched belief systems that have for so long guided educators even when they intuitively sensed this was not good instructional practice. For example, Palmer questioned the false choice represented when educators are asked "What is more important—teaching or learning?" He suggested that we hold the tension in the duality and find a way to embrace the best in the intertwined nature of teaching and learning. Indeed, it is teachers and teachable moments that open the door to learning, and it is the learner who must navigate the journey of learning. Both play important roles.

One of the most significant contributions of *The Courage to Teach* is the notion that at the core of teaching is the self that teaches, which calls for the exploration of the inner aspects of a teacher's life. Knowing one's self, understanding our purpose, and illuminating our hidden talents can give us the courage to teach, learn, and grow. *The Courage to Teach* opened the way for me and many others to find the courage to take risks, face our shadow selves, and even challenge entrenched belief systems that do not serve students well and that may indeed create harm. Teaching has its perils and vulnerabilities, as well as its possibilities and inspirations, and Palmer rightly drew attention to the what, how, why, and who of teaching.

Now comes a companion text, *The Courage to Learn: Honoring the Complexity of Learning for Educators and Students*, which focuses on the other side of teaching—the learning process itself. Like Palmer before them, the authors interrogate four key questions: *What* is to be learned? *How* do we learn? *Why* do we learn? *Who* is the self that learns? These fundamental questions form the integrating foundation to elucidate the learning journeys of over 20 learners (post–K–12 education) from diverse backgrounds. The authors interviewed these learners, who courageously shared their lived experiences in and out of classrooms, as well as their values and cultural belief systems. Throughout the book we find the beauty of poetic expressions paired with theory and practice to reveal key insights about the complexities of learning for educators and students.

A key insight for me is that the most powerful learning can occur when we are most vulnerable, distressed, and traumatized. As I reviewed the book, I thought of my own learning journey as a child who grew up in Laredo, Texas, along the U.S.–Mexico border in what was then one of the poorest areas of the nation. I thought of how my life could have gone in many different directions and how nobody really expected me to accomplish what I have achieved. As an academic now living a privileged lifestyle, I came to understand that everything I experienced from childhood to adulthood (the good, the bad, and the ugly) is and always will be a part of me. These lived experiences are what make me whole, and they have fostered what Latina feminist theorist Gloria Anzaldúa (2015) called *conocimiento*, a form of enlightenment and wisdom formed as we experience and learn from life traumas (Rendón, 2020).

Another important insight runs parallel to what Palmer asked about the teaching self: Who is the self that learns? We rarely entertain this question, and I trust that this book will guide learners across the educational spectrum to reflect on their own response. My personal assessment is that I view myself as a learner whose heart and mind are open to learning. Over numerous trials and tribulations I have learned that creating this spaciousness in our mind, body, and spirit is essential to receiving and constructing knowledge. On the other hand, if one's heart and mind are closed to learning, it likely won't mean very much regarding what is presented to be learned, how it should be learned, and why it should be learned. The learning stories of participants featured in this book reflect some of my own experiences and show the following:

- Learning is a living process.
- Learning is embodied; we feel our experiences in our bodies.
- Just as teachers and teaching moments can be found everywhere, learning can occur in diverse situations and beyond formal schooling contexts.
- Finding one's true identity and purpose is a process that can include both joyous and painful experiences.
- Taking risks, sometimes alone, requires great courage, integrity, conviction, and self-knowledge.
- Validating relationships in our lives is foundational to our growth.

Perhaps what has the most philosophical elegance in this book is how the authors contemplate and deal with the complexities of dualities, for example:

- teaching/learning
- teacher/student
- formal knowledge/informal knowledge
- theory/practice
- knowledge/wisdom
- inner knowing/outer knowing
- Western ways of knowing/other ways of knowing
- objectivity/subjectivity
- either–or/both–and

In my own spiritual journey, I have learned that Indigenous perspectives can offer insights into unlocking these dualities. The idea here is that the dualities exist in oppositional complimentarity and that, when carefully examined, can reveal a third greater reality. León Portilla (1963) noted that Angel Maria Garibay K. identified an Aztec literary device called *difrasismo* in which a pair of seemingly opposite terms were paired to reveal a single unit, for example I.You.Belong; Earth.Sky.World. In the Mayan culture, Etznab/Tijax was a double-sided symbol that, like a piece of sharp black obsidian, could cut through hypnotizing misperceptions and misrepresentations to provide clarity and focus. Engaging in the resolution of dualities is a powerful learning process that can liberate us from colonizing either–or viewpoints, which often create false choices and limit our ability to entertain multiple viewpoints (Chung & Rendón, 2018). These kinds of ancestral teachings take us to a form of radical learning that makes sense of paradoxes in our lives; shatters and liberates us from the separatist nature of the entrenched teaching and learning paradigm; and fosters a pluriversal learning competence—the ability to hold competing and contradictory systems of meaning in tension (Andreotti et al., 2011; Mignolo, 2018; Rendón, 2020).

I consider this book to be *una ofrenda*, an offering, to educators and students who seek a more spacious way to reflect and engage in the learning process. The book also offers *una invitación*, an invitation, to consider where and when our most powerful learning experiences occurred and the lessons learned from both painful and joyous moments in our lives. We are also invited to reflect on the courage it took to learn and grow into wisdom even in our most distressing, vulnerable situations. We learn that radical learning is liberating, releasing us from the bonds of outmoded belief systems; helping us find clarity; and allowing us to be fully present, fully alive. Reading this book has highlighted and reinforced that by its very nature the journey of learning is *un regalo*, a gift in itself.

Laura I. Rendón
Professor Emerita, UTSA

PREFACE

In 1998, the educator, author, and social activist Parker J. Palmer published his ground-breaking text on the inner life of educators. *The Courage to Teach: Exploring the Inner Landscape of a Teacher's Life*, is now in its third edition. It is often the central text read by individuals and communities of educators, activists, health-care professionals, faith leaders, and others seeking guidance on how to integrate the inner calling to serve with a pervasive institutional culture of efficiency and effectiveness. When considering the core message and focus of his text, Palmer (1998) summed up his intention in one question: "Who is the self that teaches?" (p. 7). This question, he contended, is rarely asked, or deeply investigated, during the formal and informal preparation of educators from early childhood through graduate school. Palmer sought to address this limitation in our understanding and promotion of good teaching, through a combination of personal story, scholarly research, and aesthetic themes from poetry, narrative, and wisdom stories.

More important, he invited his readers to move away from notions of teaching that can be systematized through the metaphor of technique and instead consider teaching as an act of vulnerability and courage. Only through the act of listening deeply to the inner life, a source of knowing that is often out of sync with Western epistemologies of objectivism, can an educator fully grow into the intellectual, emotional, and spiritual fullness of their teaching self.

What, if anything, is the relationship between *The Courage to Teach: Exploring the Inner Landscape of a Teacher's Life* and this text, *The Courage to Learn: Honoring the Complexity of Learning for Educators and Students*? Although focusing exclusively on educators, Palmer noted:

> I have no question that students who learn, not professors who perform, is what teaching is all about: students who learn are the finest fruit of teachers who teach. Nor do I doubt that students learn in diverse and wondrous ways, including ways that bypass the teacher in the classroom and ways that require neither a classroom nor a teacher. (p. 6)

Our task in *The Courage to Learn* is to examine, honor, and probe the varied and complex ways in which people learn in "wondrous ways," deep and compelling ways, that often "bypass the teacher in the classroom," the facilitator in the workshop, or educator in a nonformal setting. Given the dominant framing in formal schooling that learning is the product of teaching, it takes courage for learners to question this normalized student–educator relationship and to instead reclaim their power and agency as learners.

Learning occurs in the classroom and in other formalized educational spaces, there is no doubt about that, but what is learned and who benefits from that learning are questions we will pursue and questions we invite you to consider. What became transparent in our conversations with learners is that learning is not the sole purview and responsibility of formal educational spaces. To state the obvious, learning begins before birth and continues up to, and perhaps beyond, the moment of death. Ironically, sometimes the most potent learning happens when wrestling with the discomfort and challenge with the very system that intends to prepare the learner.

The Courage to Learn in Conversation With The Courage to Teach

Throughout this book, we make gentle references to *The Courage to Teach*. Several mutual touchpoints are worth noting as we place both texts in conversation with each other. The first noteworthy touchpoint is that two of the authors are Courage & Renewal facilitators prepared by the Center for Courage & Renewal, which includes preparation for facilitating Courage to Teach circles. Palmer is founder and senior partner emeritus of the center and continues to be an active advisor and consultant. The center is dedicated to the distribution and advancement of Palmer's ideas and commitment to the heart of teaching.

Together, both facilitators/coauthors have 24 years of leading Circle of Trust retreats and programs for teachers, physicians, clergy, faith-based leaders, higher education professionals, and community activists. Given their preparation and experience as facilitators, they draw from this foundation as an influence for the structure of this book. For example, poetry and wisdom stories are central to creating reflective spaces in retreats in which learning conversation partners can engage in conversation and reflection with respect to the deep heart of the passion to teach. Poetry and wisdom stories are woven throughout this book. They are more than artistic interludes. We consciously chose pieces that invite the reader to hear the meaning of the chapter beyond the actual words that are read. One poem in particular, "Two Intelligences," by Jalāl ad-Dīn Mohammad Rūmī (hereafter *Rumi*) anchors the *what, how, why*, and *who* chapters. It helps remind us and the reader that although learning can be analyzed in themes it is best understood as an integration of all four elements.

In *The Courage to Teach*, Palmer (1998) argued that "technique is what teachers use until the real teacher arrives" (p. 5). This book makes a similar observation but through the eyes of learners: Strategy is what a learner uses until the real learner arrives that is, strategy in the context of viewing learning as a commodity and exchange-driven process, just as teachers enamored by technique may view teaching as a series of procedural steps and protocols. In the terms developed by Patricia Cranton (2016), the emphasis on learning is individual gain and technical accomplishment. This book, in keeping with the ethos of *The Courage to Teach*, is concerned with liberating and drawing out the inner life of learners. As such, we intend to invite educators and learners to embrace a more expansive vision of learning, beyond the individual and technical characteristics of Western, objective, and neoliberal economic framing, to be courageous and try something new, to journey into new terrain and new ways of organizing experience into meaning.

Background and Context

We remember stories. Even those who are most dedicated to the facts and statistics of their trade are likely to remember and share the details of a memorable story over coffee or a meal. Like *The Courage to Teach*, this book draws from our personal narratives as educators and learners, the scholarship of learning, and the arts. Our voices as authors will weave throughout the text as background to the narratives of learners who graciously volunteered their perspectives and reflections on learning in formal and informal contexts. They describe in rich detail, sometimes painfully, sometimes with great joy, the discovery that their inner journey of learning, one often formalized in school, is no longer adequate to the task of either capturing the fullness of formal learning or guiding their current learning trajectory. Our conversation partners show that learning, even when sequestered in standardized formats, is a living process. Like water, it flows and moves, seeking new paths and ways through blocked intellectual, physical, spiritual, and emotional spaces. We have found their voices to be both compelling and moving, and we hope you do too, as their voices demonstrate how real learning entails connecting the elements of their personal narrative with the largeness of the world.

Our Learning Conversation Partners

This book lives only because of the willingness of learning conversation partners to share their stories of learning. One of the joys of writing this book was
listening to many learners, in living rooms, offices, and coffee shops, as well
as conversing by way of Zoom during the times in which in-person gather-
ing was impossible. We spoke with colleagues, students, friends, and family
members, looking to gather stories across the age span, identities and roles,
and life experience. These were informal and did not follow a set of pre-
designed questions; rather, they began with a question about the individual's
journey as a learner, followed by the process of asking open and honest questions that is bedrock of Circles of Trust, to stay with a learner's story. Our
conversations were as rich as a meandering stream, and we traveled to places
we could not have anticipated. There are stories distilled from numerous
such exchanges in this book, as well as many anonymous excerpts of student
writing, for which permission was granted. Depending on their preference,
pseudonyms may have been used. To distinguish their voices from those of
the researchers and wisdom teachers cited in this text, we use *italics* for our
learning partners and quotes for the others.

Before plunging too deeply into the structure and rationale for this
book, it is important to define a few terms we will use through the text and to
clarify the intended relationship between *The Courage to Learn* and the P–20
education system (early childhood through higher education). By *courage* we
mean the capacity of learners to both recognize the full complexity of learning (psychologically, emotionally, intellectually, and spiritually) and to act
on that dawning awareness with agency and the power of self-determination
and meaning making. This is a courageous act because it seeks to break free
of the normative frames that define much of what constitutes the taken-for-
granted lenses of formal learning. The stories we share from our conversation
partners show that, to stand alone, sometimes in opposition to the norm,
takes a type of courage that requires intellect, self-reflection, heart, soul, and
inner commitment to authenticity in selfhood.

In her text, *Understanding and Promoting Transformative Learning: A
Guide to Theory and Practice,* Cranton (2016) defined this form of courageous
learning as *emancipatory knowledge.* She drew from Jack Mezirow's (1991)
groundbreaking work in adult learning and adds contemporary framings
of postmodernism, social justice, and extrarational theories of learning
(imagination, soul, and intuition). Her integrated theory of transformative
learning includes "acting differently, having a deeper self-awareness, holding more open perspectives, and experiencing a deep shift in worldview"
(Cranton, 2016, pp. 41–42). We noted similar qualities in the interviews we

conducted with learners as they described the process of learning and believe that the stories we heard from our conversation partners mirror much of Cranton's articulation of emancipatory knowledge; both speak to the liberation and enlightenment of the self as learner.

By *educator* we mean anyone involved in the process of transformative learning, inviting learners to move from one level of knowing to more complex and integrated understandings of self and the world. We envision teachers, early childhood educators, professors, social workers, religious leaders, parents, caregivers, librarians, tradespeople, Cooperative Extension educators, physicians, and many others. We believe that teaching and learning are universal human activities that include and yet go beyond traditional notions of classrooms. Though we often default to the language of teachers, educators, and facilitators, we intend to include the full range of relationships that form around individuals with more knowledge/experience sharing their wisdom with individuals with less knowledge/experience.

We critique traditional, formalized notions of learning throughout this text, not out of intellectual or personal spite but rather to honor the stories of conversation partners, who often framed their transformation through the suffering, challenges, and disappointments they experienced in formalized schooling. We want to clearly state that this text is not intended as a condemnation of P–20 teachers. We recognize that given the current emphasis on standards, accountability, learning benchmarks, and pay for performance that traditional educators are limited in their ability to foster transformative learning. We honor the work of individual teachers, who in the face of the institutional and social limitations they routinely experience in the selection of curriculum and the creation of diverse, differentiated, and inclusive methods, still find ways to liberate learners. We are more concerned about the system of education and the ways in which it constricts the landscape of learning, not individuals who are caught up in the institutionalization of knowing.

We are pro education in its many forms. We believe in the value of structured learning, and we seek to broaden the conversation. Our book is not an either–or argument pitting freedom to learn against structured learning outcomes. We hope, through our insider lens as educators, to maintain a tone of both/and, placing these contrasting stances in conversation with one another. The Catholic theologian Richard Rohr (2011) is a strong advocate for human transformation as a blending of rules and freedom. He is a well-known critic of religious practices that lean too heavily toward form and structure. He offers this framing of institutional criticism from the inside out that we find helpful in our work: "That is probably the only way you can fruitfully criticize anything. It seems to me you must unlock spiritual things from the inside, and not by throwing rocks from outside, which is always too easy and too self-aggrandizing" (p. 75).

Like Rohr, we actively elevate the less heard voices. In our case, we center the stories of learning when that learning is released from the confines of the classroom. These are important affirmations of learning, not to negate the formal but rather to bring balance to the conversations on effective teaching and learning. We agree with Parker J. Palmer (1998) that "people who start movements do so not because they hate an institution but because they love it too much to let it descend to its lowest form" (p. 170). We *love* teaching. It is our profession and hearts' passion. As such, we believe teaching and learning can be more than a transaction between expert and novice, and the stories of our partners offer a glimpse into the heights learners can reach if allowed to soar.

By *learning* we mean the diverse, unexpected, and deeply personal ways in which people take their experiences and form them into strands of meaning. In our understanding and articulation of learning we will draw from Cranton (2016) in her articulation and expansion of transformative learning theory, featuring descriptions and analytic categories for adult learning. Cranton's work integrates the following elements, which are sometimes in tension, depending on the context of learning: individual and social learning and technical and communicative knowledge. As noted earlier in this preface, the energizing force holding the four elements together is emancipatory knowledge, which seeks to develop learner agency, autonomy, reflection, and power in the face of social and cultural injustice. Throughout our conversations, we encountered learning that is individual, social, technical, and communicative. And as Cranton suggested, the integration of these categories for our conversation partners was fluid and highly context bound. In the following pages we draw attention to these elements as salient categories in understanding the complex ways that learners turn experiences into systems of meaning.

Honoring the Journey of the Learner

In this book, we intend to pay tribute to the learner's journey in the fullness of the process and to name the distinct forms of courage that learning takes. Learning can be sad and joyful, intellectual and embodied, and immediate, as well as recognizing its fruits many years in the future. In any form, learning takes courage and integrity to self, others, and the essence of the moment. Learning can be a gift from teacher, text, nature, and self, though it may often feel like a commodity to be measured, divided, and framed through economic and production metaphors. No two learners navigate learning in the same way, even when encountering the same learning experience. This is what gives life to the learning process and is why *deep learning*, learning that is transformative of self, is inherently an act of courage. It accepts the premise that learning can facilitate the emergence of a new self who then forms new relationships with others and the wider world.

Yet, descriptions of learning in the scholarship of teaching are almost exclusively sequestered within the four walls of classrooms and favor the interests of educators and policymakers seeking to define instructional spaces in predictive and assessable ways. Although learning is currently tightly bound to Western ways of knowing that value intellect, structure, distance, and objectivity, there is a growing movement against neoliberal commodification of learning, and indeed, our learning conversation partners speak to a widely expanded notion of what "learning" means. We hope to help readers foster the courage to learn and to honor the ways in which they have shown the courage to learn by breaking through institutionalized forms.

Adult Learning Theory

Although our intention is to center the voices of many learners, part of our exploration involves examining the literature, which we do throughout this book. We agree with adult learning theorists who assert that learning is a more complex task than the ways in which it is typically framed in traditional teaching and learning spaces. The notable exception to the literature on standardized description and analysis of learning is the literature on adult learning theory, experiential learning, apprenticeships, and mentoring, which focuses on informal instruction as well as the learning and transformation of self and others (Cranton, 2016; Daloz, 1999; Daloz & Parks, 2003; Kolb, 1984; Marsick & Watkins, 1990/2015; Parks, 2000; Schwartz, 2019; Watkins & Marsick, 2021). Most formal framing of learning is transactional; knowledge as a commodity is exchanged, often at a financial and emotional cost, for another commodity, most typically a diploma or a grade. In contrast, adult learning theory is transformational for self and the wider social networks the learner inhabits. It centers the values of change and freedom over status and compliance.

Transformative learning theory, as developed by Jack Mezirow (1991) and elaborated on by others, is premised on four interlocking concepts relevant to the work of this book: (a) habits of mind, (b) a disrupting experience, (c) reflection, and (d) transformation of self as a knower. Each learner is unique based on their cultural background, past learning experiences, spiritual/emotional awareness, and skills in reflection. As such, the combination of process and individual attributes of the learner can manifest in a complex array of learning experiences, timing, and outcomes, as we highlight through learners' stories.

The themes in this book recognize the existence of formal educational environments and the ways in which educators strive to create spaces for learning to blossom. Stories of courageous teaching are being told by skilled educators and authors like Parker J. Palmer, bell hooks, Paulo Freire, Laura Rendón, Joan Wink, Geneva Gay, Gloria Ladson Billings, Mark Tennant, and many others. Our mission, with equal intensity and integrity, is to create a space for learners to speak their truths about learning, and to give voice that is parallel to Palmer's (1998) question about the teaching self, asking "Who is the self that learns?"

The *What, How, Why,* and *Who* of Learning

While Cranton's (2016) work offers a theory of learning, we rely on a second framework for organizing the chapter-by-chapter structure of the book. *The Courage to Learn* is informed by Palmer's (1998) observation that the conversations in teaching can be organized around four types of questions: *what, how, why,* and *who. What* questions focus on curriculum, which includes the content and materials with which students interact. *How* questions focus on pedagogy, or the ways in which teachers structure learning activities. *Why* questions focus on good reason giving or rationale for the *what* and *how*. They tend to fall more heavily into the realm of philosophy. *Who* questions focus on the inner life and transformation of the teacher, as well as the spiritual formation of self.

What and *how* questions dominate teaching conversations. *Why* questions are lightly present in the form of reflective practice but are mostly sidelined in the field of education. Palmer (1998) argued that the *who* question is almost completely absent in any meaningful way in conversations around effective teaching. The question "Who is the self that teaches?" (a teacher's inner terrain) frames the rest of *The Courage to Teach*.

Overview of Contents

Chapter 1 sets the stage by providing an overview of learning. We consider learning an ongoing journey, explore it within and outside of a structured school experience, consider why learning matters, and aim to connect theory and practice. We explore what the science tells us and why learning can be so difficult.

In chapter 2, each author offers a personal story of their learning journey as another way to reveal the ways in which our learning experiences frame and inform our perspectives on teaching and learning. Each narrative is an attempt to uncover the matrices of personal values, cultural beliefs, and lived experiences that inform our views about and orientation toward learning. To be as vulnerable and open as possible, we state the ways in which our social positionality, as three white-identifying authors who are engaged in higher education, informs, and obscures, our values on learning. We have tried to be as wholehearted and genuine to our conversation partners' stories of learning as possible while recognizing the inherent limitations that come with our fixed social categories.

Chapter 3 offers the foundation for chapters 4 through 7 by introducing the framing of *what, why, how,* and *who* of learning, inspired by the organizing framework Palmer chose for *The Courage to Teach*. We dedicate a chapter in this book to each of those four questions with an eye toward responding to the question "Who is the self that learns?"

Chapter 8 turns in the direction of taking a *Courage to Learn* conversation beyond individual reflection to conversing with others, who may include colleagues, learners, community members, and others.

Respect for Our Learning Conversation Partners

Despite our conscious effort to pull back our social lenses of meaning making, one of our conversation partners reminded us that in the act of requesting personal stories of learning we were leaning toward a form of Western educational colonialism. This participant invited us to consider the ways in which the stories we gathered could be a form of extractive knowledge, which could have the consequence of commodifying the lived experiences of learners in the form of the book you hold in your hands. We recognize the wisdom embedded in this challenge. Throughout the text, we seek to temper the authority inherent in our role as academics and higher education faculty by centering the voices and perspectives of our conversation partners. We cannot fully eliminate the extractive nature of our conversations, since asking questions could be perceived as invasive of personal space and meaning making. At the same time, we have consciously striven for open-ended conversations that follow the currents offered by the learning conversation partner, not a prescribed interview protocol, as well as integrative knowledge that values community gain through a power-with relationship between authors and conversation partners.

We take to heart and hope to enact with fidelity the distinction Robin Wall Kimmerer (2013) drew between a commodity culture and a gifting culture:

> It's funny how the nature of an object—let's say a strawberry or a pair of socks—is so changed by the way it has come into your hands, as a gift or as a commodity . . . I have no inherent obligation to those socks as a commodity, as private property . . . I have paid for them and our reciprocity ended the minute I handed her the money . . . But what if those very same socks, red and gray striped, were knitted by my grandmother and given to me as a gift? That changes everything. A gift creates ongoing relationship. (pp. 25–26)

Our learning conversation partners gave the gift of their stories of learning, a way of perceiving learning that reaches far beyond the confines of traditional ways of structured learning, stories we gratefully received and held with integrity. Kimmerer (2013) noted that reciprocity in this cycle of gifting carries the flow of energy back to its beginning as a gift. We hope that this book is a gift to our conversation partners as we honor their wisdom and use their voices to invite all educators to break free of narrowly defined notions of learning. We attempt to dampen the normalizing voice of whiteness, power, and privilege by bringing forth, through narrative, the critical perspectives of our conversation partners even as we hold the tensions inherent in each of our identities.

Learning as a Gift

Kimmerer (2013) noted that, when it comes to understanding the power of a gift, it is imperative to remember that "the cycle flows from attention, to gift, to gratitude, to reciprocity. It starts with seeing" (p. xii). We invite all educators, including ourselves as authors, to "see" what it means to be a learner; to answer with fidelity the question "Who is the self that learns?" For us and for our learners, an important element of seeing is recognizing the ways that Western, objective, and individualized learning can obscure other ways of knowing, learning, and being in relationship with the world. As we work to shift our lens on the teacher–student relationship from commodity to gift we are reminded of a description of knowing the world written by Barry Lopez (2019). In his reflection on his Western way of knowing in contrast to the ways of knowing his Indigenous companions lived into, he notes:

> If my companions [Indigenous peoples] and I, for example, hiking the taiga encountered a grizzly bear feeding on a caribou carcass, I would tend to focus almost entirely on the bear. My companions would focus on the part of the world of which, at that moment, the bear was only a fragment . . . They would repeatedly situate the smaller thing within the larger thing, back and forth . . . For me, the bear was a noun, the subject of a sentence; for them, it was a verb, the gerund of bearing.
>
> The event I was cataloging in my mind as "encounter with a tundra grizzly," they were experiencing as an immersion in the current of a river. They were swimming in it, feeling its pull, noting the temperature of the water, the back eddies, and where the side streams entered. My approach, in contrast, was mostly to take note of objects in the scene—the bear, caribou, the tundra vegetation. (p. 168)

The metaphor of knowing and learning as a river is instructive here. The river is free flowing and exists within a bank, a structure that provides context, meaning, and some element of direction. The bank of the river of formal education is well established, channeled, and, in many places, lined with concrete. The wildness of learning has been tamed and quantified. This book, our work, is focused on rediscovering the natural flow of the river of learning. It is always there, but not always visible as it is often channeled underground and hidden away. We are not so much interested in drawing evaluative distinctions between Western and Indigenous ways of knowing, which surely exist. We are interested in finding ways to describe learning as an organic process that occurs regardless of context, learner agency, levels of formality, and degrees of openness in the curriculum—and, as a paradox, we acknowledge how these elements may also deeply influence the way in which this process unfolds. To resist turning learning into a noun, we turn to the practices and principles of Circle of Trust work, which values listening and inner dimensions of knowing over extractive visions of learning as a commodity to be harvested, refined, and reduced to a tidy list of approved objectives met.

Reflection: The Work Before the Work

As you explore *The Courage to Learn*, we anticipate that you may wonder, so what? Now what? What are you inviting me to *do*?

The action into which this book invites the reader begins with reflection. Courageous learning begins first by turning the attention inward, considering our own learning journey; discovering unrecognized aspects of our identity; and probing the *what, why,* and *how* of learning—as well as *who* I am as a learner. We believe that even the most seasoned educator will benefit from pushing a pause button to reflect on this learning process, perhaps surfacing some surprises that will inform the way forward with a fresh perspective.

At the end of each chapter is a set of reflective questions. These correspond with the ideas in each chapter, build on one another, and set the stage for a conversation with others. We encourage you to take time to sit with them.

Best wishes on your learning journey.

ACKNOWLEDGMENTS

We offer our deepest appreciation to these learners, who generously took the time to share the stories of their learning: Dajah Abdiel, Lesley Adams, Severin Beckwith, Shaun Bluethenthal, Kathy Bond, Kristine DeLuca, Michael Eames, Carol Grove, Eric Harter, Aleena Jafri, Brooke Krasowsky, Janet McCue, Mark Miller, Andy Moore, Gwendolyn Pieper, Marvin Pritts, Susan Sanders, William Sheavly, Jamila Walida Simon, Bobby J. Smith II, Margaret Stanley, Holly Wilkinson, Susan Worrall.

We have special appreciation for Andrew Scheldorf for his thoughtful and keen eye, particularly through the lens of diversity, equity, and inclusion.

A deep bow of gratitude goes to David Brightman, our editor at Stylus, for his commitment to the vision of this book and for his fine, patient editorial guidance.

I

CENTERING LEARNING

Two Kinds of Intelligence

There are two kinds of intelligence: one acquired,
as a child in school memorizes facts and concepts
from books and from what the teacher says,
collecting information from the traditional sciences
as well as from the new sciences.

With such intelligence you rise in the world.
You get ranked ahead or behind others
in regard to your competence in retaining
information. You stroll with this intelligence
in and out of fields of knowledge, getting always more
marks on your preserving tablets.

There is another kind of tablet, one
already completed and preserved inside you.
A spring overflowing its springbox. A freshness
in the center of the chest. This other intelligence
does not turn yellow or stagnate. It's fluid,
and it doesn't move from outside to inside
through conduits of plumbing-learning.

This second knowing is a fountainhead
from within you, moving out.

—*Jellaludin Rumi (1207–1273), 2004, p. 178.*

To learn is to live and to live is to learn. These two aspects of what it means to be human are intimately intertwined. To live and learn is foundational to our identity, our relationships, and our communities. This connection between ourselves and learning is essential to the message of this book. As we note throughout, the process of learning can be both forming and de-forming in terms of what it means to be fully human, that is, in addition to its obvious benefits, learning can have negative impacts on our emerging personhood. It takes courage to learn just as it takes courage to teach.

When asked about teaching, Albert Einstein noted that "I never teach my pupils, I only attempt to provide the conditions in which they can learn." What Einstein does not say here is an important element in the "conditions" of the learning process, which is the value of mistakes and error. An old adage tells us that to err is human. A more expansive saying might be that to *learn* is human. From the time we are conscious we are learners, navigating our way through a bright, colorful, sometimes noisy, often confusing, and occasionally threatening world. Learning is as necessary to our survival as breathing, as vital to our joy as eating, and it is integrated into every facet of our lives, whether we choose to pause to reflect on it or not

As we talk about learning, we are not only focusing on the learner and the content that is being learned. We are also including the educator in our discussions. By "educator" we mean a wide range of interlocutors, including human and more-than-human teachers. This includes K–12 teachers, nature, lived experiences, texts, time, trusted mentors, parents, and higher education faculty.

Throughout the book we frequently include quotes and wisdom stories, like the Rumi epigraph at the beginning of this chapter, to center learning. Poetry in particular has the unique capacity for drawing mystery, meaning, and metaphor into the conversation. As such, it offers a wider palette for describing learning than the more monochromatic colors of standardized assessments and metrics. By its nature, introducing poetry summons the ineffable into the conversation, that which is known but is often just beyond the capacity of language to express. The poet Emily Dickinson (1976) advised, "Tell all the truth but tell it slant . . . / The Truth must dazzle gradually / Or every man be blind" (pp. 506–507). Only truth told at a slant has the potential to slide past the rational, analytical mind, which is well trained in the objective process of deconstruction, and enter forms of knowing that Rumi located in the center of the chest: the heart.

We contend that the courage to learn is a "both/and" activity; *both* the head *and* the heart, along with the body, are essential to learning. In our experiences, poetry, art, music, and wisdom stories bring an aliveness to the conversation that is not characteristic of rational and linear forms of descriptive writing. Metaphor, analogy, and imagination invite the fullness of learning to materialize. When asked about the relationship between music and knowing, David Byrne (2010) replied:

> I sense the world might be more dreamlike, metaphorical, and poetic than we currently believe—but just as irrational as sympathetic magic when looked at in a typically scientific way. I wouldn't be surprised if poetry— poetry in the broadest sense, in the sense of a world filled with metaphor, rhyme, and recurring patterns, shapes, and designs—is how the world works. The world isn't logical, it's a song. (p. 194)

The arts, like songs, are tools that help turn the noun of learning into a verb, a river flowing, changing the landscape as it is changed by the quality of banks holding it in place (Lopez, 2019). Centering *Two Intelligences* by Rumi helps frame the central themes and message of this book.

The Rumi poem draws attention to two intertwined elements of learning: the outer and inner. The former is structured and linear, while the latter is open and oblique. In the context of learning in our contemporary world, both are necessary, and they work best in tandem as a continuum, not as antithetical or in opposition to one another. You might imagine tracing your finger along a Mobius strip as a metaphor for how your inner reflection forms the foundation for your outer action, and then you turn inward again, so that your reflection upon your actions again informs further action, and so on; this is an enduring aspect of learning. Yet the outer story of learning has been told with greater vigor and focus than the inner journey of learning. This narrative, from the Rumi poem, of "a spring overflowing its springbox. A freshness / in the center of the chest" (2004, p. 178) was the most prominent description of learning for our learning conversation partners. This is the story we want to share in this book, with the hope that it will encourage all educators to see learning as something that is more than forms of knowledge that often "move from outside to inside / through conduits of plumbing-learning" (Rumi, 2004, p. 178).

Rumi wrote of "acquired" knowledge as consisting of "facts and concepts." This is the bedrock of the technical elements of learning (Cranton, 2016). It is typically perceived as more objective, and it is often assessed through tests and performance indicators. It includes demonstrations of learning that the educator can see as a score or changed behavior. The mastery of this knowledge tends to be static and can be transactional. When we master this form of intelligence, we are very often rewarded with praise in the form of certificates, degrees, diplomas, and awards that attest to our expertise.

A metaphor that captures the transactional nature of this learning is the *jug-and-mug theory* of pedagogy, the externalized wisdom of others that resides outside of us (or the text) is poured directly into the waiting mug of the learner's mind. As Rumi (2004) attested, a learner possessing externally authorized and standardized knowledge is entitled to "stroll with this intelligence / in and out of fields of knowledge" for the purpose of "getting always / more marks on your preserving tablets" (p. 178).

Credentialing agencies attach a significant level of honor and status to these institutional forms of knowledge, and we often comply as a society. There is great value to such learning. For example, when it comes to surgery, a technically skilled surgeon is preferable to one who performed poorly on an anatomy exam. And at the same time, technical competency has its limitations. When we center it as the exclusive and most important form of learning, centering outer excellence at the expense of the inner journey, quite often we unintentionally produce the kind of drive described by this young person:

> When I was growing up, my middle school and high school were . . . always trying to prepare me for the next level but never really caring about my current well-being. Phrases like the fast track to success have literally inspired a generation so demanding for speed that, in the process, they often find life passing them by. Indeed, I was one of those people. My ambition and drive to succeed had me focused on the future and blinded by the natural phenomena occurring around me every day . . . I have always demanded perfection of myself and, throughout my education, I would work endlessly to achieve academic excellence. Though I have not completely discounted the importance of academic excellence in my life, now [I am aiming to] transform my outlook on life in more than one way. . . . Not only has this class taught me about the beauty of nature and plants, but it has also taught me about the beauty and nature of human beings. . . . Many of the things I once considered important, I have found to be secondary. I realized that there is more to life than a 4.0 GPA and a high-paying job and if we don't recognize this, we are missing a huge reason [as to] why life is so beautiful.

Rumi (2004) pointed to a second form of knowing, a "spring overflowing its springbox. / A freshness in the center of the chest" (p. 178). This kind of learning is indefinable, with significant depth and meaning, and it is not subject to empirical testing or ranking. It is communicative and relational in its form and purpose (Cranton, 2016). Like a spring, it is trustworthy and has an ever-flowing quality while also containing a degree of mystery regarding its source. Learning of this kind requires a certain amount of faith, trust, and vulnerability that, if properly tended, will not dry up. A good surgeon, therefore, is both technically competent and passionate about their calling to heal. They are attuned to the ways in which their knowledge can flow through the mysterious combination of heart, head, and hand in the process of mending the body and spirit of the patient.

At the core of this book are four chapters that explore learning through the four frames of teaching offered by Parker Palmer (1998) in *The Courage to Teach: Exploring the Inner Landscape of a Teacher's Life*. Chapters 4 and 5 delve into the *what* and *how* dimensions of learning. Chapters 6 and 7 explore the *why* and *who* dimensions of learning. To bring a sense of aliveness to the chapters, we anchor the conversation in the Rumi poem that forms the epigraph for this chapter. Although Rumi was a 13th-century Sufi mystic, Islamic scholar, and poet, we believe that his framing of two contrasting forms of learning is as potent today as it was 800 years ago. His work still speaks to a dominant understanding in many educational settings of how people learn and how memorization, recitation, and the accurate reproduction of knowledge can still predominate.

Learning as a Journey

Learning is an ongoing journey. It may start from a place of curiosity, fear, and perhaps even ignorance, and then learning can move us forward. Where it moves us and how far we can go seem to depend on different variables. There are many times that learning is hard work and takes a lot of time and other instances during which we do not even realize that we are learning until we can do something that we could not do before. Learning something important is rarely easy. Richard Rohr (2020) argued that there is an essential relationship between struggle and learning. He noted that even in the midst of pain and disappointment, learning fosters growth and is part of what makes life worth living.

We often think of learning as something that happens in school. While that is certainly true, learning occurs in all areas of our lives—from how to find the local grocery store to understanding how to program a new smartphone—as a part of ongoing growth. When we learn something, it makes us think and act differently, and we cannot "unlearn" something that has been learned. If any evidence in support of this claim is needed, try to unlearn reading. Once the code is cracked, a learner can never learn to not read. Although we may wish sometimes that we had not learned a hard truth about someone, and we may want to go back to a place of innocence in which we did not have knowledge of something painful, we cannot. Learning is an essential part of who we are and what we become. How we learn often defines who we are. As we attempt to demonstrate in this book, "We learn who we are."

Learning Outside of a Structured School Experience

If you are reading this book now, there is an excellent chance that you learned how to listen for meaning and to witness another person's experience in an effort to communicate, and you began this process outside of formal schooling. You probably do not even remember learning to listen—but you did it. First, you may have heard people speaking, and if you did not have the ability to hear, then you may have used a hearing device, or perhaps would have learned to read important body language, pictorially or even by placing your fingers alongside your parent's or caregiver's throat to explore the difference in vocalizations. After a while, you began to assign meaning to the words that were spoken or to gestures and images, and this likely increased in nuance as you grew older. With time, you learned the subtleties of those words and gestures, listening to the meaning beneath what was said or how it was conveyed to you. You went through a basic process and you made it your own, providing your unique spin on each element.

You may even have pictures or videos that were taken when you first began to engage with other people and can reflect on this as a huge milestone: the first time that someone said something to you that affirmed who you were, or when someone taught you something meaningful that you still remember. You know that there was some effort involved, even though now it seems so natural. No one ever started communicating with others without making some mistakes in the interpretation, and that does not stop anyone, because engaging with others serves a deep part of our belonging and is something that has so many benefits and advantages. We seem to be genetically wired to communicate and listen. This learning impacts us for the rest of our lives, and while it took considerable energy, it did not require the same type of work as memorizing chemistry formulas or the words to someone else's poem. We learn differently in different situations, and not all of us react in the same ways to learning experiences. This is what makes the concept of "learning" so challenging to define. It is not always the same for everyone.

Learning in its fullest form challenges the structure and efficiency model that characterizes much of formal education. Consider the learning experiences of Charlie, one of our learning conversation partners. Charlie's story helps to demonstrate that learning is a process that does not always happen within a formal school system and how so much of our learning occurs within the context of family, friends, and our neighborhoods.

> My earliest learning started in church—not in the school system or some formalized school structure. In church and at home, there was a lot of emphasis on learning right from wrong and treating people with dignity

and respect. Because I'm from the South, I grew up knowing that it's "nice to be nice," ultra-conscious of how you treat people. This wasn't conveyed as a set of rules, more so, how to survive life as a child, preparing to be a teenager. And race was really big—how to be a Black child, how to be a Black teenager, how to be a Black Christian teenager, how to be a Black Christian adult. Surviving life.

Charlie's story helps us to recognize the importance of learning outside of a classroom. The lessons that we learn from our parents, family, and culture impact us throughout our lives. We learn how to interact with people and what seems to work or not work. We learn how to manipulate a situation so that we can be more comfortable in it. Or we learn that manipulation makes us feel less comfortable and further away from our true identity. We learn to avoid putting ourselves in situations that can become dangerous or difficult, and we learn what helps us to achieve. Like learning to listen and communicate, this type of learning is not usually something that requires study, and yet this learning is not easy, either.

One of the most important things that we can do is to think about who we are as a learner. Much of our early learning comes from our upbringing. We find out what works for us and what we like. We learn values, and we learn how to approach problems. Sometimes our learning will be helpful; sometimes that learning can set us up for a difficult path. The experiences that we have had growing up impact us, but that does not mean that we cannot change the way we have always approached learning if it does not seem to be working.

The learning that we do outside of formal classrooms often stays with us. Remembering Charlie, he shares the impact that his faith-based foundation had on his learning trajectory. A rising star and PhD student (at the time of the conversation with him), Charlie talks about how deeply embedded this is to him; there was the math, reading, language arts in school, certainly, and yet the way in which he was able to excel was due to the huge emphasis on an appreciation for education bestowed on him by his parents:

> I was required to study the Bible, the scriptures, and that also helped me memorize stuff, to navigate pre-K through 12th grade. We were just two generations removed from sharecropping, and my parents instilled in us to never forget that not long ago, you weren't allowed to get an education. No one can take your learning away from you. They can take away your job, but they can't take your education away from you. Not only did I have to learn what I was taught, but it was all about how to be taught. Church was a constant thing for me, used as a lens to my learning and ensuring that I'm always doing the best I can.

Learning Within a Structured School Experience

When we talk about "learning," many people think of the learning situated in the space between kindergarten and high school or college. We remember our teachers, our school buildings, and probably some of the school-based experiences such as the cafeteria or the school bus. Again, we have many types of learning, including mastering the ways our teachers taught a specific curriculum that was tested by a wide variety of exams and performance assessments. But we also had learning experiences that were not tested by a formal or standardized test. We may have figured out how to make friends and how to negotiate the social structure of schools. It is likely that much of this was difficult.

Returning to Charlie's experiences, Charlie's college years were an extension of high school as intellectual suffering and limited personal growth, "four more years of regurgitation and memorization." While he continued on and was successful after college, it is important to note that Charlie feels the way so many students feel, that learning in school is often about "regurgitation and memorization" rather than about growth and change.

Why is it that we consider learning at school to be something that feels like being sick and throwing up? Gaining facts in a vacuum does not allow us to really think about what we are learning and does not let us make that learning our own. We need to find the context of our own lives and experiences to make learning a true part of us. Memorizing facts can be difficult, and it can feel like it is not something that is meaningful. Unfortunately, there may be many "facts" that you memorized that are not helpful or useful to you now.

After graduating from college, Charlie entered graduate school, and his learning shifted. It became more about contributing to a larger conversation within his academic field and constantly questioning what was considered "truth" than about having to memorize facts and recite knowledge. Going into a PhD program, Charlie found himself reflecting deeply on contributing to knowledge production and finding his voice and, for the first time, positioning himself as a scholar. The things that he learned as a child still impact what and how he learns and experiences the world. So often there is an interconnectedness between what is learned and how it is learned. Charlie's thoughts on this exemplify the hard work of learning:

> Navigating is a huge challenge. So often people assume that learning is linear. You do x, y, and z—an already-prescribed method. Navigating that learning process and places that teach you how to learn a certain way is everything. Navigating is not just directional, but how to manage people, conversations with teachers, yourself in a new place. In part that's a

part of college in general, or anyplace going from home, it's an adjustment with transitional issues, navigating the process of learning. . . . And this also brings resilience and strength, which comes out of an actual struggle. I think it's important to create conditions where people can struggle and flourish all at the same time.

Why Is Learning so Hard?

We each learned a form of listening and communication with other people, likely at different paces depending on how accessible this was for each of us. But time to mastery was rarely the goal; learning to communicate was the goal. While that may have taken time, we may not have viewed it as difficult. So, what is it about learning that we believe to be hard? Part of the answer to this question comes from thinking about what learning really is. Learning is finding out what you do not know and then changing how you think about it. We are not just adding more information in many cases; we are changing the structure of our knowledge. This is change—and change can be very uncomfortable and scary. If you have never spoken a second language and you take the plunge, it is challenging and exciting—and also frustrating and intimidating. We might get something wrong, and that could be embarrassing. We might look foolish, and we might actually show that we do not know something. This is the difficult juxtaposition that we set up for ourselves. If we do not know something, we will show that we do not know it, and that can be a risk. We must often be brave to show that we are lacking in knowledge and demonstrate that there is something we do not yet understand. It often seems simpler to stay in our own bubble of comfort than to risk asking for the information and assistance required to learn something new. This is yet another reason for how it is that learning is a courageous act. There is a certain level of audacity in asking questions and testing our own knowledge. There is surely some level of excitement about learning, but some of that excitement can cause us to feel almost physically nauseous.

By definition, learning is challenging because to learn something new means that we have to change what we know; we have to adapt to and accommodate new information and new structures of knowledge. This can trigger the recognition that we did not know enough before. We may have been wrong. For example, Sherry Watt (2015) has, along with her students, created a *privileged identity exploration model* and a three-step process to learn and manage the skills for engaging with difference. Most of us who begin to engage with the "other" become defensive in particular ways as we encounter and deal with dissonance. Watt and her team seek to normalize this response and encourage awareness of the particular types of defenses that emerge, learning to identify those defenses and how they appear to ourselves and others. This can be difficult to admit to ourselves and even harder to share with others.

Consider Malala Yousafzai (2013), who is an activist for education, especially the education of girls. As a child, she advocated for girls to be allowed to go to school in Pakistan. Because of her public comments, she was attacked by Taliban gunmen, who shot her to try to stop her from her activism. In a speech to the United Nations, she said that "the terrorists thought that they would change our aims and stop our ambitions, but nothing changed in my life except this: Weakness, fear and hopelessness died. Strength, power and courage were born" (para. 1). Learning was so important to her that she risked her life—with impacts that were far reaching.

In Angela Duckworth's (2016) book, which focuses on the importance of grit, Duckworth tells the story of a student, David Luong. David started out in her high school algebra class. He soon demonstrated that he had an excellent aptitude for algebra and was moved into an accelerated algebra class. In that class, he struggled a bit more; his first exam grade was a D. Duckworth asked him how he handled it. His response was:

> I did feel bad—I did—but I didn't dwell on it. I knew it was done. I knew I had to focus on what to do next. So, I went to my teacher and asked for help. I basically tried to figure out, you know, what I did wrong. What I needed to do differently. (p. 19)

David, like so many of us, struggled when learning something new. He leaned in, instead of away, and asked for help. He knew that what he was doing was not working and that he needed to do something different. This took courage.

Connecting the Learner to the Learning

Do you remember what you went through to memorize the multiplication tables? If you are like many, you may have been given a table that had numbers and symbols on it, and you were told to learn them; you memorized that $5 \times 5 = 25$. Do you recall whether you knew *why*? Did you understand what that meant, or was it just a fact that you could state without truly understanding it? For many students, memorizing multiplication tables is done because it is something that we are told to do. It is unfortunate, but often, compliance to the teacher's expectation of mastery is of higher value than actually understanding what is being learned. And, if we are good at memorizing, then we do well on exams. For many, however, the simple fact of memorizing it takes away from the real purpose of what multiplication tables do, which is to provide us with a shortcut in math. It is faster to know that $5 \times 5 = 25$ than it is to add $5 + 5 + 5 + 5 + 5 = 25$. And once you understand that 5×5 actually means 5, five times, it clarifies the purpose of multiplication tables. Because much of what we "learn" in school is done by memorizing rather than understanding, we lose out on the excitement and purpose of learning.

By seeking out the *why* in the *what* is being learned, students can find their joy and their passion. They can see the connectedness of *what* they are learning to the lived experiences in their lives and those of their world. They can see that the learning that they are doing makes sense and is meaningful. Finding out the *why* is not always easy. Sometimes a student must ask for the meaning; if they are fortunate, they may discover it on their own. Wrestling with learning's purpose can create barriers that impede learning. Understanding that knowing the *why* about something makes it easier to grasp is an important part of developing the courage that it takes to keep on learning. Understanding *what* and *why* you are learning is essential.

The Interconnectedness of Theory and Practice

We all learn, but *how* we learn is often very different; it changes based on the time, the situation, and *what* is being learned. We all begin learning from the beginnings of our existence, at every stage of life, from the prenatal stage onward. To learn something new, we go through some type of process to gain that knowledge or information. This process may require no effort on our part, such as learning the words to a song that you often hear or the jingle to a popular television commercial. Any time we learn something, there is a change in our brains that will impact how we think. We can now do something or know something that we could not do or did not know before. That new adaptation allows us to make different decisions or to look at things from another perspective.

Recent research has suggested that there are seven principles that help us to understand how learning happens and why it is such a complex process (Ambrose et al., 2010). Ambrose et al. (2010) defined learning as "a process that leads to change, which occurs as a result of experience, and increases the potential for improved performance and future learning" (p. 3). Clearly, there are three parts to this definition that offer a window into the complexity of almost any learning task. The first part is that learning is defined as a *process*. This is an essential mindset to have because we are not focused on *what* is learned—we are looking at the development of that learning through an active process. The only way that we can show learning is to demonstrate it somehow.

An educator does not know that a student has learned material until that student *demonstrates* the learning. The learning may have already occurred, and it is not something that can be seen, so we show that we have learned by saying or doing something. Learning is inferred by later looking at behavior to see if it happened. By understanding that learning is a continuing process we can begin to see that it takes time and work to do. According to this definition, learning also involves some type of *change* that has "a lasting impact on how students think and act" (Ambrose et al., 2010, p. 3).

The third is perhaps the most important part of this definition: that learning is a process in which students engage and it is because of a learner's experiences that the learning process can occur. In other words, learning is not done to a student—the student does the learning. This is a crucial understanding to have about the overall process of learning. It is an active, participatory progression of knowledge acquisition. It takes time, courage, and a certain degree of fortitude and tenacity. This is another reason that it takes courage to learn.

What the Science of Learning Tells Us

I am always ready to learn although I do not always like being taught.

—*Winston Churchill*

Churchill's quote helps to remind us to make the distinction between "teaching" and "learning." While intentional teaching (often in a formal classroom setting) often does lead to learning, there are many times in which learning happens without formal teaching. Why does this happen? Are there ways to engage with the learning process regardless of what is taught? Think back to a time when you were interested in learning about a new hobby. What did you do to learn? Did you read books about the hobby, or did you find someone who was doing the activity and ask them questions or watch what they did in order to learn? Chances are that if you were interested in learning about this new hobby, you found multiple ways to learn new information and skills. You may not even have thought about what you were doing as learning. And yet, you learned something and you were engaged in (and probably excited about) that process. Many researchers and educators have explored why and how learning can occur and what makes the learning process better or stronger. The characteristics of the learner, the structure of what is learned and how it is learned, and even a learner's interest in the subject all play a role in determining how much or how well learning will happen. There is much that the science of learning can tell us about how to engage with what we are learning in both formal and informal settings.

Students' Prior Knowledge Can Help or Hinder Learning

As we acquire more and more knowledge, it is possible that our memory can become somewhat cluttered. Although some people are very good at focusing their learning, it can be challenging, and the learning that we have already done can interfere with new learning experiences. What we have learned in the past may get in the way of trying to learn something new or that contradicts a previous learning. A simple example of this might be memorizing a new phone number. If you can easily recite your old number yet have difficulties with the new number (especially if the phone numbers begin in a similar way), you are experiencing this interference from your prior learning. This can often happen when learning a new language—if you took a French class a while ago and are now trying to learn German, you might accidentally use French vocabulary in your German class because the prior knowledge that you had can interfere with the learning of new knowledge.

This can also impact learning on multiple levels. Schneps et al. (1994) produced a video that explored this topic, called "A Private Universe." In this fascinating documentary, very bright students become confused when new learning contradicts what they have already learned. In this case, the documentary looks at a ninth-grade student who is learning about the orbits of the planets around the sun. She can answer basic exam questions correctly, but when she is pressed to explain why it is colder in the winter and warmer in the summer, it becomes clear that what she learned about the orbit of the earth is being confused by her prior understanding of the distance of an object to a heat source. She answers that it is warmer in the summer because the earth is closer to the sun, and it becomes colder as the earth moves farther away. While this is clearly wrong, she cannot seem to recognize that her prior learning is wrong. This is something that happens to all of us. It is important to try to recognize this as we learn new information.

How Students Organize Knowledge Influences How They Learn and Apply What They Know

As we learn new information, we tend to make connections between what we are learning. We innately work to organize information; this helps with learning, recall, and memory. "When those connections form knowledge structures that are accurately and meaningfully organized, students are better able to retrieve and apply their knowledge effectively and efficiently" (Ambrose et al., 2010, pp. 4–5). Sometimes we learn facts that we have not yet related to other pieces of information. We may memorize something by rote rather than really understanding this. In this case, the organizational structures do not help us to learn.

Often people will think that they must memorize content to show that they have learned (and, sadly, our institutions of higher education can reinforce this). We memorize facts so that we can respond on an exam; we learn a list of terms in a formula and recite them by heart. While this content can have importance, alone it typically is not enough to demonstrate learning. Solid learning often happens because separate skills, tasks, and information become integrated. How do we make these meaningful connections? According to Lawrence Lowery (1998), these meaningful connections occur when we become engaged with and interested in something: "Connections are created when an individual becomes curious about something and is free to explore that curiosity" (p. 6). As such, learning and organizing what we learn happens because we are interested in it and we want to understand it more.

Students' Motivation Determines, Directs, and Sustains What They Do to Learn

We learn best what we want to learn. If a student feels that what they are learning has a positive value, then they are much more likely to find it interesting and remember it better. We can all recall times in which we were excited about an event, a class, or a trip. We probably remember more about them because we were motivated to learn something, and this makes the learning process much more natural. Imagine a teacher and her student walking briskly on a gorgeous autumn day, moving from one building to another. The student has taken two of this woman's classes, and they have come to enjoy one another's company, with each often mildly challenging the other. The teacher looks up at the blue sky . . .

Teacher: Hey, that is one huge squirrel's nest in that tree over there.

Student: You're shittin' me.

Teacher: No, I'm not kidding you—seriously, it's one of the larger ones I've seen. Don't you think?

Student: No, I mean, that's not really a squirrel's nest.

Teacher,   Of course, it is. Wait, what did you think it was?
puzzled:

At that moment, a squirrel neatly dashes up the trunk, across the branches and into the nest. The student stops in his tracks, looks incredulous, and then roars with laughter.

Teacher: What is this all about?

Student: I did an honors project, a 60-page paper on squirrel hibernation. But I realize now that I've never known what their nests look like.

What an amazing opportunity to learn: This student wrote a huge paper focusing on squirrels and yet had never actually seen a squirrel in its natural habitat. The student had a chance to challenge misleading information in the company of a caring educator who viewed this moment as a learning opportunity and not a moment to prove their superior knowledge or embarrass the student.

Educating is hard—and learning is hard, too. We can use some of the science of learning to better understand the art of teaching, and when we put this together with the individual differences that we each hold we can develop pathways to learning that can change the world. Learning does not happen by chance; learning is a process, and each of us has individual characteristics and interests that often guide us down different paths. When we are pushed to learn something in which we are not very interested or do not have sufficient foundational knowledge to fully understand, we are frustrated and sometimes avoid trying to learn it. If you have ever tried to force yourself to learn something that was confusing or seemingly boring, you know that forcing learning is often met with disappointment and sometimes even anger. But by understanding the science of learning, you can create better learning environments for yourself and for other learners, too.

Finding ways to intentionally plan for engagement with what is learned and ways to become interested in the new area are essential. Why is it that some people are drawn to the field of mathematics and others avoid it whenever possible? If you talk to a mathematician, you will probably find that they look at mathematics very differently from the ways that others look at it. Albert Einstein once said that "Pure mathematics is, in its way, the poetry of logical ideas." And another mathematician, Shakuntala Devi (n.d.), said that "Without mathematics, there's nothing you can do. Everything around you is mathematics. Everything around you is numbers" (para. 1). Thinking about it this way, mathematics is beautiful and almost romantic, which is not the way in which some others might describe it! But the differences within the learner and the ways in which that learner has learned or "been taught" in the past helps to explain why some learn certain concepts (like mathematics) differently than others. We can all learn mathematics, or many languages, or how to play an instrument, but *what* we learn, *how* we learn it, and *why* we learn what we do is often impacted by *who* we are and our own motivations and interests. And, while the field of education knows a great deal about the science of learning, we also know that there are an almost infinite number of variables that impact the overall process.

Why Is Learning so Important?

In the perennial dance between learning and teaching, facilitators of learning are often much more preoccupied with talking about teaching than focusing on learning. One might wonder whether our focus should be on teaching, since teachers are considered the primary drivers of how well students succeed, whether in the classroom, a weekend-long workshop for adult learners, or summer camp. When we consider the role of education in the perpetuation or diminishment of inequities in schools, we often believe it is the teacher and the teaching that make the difference. And educators do, of course, make a vast difference in ways they can be inspiring or deflating. Paulo Freire (1968/2013), in his landmark text, *Pedagogy of the Oppressed*, critiqued the dominant metaphor of schooling as the *banking model* of education. In the banking model, instead of relating and communicating, the teacher lectures as students passively receive, memorize, repeat.

Despite the most intentional desire to do otherwise, there are times when most educators feel as if they have been prepared to deposit packets of knowledge into the heads of their learners. One of our conversation partners, when reflecting on their teaching, offered this analysis of the struggle when it comes to creating space for learning:

> I have a strong tendency to over-plan and lecture until everyone in attendance is mentally a thousand miles away. It would be one thing if these were workshops I did not care about, but because I am so excited about what I am talking about I often find myself on tangents. . . . A lecture may hold a lot of information, but it usually lacks that power to inspire passionate interest. I want to share the love I hold for what I am teaching and not just the facts.

Even the most well-meaning educator can fall prey to the same tendency as this workshop facilitator. It may not be surprising, given its predominance in educational settings: Many educators were brought up in the Western intellectual tradition that values rules, emotional distance, perceived objectivity, and teacher expertise. And while these are certainly part of the teaching and learning experience, these mostly focus on the teaching aspect of this experience and not on the learning.

Power has typically resided with the teacher. Some of this power may be in place because the teacher usually has the power of evaluating student work and, often, in assigning grades. In formal educational settings, this power structure is real and can provide incentives for doing the work of learning. But what if power is shared between the one doing the teaching and the one doing the learning? How might that change the relationship? Consider what would happen if there were a transformation into a more equitable distribution of power between educator and learner. This might begin by re-forming the actions of the teacher who is charged with educating. Educators are often well prepared to be experts in their field, though not always to be vulnerable, invite wonder, or allow spaces for silence. As a result, many young people lose their excitement for learning, are distanced from the subject matter, and do not feel connected to its relevance in their lives.

Teaching and Learning and Curriculum Development

There are a plethora of books and journal articles that focus on effective instruction; visit most colleges and universities and you will find entire centers of teaching excellence and innovation. The conversation in the field of education is dominated, even constricted, by questions related to teaching. This is the case even when the learner is the focus of the conversation. For example, *culturally relevant pedagogy* focuses on the assets and strengths a student brings to the classroom, especially strengths related to culture and family (Ladson-Billings, 2014). Yet it is the educators who are usually asked to both notice these strengths and to create spaces for this knowledge to inform the instructional ethos of the learning space.

Several educational researchers have focused on the ways in which schools perpetuate, often unconsciously, the formation and longevity of social class in schools and, from there, into society. They have named this process of power and status differentiation "the great cycle of social sorting" (Tharp et al., 2000, p. 57). The power structure of schools with respect to race, class, sexuality, and gender is a major determinant of educational experience and influences nearly all aspects of life. For educators concerned with power and the role/responsibility of schools to disrupt these patterns there are many sources and solutions to pursue. Tharp et al. (2000) argued that the best lever of change is the educator and the ways in which they monitor and manage the movement of students between groups during classroom activities. The key, they noted, is teaching that disrupts the status quo of powered relationships.

The field of education organizes the research and practical conversational space around the two dimensions of curriculum and instruction. This is helpful in terms of focusing research around either the materials of instruction, broadly defined, or the ways in which teaching moves in a learning space. Yet, although learning is the glue holding curriculum and instruction together, little attention is truly paid to what learning means for learners. At best, questions and dialogue around learning are focused on narrowly defined performance indicators, frequently established through accountability measures or performance tasks. Much has been written and researched about these elements of formal and informal instructional spaces. In many ways, this has improved the likelihood that forms of learning will occur. Form and structure as outer dimensions of education are valuable and can improve the quality of the learning space. But we believe that there is more to consider when looking to improve learning. The inner dimensions, especially the *who* of learning, is less well developed and understood.

How learners respond to the instructional moves of an educator can be, and often are, quite different from learner to learner. Uhrmacher et al. (2017) divided the stages of instruction into an "instructional arc." There are three stages in the arc: intended, delivered, and received curriculum. The *intended curriculum* equates to the traditional lesson plans in teaching: the content, learning goals, and activities that are often crafted into a detailed instructional strategy with specific time sequences, instructional moves, and guiding questions. This is one of the first sets of skills that every teacher candidate learns in a teacher education program.

The *delivered curriculum* is the instruction that transpires in the classroom, ideally guided by the lesson plan, but sometimes not. It is the set of instructional moves and choices a teacher makes and can be witnessed by an outside observer. There are many factors, from the personal to the societal, that can impact the ways that curricula are delivered to learners; to reduce the variables teaching is often divided into discrete pieces and competencies that can be mapped to performance indicators. These quantified elements of teaching have spawned a robust industry that focuses on professional development and evaluation tools to ensure an efficient fit between the intended and delivered curricula.

The first two stages of the curricular arc are primarily concerned with the teacher and their actions. The third area of focus is the *received curriculum*, which focuses on *what* learners leave the instructional space knowing and being able to apply in the world. Through tests and other metrics of student learning, educators can assess the amount of learning for each student. And, given these data, they can adjust to better match the intended and delivered curriculum to the desired stated learning outcomes in the received curriculum.

In addition to the known, there also exists an unknown or "hidden" curriculum that is often operating in parallel to the formal received curriculum. The hidden curriculum does not appear on a lesson plan and is often unintended, but its impact on learners can be as prominent as the received curriculum. Prominent forms of the hidden curriculum include the ways that students learn to interact with their peers and what types of behavior are acceptable or not acceptable. Other researched forms of the hidden curriculum include ways in which gender, social class, race, and intellectual ranking influence the learning experience (Margolis, 2001).

One glaring example of the hidden curriculum that disrupts the full potential of learning is the ideology of whiteness. It can and often does infuse the classroom and instructional moves in subtle and overt ways that send messages to all learners that white ways of being are the standard by which success is measured. Educators convey an array of instructional cues that signal right and wrong ways of being in the classroom, often based on their personal opinions, learning preferences, or socialization. Because of the pervasive nature of whiteness, even a teacher dedicated to disrupting power and privilege in the class can inadvertently empower white students and disempower students of color. A teacher may unconsciously signal a preference for one student over another. They may call on that student more often, offer more support, or generally exude a greater sense of appreciation for their work.

As the scholarly examination of curriculum and instruction has increased, other troubling trends, in addition to the hidden curriculum, have surfaced. History shows that in the 1920s there was a strong and persistent movement in education toward measurement, especially related to student academic performance and behavior. This is widely accepted as the beginning of the standards movement in K–12 schools and marks the era of the "scientific approach" to curriculum design, implementation, and assessment. The science of learning fostered the formation and development of intelligence tests, which promised an objective and efficient way of sorting students into academic and nonacademic tracks. In the early 1970s the focus on efficiency shifted from student performance to "value-added" measures of teacher performance, a score indicating how much a teacher moved a student's learning along a yearly trajectory. A teacher with low value-added scores did not move a student very far, while a teacher with high value-added scores may have moved a student intellectually up several grades. The challenges associated with linking student performance to teacher performance have been legion.

From this brief segue into education we return to our main focus: learning. In this book, we advance the less told and investigated view that teaching and learning have always been twin sides of the same coin. For institutional efficiency, the ability to separate educators and learners is a convenient tool. It fosters the capacity to analyze different elements of instruction. But every educator needs a learner, and every learner needs a teacher—and the very best educators are themselves always learning. At the heart of every teacher is a learner who is constantly attuned to the educational arena at hand, reading the emotional and cognitive barometer, somatic cues, and interpersonal ripples and continually seeking feedback from students to adjust curriculum and instruction to maximize learning.

Everyone is involved in learning, and even educators are expected, through their ongoing reflective practice, to learn about their inner drivers and to improve their ability to reach their students. We can, therefore, think of learning as a more democratic process than teaching given that everyone learns, but not everyone teaches.

In this book, we intend to take the attention away from "teaching." We offer, through the voices of our learning conversation partners, a rich and varied description of learning, and we discover, highlight, and celebrate the courage involved in learning for students of all ages. Through stories and vignettes, we share how learning can be as difficult as it is exhilarating when it catapults us into unknown forests into which we would rather not stroll. As one learning conversation partner who spoke about the challenges of caring for an aging and ailing spouse shared, learning is sometimes painful:

> You want to know my story? Well, on any given day, my response would be different because it keeps changing. And in the end, it looks as if it's worse in some ways for me than for him. His Parkinson's is early onset; something you learn along the way is that everyone's response is completely different. I think of it as a constant drip of things happening. We know it will never get better. It goes slowly, but it will progress. It can make other illnesses seem easier. I thought if he had cancer, he could have an operation to get rid of it, but this one you can't get rid of and so it's a struggle to either ignore it or accept it. On any given day, it changes. I'm learning that I'm not patient or compassionate. I'm not able to deal with the real facts—until it's an emergency, then I'm right there. I am kinda mad: "Why did you need to get this?" You learn you are not as gracious as you thought. Taking a marriage vow of for better or worse seems easier when you're 21.

Learning that is solely defined by numeric indicators falls far short of the full intellectual richness, emotional complexity, and somatic wisdom involved in the tasks associated with learning. The format of this book is principally narrative because learning is such a dynamic process, involving experiences that are highly fluid and contextual.

Chapter-by-Chapter Overview

Each chapter opens with a poem or wisdom story that enlivens the chapter theme and concludes with an opportunity for reflection and practical experiences that invite the reader to weave their learning journey with the narratives of our learning conversation partners. We hope you discover a deepened gratitude for, and understanding of, the power of learning, as well as why we need to elevate and celebrate its standing.

There are many sources that underscore and authenticate the narratives in this book. We draw on the learning stories of the three authors—our experiences as students and our reflections on learning what has informed how we teach. Chapter 2 is dedicated to our personal narratives of learning. As educators, we are still learning about ourselves as learners and, as such, we felt it was important to tell our personal stories, and to be transparent in the stances we take because of our experiences of learning, since learning always exists in a context that is both indicative of the current moment of learning as well as antecedent experiences that might have occurred minutes before or years in the past. We tell our stories before we highlight the stories of a wide variety of learners to bring depth to the what, how, why, and who of learning, to which you will be introduced in chapter 3.

Chapters 4, 5, 6 and 7 draw extensively from our conversations to provide depth to the four main frames of what, how, why, and who of learning. We feature adult learners across the human life span, representing different ages, social and economic levels, and approaches to learning. We have embroidered a tapestry for our readers into which threads of learning and teaching, story, narrative, and analysis serve as warp and weft.

Chapter 8 offers a way to continue these conversations about learning and to better cultivate deep listening. This chapter concludes with some organizational resources that may help lead you to foster conversations about learning in your own community.

Throughout *The Courage to Learn*, we strive to center learning. What is the content of learning? How is that content learned? Why is it necessary to learn that content? Who is the self that learns?

Opportunity for Reflection

As you engage in your exploration of learning in both structured and unstructured ways, we invite you to think about what has made your learning the most joyful and exciting. When were the times in which you felt so engaged you may not even have been conscious of learning? What made these experiences so wonderful? Please write a few of these experiences down and think about the level of structure that they had.

Also, consider the times in which you had experiences with learning that were more difficult, mind numbing, and perhaps even felt meaningless—were these more in the structured or unstructured environments? What about them do you think made you bored or frustrated? Contrast these recollections with the ones from the previous paragraph. Do you see any connections between your experiences and the type of learning that you did?

As you reflect on these memories, you may find that your feelings have changed about these learning experiences. If so, why did they change? Did later experiences alter how you think about them? If so, how? What lingers in you from this time?

2

THE JOURNEY OF
THE LEARNER

*Everything that happens to you is your teacher . . . the secret is to learn to sit
at the feet of your own life and be taught by it.*

—*Polly Berends*

Each of us has our own stories of learning. The differences in our histories, our individual experiences, and our environments all impact the stories of learning that form us. Some of these stories include remembering people who were highly influential in ways that shape and define us; descriptions of the sometimes-mysterious manner in which we are drawn to certain subjects for which we have a passion; our various social identities and the intersectionalities among them; and how our heads, hands, and hearts act as distinctive guides, each taking us into novel terrain. Our stories also tap into our own intuition, the "extrarational" (Cranton, 2016), and can open up unexpected paths on our learning journey, such as the manner in which one day we decide to take a left turn and a whole new opportunity unfolds. The influences on our stories are quite literally countless, with possibilities as varied as the currents that flow through a river. Sometimes learning stories are joyful; other times they are painful. Rohr (2020) contended that the deepest life and personal learnings always require pain and productive suffering, which he contrasted with destructive suffering, which brings only pain. As a result of enjoyable learning, we may lean in for more. From painful experiences that deform our identity, we may construct barriers of which we may or may not always be aware. We may at times confront those obstacles with the help of a trusted guide. When we do, we often grow profoundly from the experience.

Educators, by the nature of the profession, are responsible for the learning of others. Although we spend our time reflecting on successful avenues to teaching or facilitating, the personal and professional path of educators might be best understood from the perspective of the learner's journey. This includes both the initial act of learning as well as making discoveries about how to lead in the presence of learners. Palmer (1998) noted that "We teach who we are," meaning that the inner landscape of an educator will always be projected out and onto the minds and hearts of learners. Uhrmacher (1997) referred to this aspect of teaching as the "shadow curriculum."

Whether we are aware of this or not, how educators teach has a tremendous impact on the kind of atmosphere they create in learning environments. A fearful educator may often foster an environment in which anxiety is palpable; an arrogant instructor may unintentionally set the stage among participants for condescension and egotism; and a hopeful teacher teaches the possibility of promise. Moroye (2009) called this relationship between the inner commitments and outer pedagogy the "complementary curriculum," meaning that the style of teaching, affect, and content selection can convey a general framework for learning in the classroom. This less-than-conscious framework is often perceived by learners and thus informs their approach to learning and understanding. The complementary curriculum can have equal or greater impact on learning than the stated outcomes of the academic discipline. For instance, Moroye showed how an educator committed to ecological values conveys that intent to students even when the subject matter does not inherently include ecology in the curriculum. The mindset that we bring with us as an educator clearly has an impact on how we approach any teaching situation—but it is not a mindset that is unchangeable. As educators, we can recognize what our story of learning is and how that story impacts what we bring to the classroom. By knowing what we hold in our story and thinking about how that affects the complementary curriculum, we can more explicitly think about our role as learner, teacher, and colleague. At the end of each chapter, as you have seen, there is the chance for you to reflect and think about what you have read. This invitation for reflection can help you to consider your journey of learning. It often takes courage to think about these stories, but by doing this you will better understand all that you bring to the teaching and learning experience.

In this chapter, each of us tells a story of becoming a learner, including early learning memories, impactful relationships with others, and ways in which emerging notions of learning informed our personal practices and commitments to learning. Wherever possible, we highlight linkages between our social, gender, and racial qualities and perceptions of learning. Our intent is not to offer an all-inclusive, linear story of the many impacts on each of our learning journeys (which would be quite dull!) but rather to allow for a fresh, spontaneous arising of key moments of influence and capture them in writing. In our sharing we hope to model the reflective exercises we offer at the end of each chapter in this book. We hope to show how important it is for educators and facilitators to pause, to take a reflective stance, to better understand and relate to learners. The stories we share also reflect our commitment to our own ongoing learning travels. Learning, we think, is at its best when it is fluid and generative.

Last, through our reflections we aim to offer an example of how our learning is inherently best told through narrative instead of examining data sets designed to measure an individual against normative standards. By telling our stories we hope to invite you to consider your own learning story, to provide an opportunity to deeply explore the bedrock (conscious and unconscious) for how you set up learning environments for others. As noted earlier in this text, we try, in the telling of our stories, to elevate our awareness of the normalizing voice of whiteness, power, and privilege by revealing, as much as possible, what we understand as the pairing of our social identity with notions of learning. This was not always an easy task and often involved embarrassment, vulnerability, and a willingness to expose racist tensions and orientations embedded in our white identity. We hope that our attempt at modeling the honest integration of perceptions of learning through critical self-storytelling will encourage you to write your own stories and make public, even if only personally, what is often private and obscured in the shadow of social identities, to see your learning journey with new eyes and to consider ways in which you might invite those learners in your care to understand learning as an individual and deeply personal experience. We offer our stories as examples of living and learning. In the subsequent chapters we offer the stories of our learning conversation partners as they often found ways to expand notions of learning beyond traditional measures of performance and standards.

Catherine's Journey

I grew up in a house that had a lot of books. We didn't have much else, but we had books everywhere. I vividly remember a long row of black encyclopedias that lined the bottom shelf in the living room. My mom had bought them at a garage sale somewhere, and it seemed that they were filled with the answers to everything. I was always questioning everything—and it is something that I still do. Why do the ants build their mounds in that way? How do whales swim so deep? Why do we drive on the right-hand side of the road in the United States? How were the stars mapped before cameras and telescopes were invented? When I'd ask these questions, I'd always be sent to the encyclopedia to find out the answers—and when there wasn't an answer, I would have to try to figure out an answer myself. For me, learning was always an investigation to find out more and discover the causes of things. Each new piece of information that I found always led me to more questions and more searching.

But when I started elementary school, I was disappointed by what the school thought learning was supposed to look like. We had to memorize facts without even understanding why that particular fact was important to know—or if it was even a "fact." In my third-grade math class, we focused on reviewing addition and subtraction because many of the students in the class needed that review before they could go on and learn multiplication and division. I was bored because I had learned addition and subtraction. But, nonetheless, we focused on addition and subtraction while all the other third-grade classes learned multiplication and division.

I didn't realize what I had *not* learned until I got into fourth grade. Suddenly, math was a mystery. This mystery continued into fifth grade because no one realized that I didn't know my multiplication tables. When we focused on fractions I was at a complete loss, because you can't understand a fraction if you don't understand the concept of division and multiplication. I began to do very poorly on tests because I was just randomly guessing. I remember sitting in class and thinking that everyone else was in on the "secret" and that I didn't know what this secret methodology was. It was as if they were all speaking a language that I didn't understand.

When my parents finally figured out why I was failing math, they worked to teach me the multiplication tables, and I began the horrible rote memorization of numbers in a table that made no sense to me. About a year after that, I finally figured out that multiplication was just a shortcut to addition. I could add quickly, and so I thought that I didn't need to memorize the tables—and so I never did. By that time, I was behind in math and knew that I didn't like it. No one likes to be seen as being stupid or bad at anything, so I avoided multiplication and everything associated with it. While I could memorize facts well, there wasn't the same level of excitement about *what* I could learn because I always needed to know *why* something was important before I wanted to invest time in learning it.

When I got to middle school, I found that there was always competition among those in my peer group about who was getting the best grade or the best score on an exam. I am pretty competitive, and so I learned to do well on exams and how to pass tests. The competition helped to keep me engaged in doing well, but the competition was rarely about *what* we were learning, only that we had received a high score. I still found that when I was really learning something, I would be able to ask questions and try things out, but much of this didn't happen in school subjects.

During my time in school there were a few exceptions to the need to memorize—I vividly remember growing a mealworm farm in one class in fifth grade and learning sign language in another class. But much of the "learning" that I was doing in school was to be able to answer questions on a test—and I was not engaged with learning because I saw memorization as a silly, worthless task whose only goal was to get a good grade. I was engaged with school because of the social aspects and the overall competition for getting good grades, but I didn't learn good study skills or even ways to test my own knowledge.

I did well enough in school because I could memorize quickly, and I did want to get the awards and attention that came with good grades— but I wasn't really learning what I wanted to learn, and I never really was challenged in school. Although I quickly figured out how to give the "right" answer, and would certainly do that, it wasn't really meaningful learning. When I was in high school, for example, we were studying poetry in my English class, and my friends and I quickly realized that every poem was probably about life, death, or love. While I recognize now that this isn't completely true, it was the "shortcut" that my friends and I figured out, and it resonated with our English teacher. So, my friends and I would each pick a "side" and argue (loudly) about that day's poem being about love, or death, or life. We didn't learn much—but our teacher thought that we were doing a wonderful job of analyzing and understanding what the poems meant. I got a good grade, and yet I didn't truly understand the beauty and depth of the poetry that we read.

Overall, school was reasonably fun, and I did have decent grades. But much of what I learned in school was how to be a successful student—not how to learn. I was rarely challenged by my teachers in class, and so I did what I needed to do to get what I wanted: good grades with little work. Looking back, I know how hard my teachers were working and that, because I was reasonably good at academic work, I was often not their focus. They needed to work with other students who needed additional attention and support to pass upcoming standardized tests. I liked school, but I didn't appreciate the importance of learning while I was in school. This may sound contradictory, yet for me school was a social system rather than a place to learn and grow. When I think back to my middle and high school memories, they are about events that happened with my friends in social situations, not about any excitement of learning.

Outside of the traditionally structured school system, however, I was learning a lot in many different and meaningful ways. I began to play the

French horn and was in the band and orchestra, where we had to think and learn and apply many different principles to what we were doing. There was a lot of practice required, and I made a lot of mistakes when things didn't sound the way that I wanted them to sound. I used trial and error to find out what didn't work and sometimes was able to find out what did work. I began to take horn lessons, and I gained insight into playing music and even more because of some wonderful horn teachers who would talk to me about music theory and how music could make a difference. Learning to play French horn was almost always very hands on and experiential; I discovered that this is the way I like to learn. I want to ask a question and then search for the answer—and then make sure that this answer is one that works by testing it out. I didn't get much of a chance to do this in my traditional school journey until I got to graduate school.

In graduate school, the focus from the curriculum and my professors was always on asking questions, applying theories, and questioning results. This was exciting learning, and I was able to better hone the research skills that I had gained as a child with our old encyclopedia set. Asking new questions and putting together information in novel ways was now fascinating; it led to increased discussions both in the classroom and outside of the classroom. I found that I learned best when I tried to "break" things to see why they worked the way that they did; testing failure and finding success was one of the best ways for me to learn.

I would always ask myself "What could go wrong?" and then try to find out what happened when it did. One of my graduate school mentors saw this and worked with me through a series of independent studies. He would give me a problem to solve and then leave me alone until I came up with a solution. Then, he would work to poke holes in my solution, which often sent me back to the drawing board. One time, he handed me a computer disk (back in the days when we actually used disks) with no instructions and told me to get this loaded onto his computer so that he could use the new software. This was when personal computers were relatively new, and I had to learn some basic programming skills and ways to extract data from the disk so that I could learn how to run the program. I wasn't a computer programming or information systems student; my work was in educational psychology, but because of his approach I was able to feel very comfortable with ambiguity and complex tasks.

I also became very comfortable with testing theories and finding out what didn't work. Knowing what didn't work often let me better understand what would work and *why* it would work. I looked for ways to test assumptions, and when things failed it was exciting since it opened up new ways of understanding the overall process. This led me to consider many different options for career choices, yet I knew that I was interested in why people acted the way they did and how our overall learning environment is structured. Because of the mentorship I received in graduate school and the implicit permission to find my own path in my own way, I continued to question why we did things in certain ways and to always look for new ways to do what needed to be done.

I am still very much like that (probably annoying) questioning child. I still want to know the *why* about everything. I hope to always be learning something new and appreciating the immenseness of what I do not know. I often walk into a library or a bookstore and look around and realize that I will probably never have time to read most of the books that are available and the learning that they contain. This is somewhat sad, but it also gives me something to look forward to doing every day. While this may seem like a depressing (and odd) thought, it is really an exciting one because there will always be something new and interesting to learn. That's one of the reasons that I went into education as my career choice—not only do I get to share my love of learning but that I get to always see new things and new ideas that allow me to keep asking questions.

Paul's Journey

Much like Moroye's (2009) description of being "ecologically minded," my earliest memories of learning, and therefore my teaching, are firmly grounded in the natural world. As a preschooler, my family regularly traveled to national parks in California. There are shoeboxes of vacation photos taken in Yosemite, Joshua Tree, and Kings Canyon National Parks. In the urban landscape was a park with a fire truck for climbing on and playing make-believe games. A powerful memory of that time is lying under the fire truck in the sand, smelling the shade and feeling the cool air. Nature and my emerging identity as a human being were fusing. I learned, I believe, long before my consciousness had the words to describe, that nature was a fundamental piece of the formation of my sense of self. For me, the *what* of learning at this stage meant being present to my surroundings, using all my senses to learn. There was no discernible *why* or measurable outcome; just being present to the more-than-human world was enough. To live was to learn.

There is little doubt that these early experiences of being one with nature have impacted my approach to the construction of learning experiences for students that verge on the spiritual and mystical. I strive to create a context where all the senses, emotions, and notions of selfhood can merge into a holistic learning space. What is less clear to me, as an educator who teaches social justice concepts and practices, is the interplay between my social positionality and the *who* of my ecological framing of self as learner. How much of my belief in the trustworthiness of nature as a place of knowing, that I overlap onto learning, is inherent to *who* I am, and how much is informed by the *how* of my upbringing in a white middle-class family? Unlike many families of color, we could travel to parks, forests, and natural areas without being made to feel unsafe, or like we didn't belong there, or questioning our welcome when interacting with other families. What this suggests is that the core elements of my selfhood and teaching are inseparable from my social class, racial identity, and the normalizing influences of whiteness, a shadow I continually trip over in my classroom when I forget that my story, my learning, is not always what my students have experienced.

In elementary school, we moved to Seattle, Washington. In the winter, my friends and I rode our toboggan down the hill behind the house and into the woodlot below. We learned that the more people you pile on the sled, the faster it went, which meant at times someone would fall off and perhaps get hurt. Once we went so fast, and so far, we reached the bottom of the hill only to realize that a barbed-wired fence separated the open slope from the trees. By lying flat, we slid under the fence and escaped injury. I learned that I like experiments, the *how* of learning, and that I wasn't afraid of pain and suffering as a form of embodied learning.

One other lesson, embarrassing to tell but necessary to share, stands out from my days in Washington state. I had a deepening relationship with nature but not yet a true recognition that the natural world was a teacher deserving respect and attentiveness. Nature was more instrumental, serving the *why* of my curiosity, than it was a living presence that I could form a reciprocal relationship with. There was a creek running through the woods, a place of verdant richness, mud, and frogs. I would "hunt" the frogs because they were hard to catch and because their shiny wet and hairless bodies were intriguing. At some point in my exploration of frog life I had the cruel notion that it would be interesting to see what would happen if I stunned the frogs to see how and if they would wake up. Most frogs survived this unnecessary and harsh treatment, but some didn't and died in my hands. I learned, at the expense of their right to live, that life was fragile and that frogs have value beyond their ability to entertain; I was bound to them by some mysterious energy that was related to *who* I was becoming.

Only later in life, when I studied philosophy and theology, did I begin to see the frog story through the different lenses of Western objectivism and spiritual relationalism. I learned to value agency and relationships as cornerstones to creating productive learning spaces for students. My early experiences with the pain and relational ethics as a learning tool turned out to be a good preparation for teaching about social justice and for attending to my shadows when it comes to understanding racism and white supremacy. Although I rarely like it, I value the times when I'm corrected by a student for my use of language or for not addressing racist statements quickly enough or with strong words and actions of resistance. The pain of my embarrassment and sense of betrayal of my stated commitments to equity is a good reminder to constantly question my male, white, and middle-class identity.

When I was in late elementary school, we moved to a Louisiana town on the shores of Lake Pontchartrain. The warm climate, outdoor culture, and my parent's willingness to let me roam (a freedom enhanced by my whiteness) was a perfect classroom for me. My relationship to nature, *who* I was becoming, moved toward understanding the value of being still and watching the natural world unfold in its time and pace. I learned that stillness can be more important than conversation when you really want to know someone or something. I became more and more comfortable with long periods of attentive watching; a natural form of wait time that I later employed in the classroom to invite, but not demand, student participation. There was a direct transfer of the skill of waiting for a bird to emerge from a thicket to waiting for a student's insight to emerge into the classroom.

Layered into my academic learning was a nascent awareness of power and privilege as a form of social norming in school. My fourth-grade white teacher taught me that culture is a powerful tool for norming behavior. Early in our teacher–student relationship I answered a "yes–no" question with an emphatic "Yes." I was factually right with my response, but according to her understanding of southern culture, I was wrong. She prompted me to answer again, which I did, with a slightly puzzled "Yes." She then clarified why was I wrong and schooled me in the proper answer: "Paul, the answer here is 'Yes Ma'am.'" The combination of personal shock, embarrassment, confusion, and the drive to please a teacher burned "Yes Ma'am" deeply into my psyche. Even now, as an adult, I regularly answer questions with "Yes Ma'am" and "No Sir." The *what* of culture combined with the *why* of norming to inform part of *who* I am today.

I value this experience because it provides a partial glimpse, as a white male, into the lived experience of individuals who experience the normalizing influences of schooling, not once, as I did, but on a daily basis. My brief moment of embarrassment, pain, and disorientation was socially fleeting because I could retreat to the safety of skin color and social class in other settings. But the learnings from that moment around power, privilege, and authority are lessons I look to disrupt in my classroom.

Beyond the walls of the classroom, another important learning was emerging. The lunch ladies, who were predominantly Black, taught me about love, hospitality, and marginalized centers of power. Regardless of how my classroom lessons (academic and social) were going, I could always count on a welcome smile, warm food, and hospitality as I pushed my tray along the aluminum bars of the lunch line. My favorite meal was red beans and rice with peach cobbler. The Black women behind the glass smiled, dipped their long-handled spoons into the steam trays, and gently placed the food onto my tray. If I asked, I could even get a little more cobbler.

In contrast to my white teacher, who created a dehumanizing space for learning, the Black lunch ladies offered a humanizing and safe space. At the time, I didn't see the institutional and racial power differential between teacher and lunch lady, but I did see and value their welcoming presence. I remember little of my academics where learning was circumscribed by white social norms of power. In contrast, I learned in the lunchroom that hospitality is a powerful force for fostering learning. I have a regular practice of making sure we have food to share during break time in my classes; the *why* of hospitality is a mirroring of what I experienced.

We left Louisiana when I was halfway through high school and moved to upstate New York. After graduating from high school, I attended college, where I studied natural history and ecology. It was during this time that I came to understand that the *how* of my learning is hands on, experiential, and heart centered, consistent with the ways I learned about nature and my relationship to the natural world. My grades exploded as I experienced the merging of content I was fascinated by (nature), faculty who were passionate about their subject matter, and a pedagogy that matched my learning style. I felt how joyful and engaging learning could be when my head, heart, and hands were in productive conversation with each other about emerging identity and sense of self.

I incorporate many of my *what, why,* and *who* K–12 learnings into my college teaching. I'm more interested in watching learning than manufacturing the environment in which learning happens, which includes my learning as a teacher but also, more important, sustaining humanized learning spaces for students. Hospitality is central to my teaching. It appears in the form of welcoming students as they enter class, showing interest in their lives, and eating together during the break. My most important learning is spiritual, the places where a relationship can form that is greater than self and self-knowing, the home of mystery.

Marcia's Journey

When I was little, my oldest brother Mike and I played school during the summer. We were geeky; he gave me math tests. I was small enough that as I sat at his desk my feet didn't reach the floor, and I kicked them back and forth as I worked through pages of simple math problems. As I grew older, Mike helped me with geometry, trigonometry, and calculus.

The first flickerings of my awareness of learning as something worthy of attention took place during high school calculus. My teacher's father had died, and so Mr. Briskey was leaving town for the week; he reassured us that we would be in good hands with a great substitute. The next day, I was surprised when my brother walked through the door. Mike would one day become a math professor; his teaching practice had begun. My other brother Greg went in a different direction altogether, as an auto mechanic, tapping into the experiential wisdom that connected his mind with his hands.

I no longer remember what we were wrestling with in calculus that day, only that most of the class was having a tough time. Mike asked us questions to get some clarity, then went to the chalkboard. "What if we look at it this way?" He demonstrated some things we'd never been taught. I vividly recall looking around the classroom and watching the lightbulbs go off over a few students' heads. Their faces shifted with pleasure. They understood!

The next day, half the class was still confused. My brother paused and wondered, "What if we present it this way?" Again, he offered a unique way in; at some point, I seem to recall his putting a chair on the table to demonstrate something. And the response was the same, a handful of students lighting up as they "got it."

A third day arrived, with a few of us remaining in the dark. My brother offered a final alternative to solving the problem and the rest of us were finally on board. I sat there with a dawning realization. We can learn math in different ways!

A little more than a year later, I found myself in a college that I had chosen because it offered the biggest financial package and, as such, was the only one that I could afford. It was a small private women's school in a city, and as someone whose early childhood was spent ramming around fields, farms, and creeks with brothers and a plethora of boy cousins, I was a fish out of water. One bitter cold February afternoon, I decided to take a long walk to figure things out. As I stepped inside a plant shop, the steamy air and smell of green filled my senses. I looked around and thought, "Yes," and went back to talk with my advisor about where to study horticulture in a setting much more suited to my grounded-in-the-natural-world sensibility. I have never looked back.

My journey has taken many different twists and turns since these three early vignettes, yet there are some key themes hidden here that speak powerfully to my path as a learner. I think of my oldest brother as a consummate teacher, and I am a perennial learner and educator-as-facilitator. Some of my best insights have come through my interior, not through something I was taught formally. Though two of these recollections involve math, I have been more interested in the arts and life sciences. I managed to get all the way through graduate school without taking a test, and I have never given so much as a quiz in my long career as an educator. My relatively small classes require significant project work, reflective and creative writing, presentations, and other methods of assessment that, while more time-consuming to review, seem more multidimensional and interesting to review (and, I hope, to create as well).

With respect to the *what* of my learning—that is, my disciplinary focus—as much as horticulture matters, reflection, integration with other subjects, and tapping our own inner wisdom lies equally at the center of every course experience that I offer. My courses weave the arts with horticulture, plants with human well-being, gardening with social justice, and community development with food systems, and throughout all of them are questions that take students into the heart of who they are. I am both a teacher in a classroom and an outreach educator; my Cooperative Extension and outreach activities predate the formal classroom by 15 years and, as such, have deeply formed my relationship to participants' learning.

Learning *must* be meaningful to make sense to me. In terms of the *how* of learning, as an experiential learner, I appreciate alternative ways of knowing, and I need to try something out, I hope with a compassionate guide alongside me (Catherine's earlier story about figuring out how to access the computer disk with no instructions would have daunted me!). Long presentations and dense instructions make it hard to focus, and a sure way to kill my love of learning is to tell me that I "should" do something.

I try to teach the way I prefer to learn, as a guide on the side, not a sage on the stage. I do not "lecture" much, though I might offer some imagery to spark new ideas or ground a class in a 10- or 15-minute presentation to make sure we are all on the same page. I favor longer, 3-hour class times over shorter 50-minute periods to give us the chance to reflect, interact, plan, problem solve, discuss, and, depending on the class, to garden, engage in art making, or talk with community members.

Creativity and collaboration are more important to me than being perceived as an expert. My favorite class that I have ever taught was a course in which I was so excited about the topic—healing plants and the people who use them—that it was not until I had gotten funding and begun to create the syllabus that I realized just how little I knew about the subject, at least from an academic standpoint. I invited three graduate students in anthropology, plant biology, and horticultural science to be content experts. My role shifted from teacher to lead conductor, managing a complex symphony of learning that involved an exploration of plant medicine, tender reflection on our own healing, and international travel to work with colleagues in southern Belize, where we collaborated with six shamans who had reached out through our program partner to seek a particular partnership with our students.

If I am willing to risk not knowing, when I reflect on *who is the self that learns*, I am also increasingly comfortable with being a vulnerable learner. At the end of a recent workshop, one of my colleagues said that he values my fallibility. I was surprised and relieved, since in the past I have been more of an earnest achiever with a protective coating than I would have wanted to admit (and, frankly, could not even see). My most courageous learning has involved shadow dancing with my ego identity, turning a compassionate gaze to my shortcomings and the hidden fears that serve as powerful drivers, such as the not-enough-ness that I didn't know lurked constantly just below the surface. I needed guidance for this exploration and found it in the Enneagram, a system of personality exploration that describes patterns in how someone interprets the world and manages emotions, inviting one into the mysteries of one's true identity. It initiated a process of inquiry that led to a more profound truth about myself and my place in the world, and as such, has been a learning tool that has provided both the language and practical tools for peeling away some armor and poking into the depths. Nowhere is that more vivid than in my family life, in which a deep dive into some formerly invisible patterns (invisible to me, not others!) revealed certain ways in which I unknowingly repeated unhealthy generational behaviors—a voyage that has been uncomfortable at best, scary at times, and a liberating relief all at once.

My courage to learn has also arrived in the form of self-examination with respect to unconscious bias; the intersections of my social identities; and stepping up and into action around race, equity, and inclusion in the workplace and in my village community. For a long time, I shied away from talking about racism. I struggled with the language, too; since I grew up in a working-class family with a history of poverty among our ancestors, I flinched initially when hearing about "privilege," since that was not a term I would ascribe to me, someone who put myself through college, and so on, and so forth. With time, it was evident that I had a lot to learn.

As I began to try to make sense of what I was discovering and experiencing, I experienced shaming by well-intentioned white-identified colleagues. Several years ago, I attended a powerful Circle of Trust retreat on healing the wounds of racism. In this trustworthy space I was better equipped to move past critical analysis and make the long journey from head to heart, peeling back old layers to probe my experience of whiteness and its impact on pretty much everything. Participation in Circles of Trust encouraged me to break the silence, initiate conversations, risk making some mistakes to fumble a bit and engage in an ongoing exploration of the influences of our racialized society, eventually bringing this dialogue into the heart of my classes.

As I reflect on *why* I love learning, I realize that all true learning is deeply personal and intimate and culminates in these kinds of powerful understandings. I place such a high value on personal growth that it surely makes some students uncomfortable; some seem to be uneasy as they figure out that my classes might be different from other horticulture courses, especially when they find themselves deeper in reflection than they might have expected. Admittedly, when students discover during the first day of class that there is no way they can be invisible, a few tend to drop. I'm OK with both their discomfort and with their making this choice.

Last, reflective practice is bedrock to my learning journey. Reflection is integrated into all my course experiences—indeed, into my daily life—and it is vital to my well-being. There is a part of me that constantly searches for ways to integrate self with the contemplative wisdom traditions of the world, the ongoing examination of meaning and purpose. As I look toward retirement from my current position at the university, I am curious as to where this part of my calling is going to take me.

Learning as Intricate Interplay

Catherine is an experiential learner who likes to investigate, ask the bigger questions, and seek insights. Her commitment to inquiry has led her to a passion for educational psychology and a penetrating desire to understand how people learn. Along those travels, she has become more comfortable with making and learning from mistakes. The woods, creeks, and fields in which Paul grew up embedded in him a deep nature ethos; layered onto and into this bedrock is the way in which he has learned about power and privilege. He learned important lessons of hospitality and kindness, and it has become important to him to meet his students from a path with heart. Marcia began her learning with people she cared about; she also grew to trust her intuition and imagination as important teachers. Whether she is exploring topics as varied as art, plants and gardens, or social justice, she names creativity, inner work, and collaboration as vital to her learning experiences.

For each of us, the *how* and *why* of our work is as critical as the content of our learning and teaching. *Who* we are as learners has profound impacts on how we live, lead, and make new discoveries and insights—as well as how we relate to the learners to whom we have responsibility. Our *who, how,* and *why* are more important, in many ways, than the *what* of the disciplines with which we engage.

Each of us is also white identified, heterosexual, able, and engaged as a professional in higher education, the intersections of which deeply influence our learning stories, unconsciously and consciously. In her essay, "The Complexity of Identity: 'Who Am I?'" Beverly Daniel Tatum (2000) offered questions that begin to explore how we experience our identity and form a deep, core sense of self:

> Who am I? The answer depends in large part on who the world around me says I am. Who do my parents say I am? Who do my peers say I am? What message is reflected back to me in the faces and voices of my teachers, my neighbors, store clerks? What do I learn from the media about myself? How am I represented in the cultural images around me? Or am I missing from the picture altogether? (p. 9)

This amazingly intricate interplay of what we receive from our external environments, those pivotal learning events of our lives, and our internal processes of reflection all offer tremendous influences to what we perceive to be "us" as learners and who we are. Whether or not we are aware of it, they are drivers that have a huge impact on the complexities of our learning journeys. In the opportunity for reflection that follows, as we invite you into your own story of learning, we encourage you to linger here awhile as you explore your passions, interests, social identities, and the diverse influences on you as a learner as a part of your reflection.

As authors, we have nodded to the content of our learning, how we have learned, what has motivated our learning, and how it has shaped us into who we are today. In our next chapter, we center the foundation for the *what, how, why,* and *who* of learning that lies at the heart of this book.

Opportunity for Reflection

To reflect on your own learning journey, you might set aside a full half hour or 45 minutes for this exploration.

We invite you to take some time to sit with your life. You might close your eyes and allow people, insights, events, passions, discoveries—anything that has been critical to your learning journey—to come to mind. What are the meaningful choices, people, events, and life experiences that have led you to where you are now, to what you are doing today? Please make a few notes.

What are your various identities? As you reflect on your various identities, you might consider including race and/or ethnicity, gender, religion, sexual orientation, socioeconomic status, age, physical or mental ability, or any other social/group identity that is important to you. Consider, too, which identities fall into dominant culture (e.g., white, male, educated, heterosexual) or excluded cultures (People of Color; female, nonbinary; educated by life; gay, lesbian, bisexual, questioning). How have your identities shaped you? What experiences come to mind that were powerful, memorable moments in the development of your social identities? What role do you think these identities contributed to your socialization in the work in which you are engaged today? There are many outstanding resources available for identity exploration. An exercise called "Identity Pie" can provide a graphic depiction of this part of your story, through creating a pie chart that illustrates the roles and social identities about which you are most aware, which can be particularly helpful to consider in your role in teaching or facilitating groups. However, a word of caution is helpful here. Often, when identity is taught or when privilege and social standings are discussed, we might portray it as puzzle pieces or parts of a pie. Identity is more complex, and the theory of intersectionality is not truly additive but maintains that each intersectional identity has its own unique position, privileges, challenges, and experience. This exploration will likely take significant time—indeed, the rest of your life. If it is your first foray into identity, we encourage you to consider this as an ongoing discovery.

As you continue to reflect on your learning experiences, you might want to consider what you stand for. What is the foundation that supports your day-to-day life? What are you passionate about? How has this driven the learning you have pursued in your life?

After you have reflected for a time, select a few vignettes of your learning that seem significant, and jot them down. This does not need to be linear, as with a timeline—this is more of a collection of significant people, events, discoveries, passions, and identities that are linked to stories. If you are inclined to work with images instead of words, please do so. When you have a handful of items, you might want to write down a few sentences about each one.

Now, consider a wider perspective and notice if there are any themes or "through lines" running among them. They might be gifts or skills, how events and changes have occurred, core values, people you have been drawn to as mentors, how your various identities have influenced your journey, or other connecting lines of congruence.

As you consider what you have written or drawn, what have you discovered or learned about your learning journey—how you got here—what has been important to you through the lens of learning? How, or in what ways, do you appreciate learning? Why do certain things matter to you?

If you are an educator or facilitator, what aspects of your learning story are apparent to others? What remains hidden? Why might this be?

How might you respond to the questions "Who is the self that learns? Who are you as a learner?"

3

AN INTRODUCTION TO THE *WHAT, HOW, WHY,* AND *WHO* OF LEARNING

*Learning is not attained by chance, it must be sought for with
ardor and attended to with diligence.*

—*Abigail Adams*

Thomas Merton (n.d.) is known for his observation that "The solution to the problem of life is life itself. Life is not attained by reason and analysis, but first of all by living" (para. 1). For Merton, one route to deeper levels of self-discovery is to live life. In the crucible of pain, joy, and decision-making that constitute life, we begin to know our inner self and the gifts and dispositions that make us unique. Instead of running away from the uncertainties of life, Merton suggested plunging in and living soulfully. Merton's advice is good guidance for learning. The invitation to all learners is to live the fullness of learning, to resist the temptation of defaulting solely to external strategies of effective learning defined by educators.

Throughout this text, we place an emphasis on the fullness of learning as a complex creature, which is why we employ nonlinear tools (poetry), analytic tools (the literature on learning), and personal narrative tools (learning stories) to address why learning is inherently courageous. As Adams's quote tells us, it does not happen by chance, and it must be attended to firmly and passionately.

Part of this passionate approach to learning involves stretching it for all its richness—which includes more than the content of learning or how we go about it. Here we introduce the four themes of learning, *what, how, why,* and *who,* that will provide the foundation for the remaining chapters.

The *What* of Learning

> I have learned that no matter how strongly you disagree with someone, you still need to see and understand their truth. Especially at a political time like this, we need to understand where our opponents (not enemies) are coming from. This class taught me to try and understand what life experiences may have shaped someone's perspective, especially if it's different than your own. Fundamentally, no truth is more accurate or "true" unless we collectively say that it is, so it's imperative that we keep conversations going with those with whom we disagree. . . . To that end, I learned you can't just throw facts at people, expecting them to listen and change their beliefs without first understanding why they hold those beliefs.

Indeed, throwing facts at people can diminish both their learning and their desire to learn. And yet, we often focus on the outermost layer of learning, which is often conceived in a technical frame. Most learners were students in K–12 education at some point in their learning journey. As such, they are often well trained in the art of "doing school." Students learn the tricks and skills of mastering the content and meeting the teachers' expectations for demonstrating that learning occurred—oftentimes, this involved learning the particulars of information. This is a valuable skill and fits with Rumi's (2004) first form of intelligence, which is associated with memorization and mastery of concepts and facts. In one class a student is a model learner, actively engaged in learning. When the bell rings and the student moves to a new class they may be passive and resistant; living and learning are intimately negotiated as learners encounter pleasure, confusion, or dissonance with the subject matter and the educators who offer it. Learners in formalized learning spaces can become adept at "reading" the educator to the degree that the student's personality can change from classroom to classroom, the reasons for which can range from pleasing the teacher to survival. Code switching, for example, is a now-familiar term that originated in linguistics, referring to the practice of alternating or "switching" between two or more languages or varieties of language in conversation. Currently, the term is often used with regard to the practice that people in marginalized identities employ when they believe they need to conform, such as a student who engages in African American vernacular English at home and community spaces, who may learn to believe that they must speak differently in the company of white-identified people in places such as at school.

As valuable as the technical elements of learning are, there is another aspect of equal importance. The limitations of technique become transparent when the lived experience of the learner meets the unexpected and unpredictable. It takes courage to accept the limitations of technique and to follow the rivulets of body- and heart-knowing into a paradoxical space of certainty/uncertainty. The *what* of learning also centers on the second form of intelligence that Rumi identified in relation to the flow of knowing. This inner form of learning is more mysterious and harder to define than the external and technical version of *what*, a complexity we explore in greater detail later in this book. Here we will simply state that it is at the point of limitation of the external that the internal learning becomes more robust and definitive. This is the less-told story of learning not often featured in the literature of learner and educator interactions. Learning, in this expanded sense, requires the clarification of old, often unconscious frameworks of meaning and establishing new, more holistic patterns of meaning (Cranton, 2016).

As Rumi described, the heart and our emotions create a form of intelligence capable of guiding behavior. To access that knowledge requires a quieting, a settling of the soul. As Palmer (2017) noted, the educator's heart is shy and easily scared into the wilderness. This could also be said about the learner's heart. To achieve this state of quiet openness takes practice, intention, and trust, and it can be achieved even in the midst of a mind-maddening scramble for solutions. It can also require some element of vulnerability and suffering as the old drops away and is replaced by more holistic understandings of the self as a learner.

Expanding From *What* to *How*, *Why*, and *Who*

An interesting part of my aging process is thinking of all the surprising twists and turns along the way. I know this may seem mundane, but I was just thinking yesterday about learning to type on a typewriter. I was a first-generation college student, although we didn't call it that then, and honestly, in high school, I didn't give college much thought. My junior year my close friend talked me into taking personal typing, matter-of-factly telling me that I'd need it for all those college papers. I didn't even know what she was talking about, but I went along for the ride, since she was taking it and I wanted to be in a class with her. I learned the touch-typing techniques and it was a pleasure to type like the wind without looking at the keyboard. She was right—it made writing college papers a breeze. It would be years before I used a computer, and I couldn't have imagined then the ways I'd use it later on. It's like an extension of me now—as a writer, although I love the feeling of having paper and pen in my hand, when I'm working, my hands are moving so quickly that they can almost keep up with the flow of my thoughts. What an incredible skill—one that I take for granted unless I pause to think about it.

This scenario might be familiar to some older adults. At first blush, it is a straightforward story about learning to type; that is, the learning content is typing or keyboarding. However, unpacking this brief vignette offers some interesting layers. This learning conversation partner learned a particular method in learning *how* to type by using touch-typing, allowing her to take her eyes away from the keyboard, increasing her speed. Her motivation, or *why*, morphed from taking the class to be with her friend, to the recognition of a useful college skill, and then, later, to how necessary it has become to her as a writer, indeed, an extension of her. It is the latter, most interestingly, that is intriguing, the way in which it became a part of *who* she is—a writer who can express herself with an immediacy because of the way in which her body and mind are in sync.

A Composite of Learners

To expand on *what*, *how*, *why*, and *who*, we reflected on students we have known, some very well, many over long periods; we have created collective composites, vignettes of their learning here, weaving the stories of a number of learners into some vivid characters who, although fictitious, are still very much true. As such, the elements of each of these vignettes are particular to several learners, integrated into one voice.

Ava provides a concrete description of the powerful hold the *what* of learning can have on a student. Ava is taking a class on nutrition and begins by describing her frustration with the current trajectory of the course. In her opinion, it is moving away from Rumi's first form of intelligence, the technical acquisition of knowledge, and into his second form of knowing, which involves the social emotional aspects of learning. For Ava, the *what* of learning is shifting from abstract forms of knowing to concrete inter-personal framing that leaves her feeling uncomfortable and frustrated. She took this class because of its emphasis on global issues in nutrition. She hoped to master the content of global nutrition. As the course conversation begins to shift to cultural competency and social emotional learnings in preparation to better understand the people with whom they will engage abroad, the more uncomfortable she begins to feel, privately expressing to the teaching assistant, "Is this a conversation, are we supposed to talk about our feelings? Someone is talking about cultural humility and I just want to gag." For Ava, the *what* of learning is a noun and thus requires the external acquisition of knowledge.

The *what* of learning is rarely static, even in formalized spaces. For Ava, learning becomes a verb when a classmate, Tristan, begins to speak. He had previously defended Ava when another student was criticizing her for not performing well on a standardized test. Because of his kindness, she wants to listen to his views. She suppresses her usual eye-rolling as Tristan describes the activity he is about to lead, which will put classmates into situations designed to enhance awareness of their underlying perspectives. He begins with a story of growing up:

> I grew up in a small city in Michigan before moving here. I experienced some lifelong pain around the simple question of "So, where are you from?" Although I live in the Wolverine State, I knew by fifth grade that people were not talking about East Lansing! "Where are you from?" invariably leads to: "No, where are you really from?" My grandfather is from China and his dad is from Thailand, so people make all sorts of assumptions about me based on my appearance. If it happened once, it might not be a big deal. But it happens every day. I get tired of it. It happens year after year, and I start feeling defeated.

Ava has been listening intently to Tristan's testimony. As his story unfolds, she finds herself sitting more and more upright; learning is becoming an embodied experience. She is flooded with recollections of the things she has said—those small assumptions she has made about people, the slights and insensitivities. She remembers having a moment, "a vivid, intense realization about the nature of reality, in this case, that it isn't what I thought it was." As she later reflects in her reflective writing assignment on what happened in the moment Tristan began to speak, she writes:

> I thought I was taking a course in nutrition. I know I still am. But I realize now that this is going to be a different journey, not one I planned on. I guess I'd better get used to being uncomfortable.

To accept this transformation of learning from noun to verb, from passive to active participation in knowing, is an act of courage. It requires a reconfiguration of living and learning that can lead the learning into unexpected terrain (Cranton, 2016).

The *How* of Learning

The interconnected nature of learning is foundational to an understanding of the *how* of learning. Although for analytical purposes we explore learning through the four lenses of *what*, *how*, *why*, and *who*, we also recognize that all the elements are connected and integrated. The *what* of Ava's learning also contains some elements of *how*, such as the role of suffering and discomfort that are important elements to her *what* of compassion and humility as important course learning outcomes.

Jayden's description of learning adds another dimension to the *how* of learning, an embodied perspective. His vignette sits in strong contrast to Rumi's (2004) description of the first form of intelligence as "one acquired, / as a child in school memorizes facts and concepts / from books and from what the teacher says" (p. 178).

Jayden is a high school senior with a passion for environmental stewardship. He is leading a session for community members on sustainability projects taking place on the school grounds. He believes that permaculture methods will support human needs, addressing such critical matters as food production, house cooling, energy conservation, and stormwater management, while at the same time regenerating the native landscape. Although Jayden is not what the academic system of assessment might call an academic high achiever, he is steady and reliable.

As he talks about the benefits of this philosophy of working *with*, rather than *against*, nature and the thoughtful observation that undergirds it, he seems calm and confident. His commitment, growing from his knowledge of permaculture, is mirrored in his body. No one doubts his expertise and passion as he passes the handful of soil around the cluster of attentive listeners, holding out their hands to feel and smell the warm earth. Jayden literally has the *how* of his learning cupped in his hands, a mutual relationship between self and soil. As Kimmerer (2013) noted, "Reciprocity is a matter of keeping the gift in motion through self-perpetuating cycles of giving and receiving" (p. 161). Jayden has received the gift of learning about permaculture from the soil and a knowledge of science, as well as by learning through handling and being in relationship with soil, "For what good is knowing, unless it is coupled with caring?" (Kimmerer, 2013, p. 335). And as Kimmerer suggested, Jayden now has a responsibility to pass that knowledge along to others, both as understanding about permaculture and as an embodied experience of care for the more-than-human world. His story of learning speaks to the way in which the *how* of learning is informed by relationships with soil and others.

Isaiah's story proposes a different response to the *how* of learning. Whereas Jayden demonstrates a physical, embodied manifestation of learning, Isaiah's is more ethereal. His vignette begins when he looks up at the clock and is startled. How did 2 hours pass? He is going to be a few minutes late for lacrosse practice, but he doesn't care; it was worth it. Isaiah just completed an intricate drawing of a small vase of daffodils for his mother's birthday. He knows she is not going to believe it when she sees how delicate and beautiful it is—and he made it! Isaiah is in his second year of studio art—something in which he admittedly enrolled only because some of his friends had also signed up for the class. And as Isaiah describes the *how* of his learning, we see that he is learning more than how to draw lovely and caring birthday gifts of daffodils:

> In the beginning, drawing was strange and completely not what I had expected. I thought we would start out drawing—well, things, like bowls of fruit, but we did the most bizarre exercises, such as drawing my hand for a full 20 minutes without looking at the paper. When I finished the paper was covered in strange, spidery lines that didn't even look like it came from me. My teacher talked a lot about drawing as the foundation of learning to see. Making art begins with observing the world through new eyes, about being present to noticing. At first it was a little strange, but it was fascinating.

The *how* of learning for Isaiah unfolds, like the daffodils in his drawing, in discernible but unexpected and unplanned ways. He took that art class mostly because of his friends, not for the purpose of learning to draw. But in surprising ways he found himself enthralled with both drawing and the techniques his teacher employed. As his skills improved, he also learned that the *how* of learning went beyond technique to include learning to see . . . being present to noticing. As Isaiah continues with his story of learning, we find that his *how* goes even deeper, that being present is a gateway to a state of mind:

> In psychology class, they talked about this guy, Mihaly Csikszentmihalyi. The teacher was going on about happiness and creativity, but when she started talking about flow—a state of fierce concentration, accompanied by states such as distortion of time, and a loss of awareness of the self, my eyes got big and I started to lean in closer to listen. That was it! I knew that state. I experienced it with drawing, exactly!

Isaiah's *how* of learning is consistent with Csikszentmihalyi's (1990) theory of flow. As his vignette suggests, he knows the feeling of losing time and just becoming one with drawing. The benefits of tapping into this state of being are multifaceted for Isaiah. He ritually prepares himself for the experience of drawing:

> I do this little preparatory dance, walking through the house, putting away my backpack, making a snack—like a dog walking in circles before lying down, it's like everything has to be in its place. Then, I settle into drawing.

Ritual, as we will show in subsequent chapters, is an important aspect of the learning process, both in the ways it can open, or close off, the depth and complexity of learning for students. For Isaiah, ritual prepares him emotionally and physically for the learning that occurs through drawing.

Isaiah's *how* is a combination of skilled instruction, noticing, flow, and ritual preparation for the work. When it all comes together in the mysterious ways of learning that are rich and deeply complex, he experiences, as Rumi (2004) noted:

> A freshness / in the center of the chest. This other intelligence / does not turn yellow or stagnate. It's fluid, / and it doesn't move from outside to inside / through conduits of plumbing-learning. / This second knowing is a fountainhead / from within you, moving out. (p. 178)

The outward flow of learning for Isaiah is evident to others. His grades have gone up in all his classes—not by a lot, but it is noticeable. His uncle said to him the other day, "Isaiah, my man, you're no longer living life in the shallows." Although he is not entirely clear what his uncle means, he feels something different in his bones. Settled. Focused. Flow.

The *Why* of Learning

What purpose might the *what* and *how* serve? In short, *why* are Ava, Jayden, and Isaiah learning? Is there a rationale or justification for learning the technical, quantifiable, or embodied forms of knowing? In philosophical and metaphysical terms, questions of *why* lead to a conversation about the elements and features of the good life. Why did Ava open herself to learning in that moment of discomfort and uncertainty? Why did she slow down and listen instead of returning to tried-and-true techniques designed to pass the course based on content expertise? Why did Jayden use experiential and embodied strategies to make his argument for permaculture to community members? Why does Isaiah's art begin with ritual?

Like the *what* and *how* of learning in Rumi's (2004) poem and the stories of our conversation partners, the *why* of learning is framed by the seemingly contrasting goals of outer competence and inner awakening. Laticia's story is emblematic of Rumi's first form of intelligence in which learners can be "ranked ahead or behind others / in regard to [their] competence" (p.178) though in this situation the ranking and evidence of competence goes beyond the more typical measures of grades or higher test scores.

Laticia is a high-performing student, but as she sits in class she wonders, "How on earth will I get it all done?" As the math teacher talks about sines, cosines, and tangents, she drifts into a tangent of her own. She has two exams for which she needs to prepare, and then there is concert band practice, volleyball, and the school play. She is the president of the student assembly, and some concerns have arisen related to a hazing incident with the soccer team. Laticia is responsible for hosting a conversation with faculty to prepare for an upcoming meeting to address the hazing. All that, and she still must complete two of her nine applications for college. Her parents have been riding her about cleaning her room, and she is supposed to drive her brother to an out-of-town youth group meeting for their church. "How on earth will I get it all done?" is a constant refrain in her head. It feels like there is little room for learning math today.

Laticia sits staring at the whiteboard in front of the classroom, her face a carefully arranged mask of concentration. Years of practice have honed the image of the attentive model student; only her bitten-to-the-quick fingernails and rapidly bouncing leg betray her perfect exterior. But her insides are consumed by the ever-present question, "How on earth will I get it all done?"

The *why* of learning for Laticia is contingent on the *what* of learning. We hear in Laticia's story that *what* she is learning is associated with becoming a model student, a learner who fits the social framing of school as a high performer and willing participant. *Why* is she learning these skills? It could be in response to external authorities at school and at home; in addition, she may likely struggle with overcoming stereotypes and pressures to perform to surmount societal expectations. For someone viewing Laticia without knowing her well, the *why* behind her actions might indeed appear to be about compliance, respect, or wanting to show appreciation for the care of coaches, teachers, or her parents; it could also be assumed that her *why* is reinforced through parents who have emphasized the importance of showing up a certain way or adapting to a dominant culture. Regardless, much of her *why* is bound up in the external world of ranking and competence.

Laticia's bouncing leg and bitten-to-the-quick fingernails suggest a certain level of unease around *why* she is learning to be a model student as defined by the social parameters of perfection—perhaps she senses the challenge of adapting to a dominant culture that she does not fully respect. We cannot say what might constitute other motivations that are yet to be fully expressed (and it is always wise to challenge our assumptions about learners!). As we will note in later chapters of this book, the *why* of some learners is closely aligned with the heart and soul of the learner. A goal for these learners is to allow the "freshness in the center of the chest" to flow freely and merge with the great wisdom of living a full and rich existence, a form of learning that is enduring and "does not turn yellow or stagnate" at the end of the class period or with the assignment of a grade. It has a living quality that reveals the true nature and responsibility of learning. The most enduring forms of *why* are long lasting and subject to modification and deeper understanding over time. In purely speculative terms, what might Laticia's life look like if her *why* was connected to the depth of her heart's longing? Without knowing Laticia's heart, it would be difficult to infer.

The *Who* of Learning

We now turn to the *who* of learning: Who is the self that learns? While it may seem obvious in the context that the *who* is the person doing the learning, our conversations with conversation partners suggest that the *who* of learning is more complex. It often involves an emergent and latent sense of self that goes beyond the three-dimensional form of the learner. *Who*, like Rumi's springbox, is often fluid and amenable to change over time and context. This is consistent with the observation of Sharon Parks (2000), who noted that "every institution of higher education serves in at least some measure as a community of imagination in which every professor is potentially a spiritual guide and every syllabus a confession of faith" (p. 159). The *who* of learning is in many ways a confession of faithfulness to the inner learner. When attended to with fidelity, the development of the *who* of learning means increased validation of one's identity and lifelong calling to wholeness.

The purpose, the *why* of learning, is much debated and contested. Is the purpose of education to improve individuals, to enhance the functioning of society, or to create an obedient work force? Should learning confirm existing value stances or provide the skills to challenge the status quo? What is of greater importance, homogeneity of learning outcomes or individualized instruction? The *who* of learning seems equally complex yet less well developed conceptually and practically in the literature on learning.

We begin with an examination of the root meanings of education. The word *educate* has its roots in two Greek words, *educare* and *educere*. *Educare* means to train or form to an ideal form, and *educere* means to bring forth (Bass & Good, 2004). *Who* questions are more closely associated with the *educere* goals of education in the sense of drawing out the inner wisdom of the learner. This kind of deep listening, for the true self-as-learner, requires courage because traditional notions of student are framed in static images of acceptance to external sources of authority (text, teacher, and tests). As we see in Laticia's story, many students learn through years of observation and experience that to be successful means yielding the formation of core elements of self to those who are crafting the learning environment, whether in schools, homes, or communities. This notion persists even when an educator invites students into learning approaches that are grounded in agency, self-exploration, and empowerment.

Silvia's story offers another vision of learning that is free of external parameters and perceptions of *who* she should be, in contrast to *who* she is. Her epiphany comes not from a formal educational experience but rather from the simple act of knitting. Her story reminds us that learning is a more complex experience than the interaction between educator and student. It involves the full circle of living, learning, and changing. This is especially the case when it comes to the *who* of learning.

> My interest in knitting started as an idea for a gift, a scarf for my aging mother who lives in a nursing home several cities away. But somewhere along the line in the last few weeks or so, I got hooked. Despite all of my pressures in life, the difficulties of having so many bills to pay, my cranky supervisor, the challenges in my marriage, worry over my younger daughter, I found something soothing in knitting.

Silvia is sitting in her living room with no agenda, no one to take care of, nothing expected of her, listening to the rhythmic click-click-click of the needles. Her fingers savor the soft wool as it glides between her fingers. There is a tactile and embodied feel to her process of learning to knit. She is alone, and although the apartment will soon explode with activity, right now she isn't even lost in thought—she is just *here*. She is learning to be present to herself, *who* she is. She notices the growing rows of stitches, neat and tidy, forming little hillocks of maroon. When reflecting on what she learned from knitting, Silvia observes that "Each stitch is a tiny mountain, exactly like all the others. And all it once it hits me: Every stitch is absolutely ordinary, and yet, without each individual one, the whole of it would all unravel." Her smile widens into a grin and for just a few moments, everything shimmers.

Silvia realizes, through the metaphor of knitting, how important she is as an individual. She is part of a bigger whole that is enhanced by the fullness of being present to self, task, and the world. Everything makes sense, if only for a moment—a moment she will likely remember.

As we continue to develop the *what*, *how*, *why*, and *who* of learning in *The Courage to Learn*, we invite you to consider these frames with respect to your personal journey as a learner as well as the experiences of learners under your care, or with whom you engage. At times we anticipate that the stories we share will overlap with yours. And in other cases, the *what*, *how*, *why*, and *who* of learning may feel challenging and awkward. Regardless of which emotion you feel, we hope that you will remain open to surprise, delight, or challenge around your current perceptions of learning.

Opportunity for Reflection

Please take a recent learning experience, such as a workshop, online class, study group in your community, or other situation for which you enrolled or registered. Pause for a moment to bring it fully to mind. It may be, too, that the experience was not comfortable. As Rendón points out in the foreword of this book, sometimes the most powerful learning can occur when we are most vulnerable, distressed, and traumatized.

What was it you hoped to learn, what drew you to the experience—or, if it was an experience you were not drawn to, but found yourself cast into, what brought you there? What was the "content" that you actually learned in addition to the "content" that was promised?

How was the learning actually structured? How did this integrate or fit with the how of learning that is most comfortable or familiar to you?

Why were you motivated to enroll in this learning experience? Upon reflection, are there subtle motivations about which you may not have been aware at the time?

As you reflect on this learning experience, what have you discovered about *who* you are as a learner? What else have you uncovered through this reflection?

With this introduction to an expansive view of learning that encompasses *what, how, why*, and *who*, what might be helpful to consider through the lens of learning experiences that you create for other people?

4

THE *WHAT* OF LEARNING

I had a kindergarten teacher who made me believe in myself. I can still picture her, hear her voice, see her. I was lucky that it was how I began my school path, because after her, it was completely different.

—*Krystal, math teacher and doctoral student*

As we know, learning occurs in as many places and contexts as there are human beings asking, seeking, and unraveling questions of meaning and purpose. Learning is what we do and how we grow! We learn language, culture, and ways of being from the moment we are born. As such, the content of *what* we learn is quite literally "everything." Learning happens everywhere, all the time; it is ongoing, far outreaching the narrow confines of academic disciplines that study learning. For most people, learning is the principal domain of education in spaces that are formalized and structured, as in classrooms and schools. Because of this, it is quite easy to confuse learning as something that takes place exclusively in formal education settings rather than considering how it impacts all aspects of our lives, before, during, and after schooling. One goal of this book is to decouple learning, at its best and worst, from K–12 and higher education classrooms and consider learning more broadly as an all-encompassing human endeavor. While we do often learn in classrooms, we spend more time outside of them—and the learning, while it may be more informal, can be just as powerful and lasting, sometimes even more so.

Jean Lave and Etienne Wenger (1991), in their classic text, *Situated Learning: Legitimate Peripheral Participation*, offered a detailed analysis of activity theory and the multitude of ways in which informal educational spaces structure and inform the nature of learning. They spoke to the central nature of "legitimate peripheral participation," meaning the ways in which newcomers learn from more experienced members of a community and move from less knowledge to expertise through increased levels of coparticipation.

This includes the ways in which, at times, more experienced practitioners can thwart the learning of novices by denying them access to the central activities of the community. In this sense, participation in the learning process is more peripheral and less legitimate, as the activity of the novice is less central to the functioning of the community. As we aim to demonstrate in this chapter, the role of newcomer can be as encompassing as entering a new cultural setting and as micro as human-to-human interactions in a classroom. The *what* of learning, as Lave and Wenger indicated, is highly contextual and power dependent wherever newcomers encounter communities of practice that have established norms, protocols, and ways of being in the world.

What Is Worth Learning?

As we consider that learning happens all the time and in a multiple places and contexts, we must ask a question: Is "everything" worth learning? If "everything" is important enough to be learned, how can we possibly organize knowing into a coherent conceptual scheme? What happens when the learner is provided experiences that are less than "everything" both inside the classroom and beyond? How is learning enhanced, and how is it stunted?

Often, these types of questions are answered from the perspective of teachers empowered with the responsibility of organizing, delivering, and assessing learning in the classroom. Uhrmacher et al. (2017) noted that there is the *received curriculum*, which is what a learner learns. This may be different from what was intended by the educator, which is often considered the *delivered curriculum*. The gap between the delivered and received curriculum can be enormous and not always evident to the educator, because what an educator sees or thinks may not match what the learner is experiencing. Formal assessment of student learning, for example, is geared toward the task of quantifying the distance between the intended goals of learning and what students ultimately acquire or remember. Based on these data of "success or failure" the educator can make decisions about what to reteach or to cover in the next lesson. But formal assessments, by their nature, are designed to measure only what is expected and intended in a learning experience. They are not well suited to the task of uncovering other, less quantifiable, elements of the learning space. As we explore in this chapter, there is much that is taught and learned that falls outside the parameters of traditional notions of assessment. As Krystal's quote in the epigraph that begins this chapter suggests, the *what* of learning is more than multiple-choice answers, bubble sheets, or essay questions chosen by the educator.

Sometimes, in a classroom, the *what* of content that is intended to be taught may not match the *what* of what was actually learned. For example, an instructor may intend to use poetry to help young people learn the value of language to express emotions, but if the poem is too obtuse, a cultural mismatch, or stereotypical, what the student may actually learn is that poetry is inadequate for the task of describing their current lived experience.

Outside the formal classroom, we are still faced with this important question as educators plan learning experiences for students of all ages. For example, an eager camp counselor may use lively icebreaker games, and yet if introverted campers feel embarrassed and excluded by their more enthusiastic peers they may learn that icebreakers are distressing and something to avoid. Worse, in times of deep stress and uncertainty, the brain's amygdala, which is keyed to emotional, physical, and spiritual safety, fires up the fight, flight, or freeze response. In this heightened state, learning becomes secondary to locating and moving (emotionally or physically) to a place of safety. And in the case of the camper, what is learned might be to never risk, push boundaries, or share outcomes that may differ from the intention of the camp counselor. John Dewey (1938) noted that "every experience is a moving force. Its value can be judged only on the ground of what it moves toward and into" (p. 38). As such, Dewey invited all educators to pay less attention to their intentions, what they believe will happen, and more to the actual learning that is forming in the minds and hearts of learners. Through this framing, the *what* of learning becomes more complex than traditional notions of content that are offered and assessed through various forms of rubrics, standardized assessments, and measures of academic success. Formalized assessment of learning is an important educational tool. It offers educators a glimpse into whether or not their hopes for a lesson are realized. But, as we argue, there is more than meets the educational eye to the question of what is being learned.

Learning is a complex process, and the *what* of learning, in both formal and informal settings, often overlaps as learners bring their own experiences, prior learning, and funds of knowledge to every new learning situation. This is particularly the case for culturally and linguistically diverse learners who are entering into learning spaces in which there is often a cultural mismatch between educator and learner (Hammond, 2014). To demonstrate the role of background knowledge in learning, let's take a moment to meet Mike. Mike is a math teacher at a community college and has many years of experience teaching in a variety of institutions. He says:

> My first discovery teaching in a community college was the realization of different levels of preparation in the students. If you talk to admissions folks, they will say it's not open enrollment, that students have to meet certain criteria, but the level of threshold may be quite low. It's the next

best thing to open enrollment. In the other settings I taught, there were certain criteria, testing scores and so forth, and because of that, a more level playing field. Here there is a wide range of students. Some have graduated near the top of their high school class and they come to take their general education courses while paying a lot less money. In addition, there are some students that would be considered lower ranking and part of this is simply due to a wider age range.

When I taught at the other three places, I taught primarily freshmen and sophomores. Now what I'm seeing are the 18- to 19-year-olds, alongside the 45- to 50-year-olds. The older students have gone out and lived life, and the place to start their education is a community college and they struggle since they haven't used these skills. They may have the discipline of going to work every day, but they don't have the discipline of studying.

That wider age range might make for a rich discussion in a class like sociology. But when you come into a math class and I ask, "How do you solve this equation?" older people say, "I haven't seen an equation in 30 years." I've had to spend a lot more of my time getting my hands around the notion of taking people back and saying, "Somewhere in the past you had this, and now we've got to bring it back."

Mike's experience and expanded understanding on how to decide what or what not to teach is important because his decision is not just about the content of math and material of curriculum. Some of what he needs to include in his teaching is how to learn (as we will explore in chapter 5), and the interplay between *what* and *how* can be important to the overall process of mastering content. Mike's story shows that as educators consider *what* is learned, they often must decide *what* will *not* be learned. The implications of framing learning as not learning what the educator is offering, but rather learning as the subject of the student's focus, are significant. Imagine, if you will, an assessment that targets what a student chooses not to learn because it did not advance their understanding, instead of assessments that are aimed at what the educator thinks should be valuable for the student. For learners it takes intention, courage, and reflection to sort through their learning experiences to decide and decode what is core to their emerging sense of selfhood and what is not, especially if educators expect mastery of everything taught.

Mike goes on to share a story of a student in class whose parents seemed to assume that because they lacked advanced academic knowledge of a subject, they could not learn new material, or help their daughter with college-level content.

A young lady said to me yesterday that she had asked her parents for help on a problem she was working on. It was about how Company A rents a truck for $30.00 a day and $.50 a mile, and Company B rents a truck for

$60.00 a day and $.10 mile: how many miles would you have to travel so both companies had the same price? This student went to her parents and asked for help. They said they couldn't help her since it was college math. I said to the student that they might want to imagine a U-Haul and Ryder with those same fees, and they have to move you to college and decide which is more affordable, so which is going to save you money? This is not a college math problem; this is a life problem. We typically don't spend time in high school teaching people how to—how to balance a checkbook or how to figure out the best mortgage rate. Once they graduate from high school, that's the kind of math they need. So when they come back at 45 [years of age], I try to take it and turn it into a U-Haul versus Ryder problem.

Again, Dewey (1938) stated that the *what* of learning, when framed as an experiential continuum, can ripple through time. In the case of Mike's student, it appears that, for her parents, the *what* of learning is likely bound up in the perceived limitations that the learning of math stopped with high school and therefore lacked application to college curriculum. The *what* of learning, in this case, is time bound rather than transferable to other contexts, places, and challenges. Transferability, according to Grant Wiggins and Jay McTighe (2005), is the cornerstone of learning. It demonstrates the understanding of deep meaning behind concepts because it shows that a learner can take the discrete forms of *what* (facts and content knowledge) and transfer them to multiple contexts, situations, and problems. Mike is struggling with the challenge of helping his students embody math as a life lesson, not a college academic problem to be solved. The *what* of learning for Mike reaches well beyond the discrete boundaries of facts, concepts, and algorithmic formulas; it is literally life enriching for learners.

Sometimes, the *what* that is received, the ideas and images associated with learning, can be accidental, as is the case with the following story of a student who unexpectedly learned how to better observe the natural world while engaged in drawing. Their experience supports the claim that every new situation brings learning opportunities and that learning, even when unanticipated, can be life changing:

It has been far too long since I have had to examine anything for extended periods of time in order to capture their likeness, or even simply understand what they are. I have gone out of practice . . . and as I began to shake down my stiff, rusty artistic state of mind, I am reminded of the complexity in the world around me. There are things lost to the ages and things lost to one who stops seeing.

I did not actively look for the small scale. I was so busy, I only appreciated what fell into my lap—the sunsets that happened to coincide with my walk home, the opening in the clouds that light up the engineering quad during my morning walk to class. I became too busy last semester to stop more than once or twice to appreciate what I saw. That was disappointing, because I distinctly remember telling someone that "People never stop to look around them." I wonder if I knew at the time that I would stop looking as well, so consumed by the false idea that I was too busy to stop.

This class has reminded me that I need to slow down again. What's the rush? I try to take in more during my walks between classes again, and it lengthens my day appreciably. I have begun reading my books again. I see the wood pulp, the fiber, the tension of the ink.

I am looking forward to seeing again.

"Seeing again" is such a powerful metaphor for an expansive and inclusive understanding of the *what* of learning. As this student so elegantly demonstrates, learning to draw again, rather than just putting lines on paper, suggests that the *what* of learning is best framed as a both/and experience. Drawing is both a technical process of skill development and the more ineffable process of seeing behind the real world to the mystery that energizes the object. For this student, the formalized structure of a class, instead of confining learning as it apparently did for the parents in Mike's story, facilitated slowing down and remembering the ageless gift of deep observation of the natural world. The course invited shaking off their "rusty artistic state of mind" and seeing "the wood pulp, the fiber, the tension of the ink." Becoming fully connected to self, the world, and their artistic gift is the *what* of learning for this student.

Accidental or unintentional forms of learning can work the other way, such as learning to despise math because the teacher has dampened the student's enthusiasm for learning by using antiquated approaches of lecture and rote memorization to teach mathematical concepts, engaging in teaching strategies that confine the beauty of mathematical patterns and ways of knowing to discrete numbers and testable formulas. The learning here, to dislike math, is unintentional but deeply impactful. It becomes a form of hidden curriculum that can be as powerful in shaping thinking and being as the explicit curriculum of learning exemplified by the art student.

The Hidden Curriculum

The concept of the hidden curriculum encompasses all those implicit learnings embedded in the rituals, practice, and traditions of formal and informal places of learning. A good example is how students learn through school curriculum one meaning of gender (that gender encompasses the binary male or female) instead of encountering a fluid range of gender expressions in the books, assignments, or in-class conversations in which they participate. While this may not be explicitly taught, the concept of gender is also learned by watching family and community members' behavior, which is framed by the binary choice of male or female. As such, different situations and cultures can produce very different learning and understandings. Scholars and practitioners who examine these and other questions that support normative perspectives on language, culture, and behavior note that through the hidden curriculum, students learn only what society or the educator wishes to teach them. In addition, the content of the hidden curriculum can vary from place to place, educator to educator, or from informal to formal educational spaces. When all the images in a textbook correspond to the gender-specific roles of male or female, or a parent reinforces gender norms, young people learn one way of thinking about the *what* of gender. The educator does not have to say anything; the gender message comes through and is reinforced by the images.

Through the hidden curriculum, children and youth learn about race, social class, and who in society is granted more or fewer opportunities to form the types of relationships and social networks that provide the context for social advancement. In Mike's story, he seeks to unravel the hidden curriculum that teaches that math is a grade-specific phenomenon and is not transferable to other contexts in and outside formal schooling. The art student wrestles with the hidden curriculum in the form of the Siren's call to speed up and abandon deep seeing and to instead embrace the myth of being too busy to look at the fullness of life. These messages that normalize learning behaviors can be ongoing. Throughout our lives, we encounter the hidden curriculum and unintended learnings, often in surprising settings.

An educator may also experience the hidden curriculum in the midst of teaching or facilitating. Marcia, one the authors, became aware of one of the most sobering and unplanned lessons of her life while facilitating the Prison Mindfulness Institute's *Path of Freedom* curriculum, a mindfulness-based emotional intelligence model for incarcerated youth and adults, through the Cornell Prison Education Program. She facilitated the course for incarcerated students with the intention of sharing the joy and meaning of mindfulness with a group with which she had never engaged. At the same time that she was spending 3 hours each week in a maximum-security prison in upstate New York, she happened to be simultaneously reading *The New Jim Crow: Mass Incarceration in the Age of Colorblindness* by Michele Alexander (2012), which addresses the devastating account of the rebirth of a caste-like system in the United States—one that has resulted in millions of African Americans becoming incarcerated.

Marcia anticipated one outcome—sharing the benefits of mindfulness and meditation with incarcerated students—and yet had no idea how much of her own impactful learning and growth she would come to realize through uncovering this often-concealed facet of American life. Initially, she experienced guilt, shame, and bewilderment. Despite a hidden curriculum of white supremacy culture that encourages a normalizing gaze of defensiveness, either–or thinking, fear of conflict, and urgency—which could translate to trudging forth without the painful reflection—Marcia ultimately learned to keep her eyes open to "be with" what she was witnessing, alongside her students, who were learning the same practices, and to deepen in her own learning on the subject of racism. Watt (2015) and her students addressed the enduring challenges of racism, while they emphasized a commitment to difficult dialogue, and encouraged making room for those missteps that naturally develop along the way. This learning would have significant implications for Marcia's teaching and facilitation, and is, as Watt named, ongoing—and the dialogue is both internal and with others.

Beyond the hidden curriculum, the *what* of learning can entail a shifting from what a person thinks they are learning to something completely new and different. This change in learning direction, unlike the negative aspects of the hidden curriculum, can be a welcome reality. Consider Sarah's story. Sarah decided to take on a new volunteer role. During the years she was actively working, Sarah was a successful software consultant, involved in technical sales, providing guidance as to the best fit of product to match client need. When she retired, she was ready to do something completely different:

> I always knew I wanted to do something with seniors. I think I got that from my father. He was always kind to older people, and I enjoyed watching the way that showed up in his life. And hey, I like kids, but volunteering at the schools did not appeal to me at all! I heard through a good friend about elder services with all their different programs, and somehow that just felt right. I wanted something to keep my mind active, too. And so now I help elders figure out Medicare, Medicaid, and what, if any, programs they might qualify for to get extra assistance.

To prepare, Sarah entered a twice-weekly, 3-month training program hoping to learn about the ins and outs of medical insurance. She was amazed at how much she did not know, each day offering another wrinkle, wading through the murky waters of health insurance. She kept meeting new people and encountering different situations, and she experienced a steep learning curve. There were different rules and regulations for various programs based on such things as citizenship and marital status. Sarah's response:

> This just doesn't make sense. For example, the first year I was involved in this service, gay marriage was legal in my state, but not legal from U.S. government perspective. A couple came in to see me; they were married. One woman had a very good job, made good money. The other didn't make much beyond minimum wage. In my state, because they were married, we looked at both their incomes. Because of the higher income, they couldn't get any assistance. But because it was a same-gender marriage, they also couldn't get the benefits from the U.S. government, so the one with the lower income wasn't able to get anything. It was a mess. That changed later, but it gave me an intimate view of something that isn't right at all. I was able to witness unfair, awful, unjust situations just because of what was deemed illegal.

In addition to learning the technical aspects of insurance, Sarah learned to trust and apply her software consultant skills, something she did not expect. She learned that her ability to come up with innovative solutions by looking at problems from a variety of angles was an asset for her elder clients. For example, she works with many widows, some of whom have had the same health insurance for years. They are often paying for more insurance than they need, but they keep the policy because they believe their husband made the right decision, and so they keep paying exorbitant fees. Navigating this very personal space with grace is a challenge, but it is satisfying for Sarah as she guides people toward decision-making that can help make their lives easier and more independent.

In addition to learning that her old professional skills can be repurposed into a new context, Sarah gained another unexpected learning outcome from her new role as an insurance advisor. She often assists people who earn just above the poverty line, therefore not qualifying for any form of assistance, yet she witnesses the way in which they are barely making ends meet. She works with people who struggle to pay for food, rent, and utilities. They often quite literally haul in a box with all their bills, lay it down on the table, and ask her for help managing their complex financial situation. Her role is to look at their income and search for assistance for which they may qualify.

> Some people work two or three jobs their whole life. Now they're old and they are still scraping by. There are other people in their fifties who are not working and who are getting benefits, but who suffer from serious issues with mental health, such as debilitating depression and anxiety. If they were getting better treatment, I'm certain they would be happier, more

functional and productive—but then, that isn't my job. Another major learning for me is that I believe we are doing people a disservice by making excellent mental health care so hard to get.

Sarah concludes with this: "I thought I was going into this to learn how to help people with insurance. When it comes down to it, what I have really learned about is disparity." For Sarah, the *what* of learning was not hidden from sight, though it was fully evident in the lived experiences of her clients. She learned to lean into that space and see the challenges of her clients not as a process of finding the right fit between programs and needs but rather as a larger problem of social and economic disparity.

The Complexities of Learning the *What*

How can the *what* of learning result in such different outcomes and purposes to education, whether in school, a workshop, or a program such as the one with which Sarah is involved? Often, our learning is steeped in complexity: Simply put, given the complications of a situation such as Sarah's or Marcia's, more is happening than a program leader or educator/facilitator can plan for. Add to this the additional nuances of difference, and the complexities continue to become multilayered and often quite challenging. Consider Mark, a man who self-describes himself as gay (an identity central to his learning journey). This short passage speaks volumes and contains both the ways in which he learned to frame his identity around being gay as well as navigating social spaces:

> In high school, I wasn't "out" to myself or anyone else, but it influenced me. I felt like I had to be as perfect as possible. I knew I was different, and I used being smart as a defense mechanism. And I still do. My sister recently said, you use your education like a club.
> I came out as an undergrad. Again, I would say that being different propelled me to be an excellent student. I competed with this woman for the top grades all the time. I also had to learn how to be OK with my sexuality, learning about the social network within the gay community—what was and wasn't appropriate, what was and wasn't safe. I had to learn how to come out to my family and friends.

Mark's experience of feeling different from mainstream heterosexual culture required a parallel track of sorts, learning new ways of being "OK with [his] sexuality" alongside learning the rules of fitting in, by being "perfect" in the eyes of peers and society. Mark's back-and-forth boundary crossing impacted many aspects of the *what* of his learning. In addition, the layers of knowing deepened for him as the cultural complexities around his sexual identity continued to surface as he learned from the gay community "what was and wasn't appropriate . . . and . . . safe" and as he moved beyond formal schooling and into the world of work and professional life. The *what* of Mark's learning was highly contextual and dependent on his emerging notions of self.

The lack of equity between the learner's identity and the deforming social norms of society are evident in Mark's story. He is forced to constantly find his footing as his sense of self and the expectations of society collide. His story invites educators who care about their learners, whether in the formal classroom, faith-based settings, corporations, or homes, to reflect on the *what* of learning and the various ways in which the learning environment offers different content for different learners.

Looking to Rumi's (2004) wisdom is again helpful here. In the first part of Rumi's poem, he speaks of knowledge as the ways "a child in school memorizes facts and concepts / from books and from what the teacher says, / collecting information from the traditional sciences / as well as from the new sciences" (p. 178). Many contemporary scholars of education would recognize Rumi's description of facts, concepts, and traditional sciences as the hallmark of the liberal arts tradition. The liberal arts are perhaps the most well known and most widely accepted of the traditions in education concerned with the *what* of learning. According to this way of understanding the purpose of schooling, the goal for learning is the intellectual development that is needed for the preparation of an educated public, to get training for a job, and to be prepared for life.

As such, to accomplish this goal a premium is placed on a set curriculum; a canon of accepted texts; and a pedagogy that often prioritizes memorization, didactic instruction, the Socratic method of dialogue, and rhetorical abilities. Learners are encouraged to develop a capacity for free thinking, synthesis, and novel solutions. These are important skills, but they are often situated within the social and intellectual norms of the time. And this dichotomy can be stunning: Critics of this tradition will ask, How can we expect learners to be "free thinkers" if they are provided a set curriculum that is given to everyone? Where is the opportunity for the learner to bring their interests and background knowledge to the learning process? At the same time, perhaps an even deeper question is embedded here, a question pertinent to all forms of curriculum: Do society and the public education system provide all learners with the same curriculum? Unfortunately, the answer is no, in big ways (the lack of a national curriculum) and in small ways (unequal resource distribution between schools), and this certainly adds to the complexity of what is learned in any form of curriculum. Let's go back to Mike's story:

> Another big difference between my experience teaching four-year colleges and community college—in the four-year colleges, the mentality always seemed to be that if you were a student, that was your job, your primary focus. Here, students are going to be unhappy if courses conflict with daytime work hours, for example, since there are only a few students who aren't working. We offer courses in the day, evening, Saturdays—if we have demand for 10 sections for a course, we'll put 20 of them out there and let the students determine when they run, and then cancel the ones that don't get populated. Even younger students have part time jobs. A lot of students come in under the auspices of DSS [Department of Social Services]—with DSS housing and vouchers—and they are working since many of them have children.
>
> As a result, I have become much more flexible. It used to be that a student would say "I can't get it done because I have to work," and I'd say "It's your job, get it done." A while ago, before the pandemic, I announced that I was going to set up a course using software called mymathlab. A student raised their hand and said, "Does this mean I need a computer at home?" Another student said, "But I work." Another said, "I don't have internet." And still another said, "I have internet, but only with dial-up." By the time I got done, three-quarters of the class said that they wouldn't be able to manage this software, and what started out as a great idea turned into something I realized wouldn't work. There are certain things that I have taken for granted that some people just don't have access to. I've had to learn to adapt.
>
> Students are dealing with jobs, technology and fighting a lot of battles in their lives. Why would I want to make it harder? Yes, there is a certain level of accountability I have to hold them to and I try to tell them—there will be deadlines. On the other hand, if a student has four children and is trying to go to school at the same time, you can't really talk with them about levels of responsibility—they've got four kids! Their hardest time is balancing the responsibilities of job, children, home and school. It comes down to understanding.

With time, Mike has learned to be much more nimble, sensitive to the nuances of the needs of his students, integrating learning about math with learning about life.

Mike's example of an integrated curriculum of human needs and academic learning takes time and energy, sometimes requiring swimming against a powerful current that can dominate instruction and assessment.

Consider the story of Paula, a passionate teacher who identifies strongly as Argentinian. She shared a powerful story about her discovery of unintended lessons, how she ultimately navigated them, and how her learning impacted her teaching. She came to the United States when she was 21 years old, yet kept strong roots in Argentina, trying to spend as much time as possible going back home.

Paula came from the professional middle class and felt very fortunate to grow up around books:

> For me, school has always been my water, even more so than my own house. My family's life was stormy, so going home was going to school. Since I can remember, there was so much freedom at school! I could be myself, detached from my family of origin. School always gave me the space to be who I wanted to be, without attachments.

School was safe, a home away from home—and her peers became her family and her teachers, second parents.

Given this stability and foundation for learning, Paula had a recent epiphany about teaching and learning that deeply informed her commitment to students. It began with a recollection:

> I remember looking at the only notebook that my mom kept from my K–12 years. There was a test on parts of a bird and 35 years later, I couldn't answer a single question, but I was able to successfully pass a test when I was 8. So I wondered, what is the purpose of learning if I can't remember anything from this time? This [question] has impacted my own teaching. I don't think you learn content per se. I think you learn and evolve how to be a better learner of life, a more acute reader, not just of pages, but of the world, of culture, of experiences—and what can you learn from them. And they don't just have to be in the classroom—we go to school to become better people; school is the preparation to be better outside of school. That's what I got out of school. I learned that the teacher can be a role model that leads you through life, and it has nothing to do with the content you teach. It has to do with how they make you feel, how they believe in you—spotting something in you that you didn't know you had. They make you see possibilities when you thought there were none. That has to do with the way of teaching more than the actual content you happen to teach.

For Paula, the unexpected learning from an old journal shifted her sense of what is actually learned in an academic space. As her story of learning unfolds, she shares another unexpected learning. As an undergraduate in the United States, Paula's early experiences were astonishing and utterly unanticipated:

> The first class that I took as an undergraduate was education. The first learning experience I had was that everything I thought was important when I read a text was not important for assessment purposes in the U.S. I was the valedictorian of a 2,000-person high school, and yet I got a C on my first test on theories of learning in the U.S.—and I studied really hard. I read it, I understood it, my mom had taught it—I loved it—and yet when I faced the test, the first multiple-choice test I had ever taken, I had no idea what they were asking. Everything I was asked about were all the things I had left out, because I didn't think they were relevant!
>
> For example, I found it fascinating that most elementary school teachers were female—for me, that was the interesting concept. Why would this be; what were the cultural connotations? Yet, the question on the test was what is the percentage of female versus male teachers in elementary school? The answers were something like, 80, 85, or 88. I'm like, wow, how is this even relevant?

Faced with a new situation, Paula learned to adapt to the content of the exams in a strategic manner. After her first C, she changed her approach to studying altogether, even though it meant memorizing content that did not matter to her:

> It was kind of sad. It was hard to memorize small pieces of information without context; it would take away from the most interesting things—the bigger theories, ideas—but I didn't have time, so I just focused on memorizing. I got an A on my second text, but it was ridiculous! I learned to play the game. It was very flattening. I felt I was stripped of my best tools.

As learners constantly attune their antennae to the pulse of expectations and assessments, they may find themselves adapting to the nature of the learning space, whether they have Paula's keen self-awareness or not. In addition to the struggle with *what* is required, there are examples of extreme cases of disconnect between the learner's reading of an educator and the educator's expectations for the learner's behavior. For example, a student may learn how to resist the actions and instructions of the educator. This is particularly the case if the learner feels that the educator's efforts at structuring learning are inconsistent with the learner's image of themselves or of how they think the learning environment should be structured. This often happens when the learner's behavior or affect does not fit the educator's biased perceptions of gender, social class, race, or intellectual ability, and it can result in conscious forms of resistance to the educator and to the entire learning opportunity.

Active resistance provides the learner with some sense of power and agency, but it can also be perceived by the educator as defiant, antisocial, or disengaged behavior—values that often result in increased tension between the educator and the learner.

Outside the classroom, there can be the same kind of impact on learning. A child often develops one friendship over another and may choose a particular friend group because they have things in common with them. This can lead to a lack of diversity among our friendships outside of more formal settings and can explain why we often choose others who are very similar to us (in age, nationality, race, and social and economic standing). We also tend to reduce diversity in our circles to avoid challenges and discomfort that can come up when we encounter people with contrasting viewpoints. Since we choose whom we will befriend, those are often the peers who impact what we learn. If a child has a friend with healthy, skillful habits, those will probably be the types of habits that the child learns and uses. However, if unhealthy, less skillful habits are shown in our friends, these are the ones that we are more likely to learn. These, in turn, will often determine who our next friend group is as we continue to grow and develop. No matter how many good role models are placed in front of us, we will choose to learn from the person whom we perceive as most similar to us, or whom we think respects us, before we will turn to a role model with whom we do not have much in common or that we feel does not treat us (or those like us) well (Hammond, 2015).

Paula's bewildering experience of adapting to the new expectations for learning as she moved from Argentina to America—and the ways she had to change her ways of demonstrating learning—could have resulted in cynicism and despair. And yet, as an ardent teacher invested in the learning of those in her charge, Paula's experiences altered her perspectives of course content for the better. Her learning struggles, not of her making, paved the foundation for a teaching style that would eventually foster a more life-affirming classroom space for her students. In a relational model, knowing the intellectual and social–emotional moods of learners allows the teacher to form a caring relationship with students (Noddings, 2015). In Paula's case, offering a warm, positive, relational atmosphere brings out the best in her students:

> When I think about the *what* of learning, I think about the content I'm passionate about, and how it comes together with community—the image that comes to mind is spark—something, whatever it is, that I cannot wait to read. I consider myself a good teacher and then I learn something and I think, how have I taught all this time without knowing this? It's like a self-boundary pushing, an expansion of the self—ever expanding your heart, mind, and abilities. Once you notice how much you can expand, how can

I stop? Would it even be responsible to stop? There is so much learn, it's wasted time to be in this life not learning more.

Being a constant learner has made me a much better teacher. The more I feel I know about learning, the less I'm concerned about the details of the curriculum. It's almost anecdotal. I'll have curriculum discussions with colleagues—should we do this, that—and it's almost funny, I don't think it comes down to that at all. Of course, there is a curriculum! But if we are loosely there, there is so much more learning that can happen that is not tied to the bullet points, and the bullet points under the bullet points, and covering so much on the page. When I walk into a classroom, I want my students to feel seen and cared for. They are so much more than this tiny self they show—that's my big thing! We'll learn Spanish together as we go along, but moving the focus from the details of the curriculum to the big picture has made me, ironically, a much better teacher. This approach works and people don't take advantage of you when you care, when they feel truly seen. Seeing the humanity—that's it. The what becomes that. Learning to become better humans together.

Learning as Dehumanization: The *What* of Not Being Seen

The *what* of learning is frequently considered within the narrow confines of curriculum or what the teacher deems most worthy of learning. But for some academically focused learners, being well prepared and high achieving cannot erase the conscious and unconscious bias of teachers that can obscure a learner's sense of self and cloud their understanding of the *what* of learning. For instance, it is well documented that, for many students of color, teachers often assume they are not capable of performing at high academic levels. This often results in students learning to be dependent learners instead of independent learners who can expand their knowledge through self-efficacy and agency (Hammond, 2015; Ladson-Billings, 1998). Krystal, a math teacher who is currently in a doctoral program (the quote about her kindergarten teacher appears as an epigraph at the beginning of this chapter) experienced the way in which the *what* of learning can include internalizing her teacher's destructive prejudice. For Krystal, who was born in Colorado and identifies as Mexican American, learning became important to her from her earliest experiences in kindergarten, and it was there that she knew she wanted to become a teacher. However, after kindergarten, everything changed for her:

> School for me became all about having to prove myself. I went to a very white school district. My brothers and I were one of the two families of color. From a young age, it made me feel unsafe. I used to have to work five times harder to just be seen by my teachers. "There's no way you could

have scored this high," or "No way you could be in this higher reading group"—it happened all the time. I once scored well on a test and my mother was called in. They said, "She couldn't have gotten this high score, she must have cheated." I remember walking into science classes and the other students said, "Why are you in here? You'll fail quickly." I have distinct memories of having to score the best just to be seen as a student, it became the driving force behind needing good grades. It made me feel that I had to be at the top. The only way to do that for me was scoring well—so my learning became centered around that.

Krystal graduated from public school mastering two very different forms of *what*. She demonstrated deep understanding of academic content knowledge, and that high achievement was necessary to overcome racial prejudice and to be valued as a human being. In fact, she learned the lesson of not being seen so well that she now focuses much of her post-schooling life trying to regain a core sense of self. Only recently has she felt comfortable recognizing the fullness of her humanity, even though elevating the humanity of her students is a central tenant of her teaching. In addition, it took her a long time to accept and value other forms of learning than grades:

> Part of my what of learning became about learning how to please my different teachers. I was trying to alleviate the sense of being unseen with scoring well. "If I just do well enough, I will be seen as a person, equal to the white students in the class." It became more about chasing the grades to get my teacher to like me, to talk to me.

It took a long time and a deep act of courage before Krystal was able to disengage from the racist messages that she did not belong from her teachers and other white students. The sense of alienation from her Mexican American identity was so intense and the messages of whiteness so normalizing that she even tried to become white to fit in and be seen. The *what* of learning was a wholesale abandonment of her cultural identity and the acquisition of cultural norms that she could never attain:

> Around this time, I experienced a time in which I really wanted to be white. I went so far as to cry to my mom. I pointed to my skin and said I wanted to be white and for everyone to call me Jessica! Later, I started to identify as Mexican-American. As I've continued, my sense of identity has strengthened, for sure. It's coming to accept learning how to accept me, and what do I want that to be.

The LatinX scholar and teacher educator Maria del Carmen Salazar, in her book *Teacher Evaluation as Cultural Practice: A Framework for Equity and*

Excellence, coauthored with Jessica Lerner (del Carmen Salazar & Lerner, 2019), shared a story of marginalization and boundary crossing that mirrors much of Krystal's experience. She described her first-grade teacher as "harsh, cold, frightening, and lonely" (p. 31). Her teacher was relentless in her diminishment of Maria's native Spanish and vigorously promoted English. Over time, the *what* of her learning became a form of dehumanization: "I deduced that my native language did not have value, my culture did have value, my parents did not have value; thus I did not have value" (p. 31). Much like Krystal, Maria also learned to dislike her cultural and linguistic self and wanted to "reject all that was native to me . . . I wanted desperately to be White and worthy" (p. 31).

Krystal struggles, as a person and as an educator, with this conundrum of being brown skinned and academically high achieving. She wonders if she came to love learning because achievement provided access to the attention of her teachers, or for the learning itself. Yet, despite her personal experiences of not being seen, she could not be clearer about what she intends for her students. She wants them to think critically about math, to develop deep understandings, and to know that she cares about them as human beings. As she notes in this passage, the gift of grace is something she gives to her students more than she extends to herself:

> I want to be a teacher for students who look like me, so they don't feel what I felt growing up. This is why I drive an hour to work each day. I try to instill in my kids that the scores don't matter—it's about what are you thinking and how did you get there? The correct answer is great, but I want to see your thinking—and I didn't have that. I give different goals and even a different sense of grace to my students than I've ever given myself.

Krystal names achievement and critical thinking, the student's personhood, the content and the skills, personal agency, and voice as what she values as the outcomes of learning in her classroom. She reminds students that it is *their* class and that they have choices regarding how the experience of learning will materialize for them. This freedom to learn, according to Krystal, is vital preparation for the world in which we live. And yet, the negative lessons she learned regarding achievement continue to impact her learning in graduate school. She notes that even as she realizes that she would be upset to see a B as a grade for herself, she hopes her students will have a healthier sense of self than a grade from a teacher:

> Yes, I want them to achieve well, but what does that mean? I worry about their focusing on the score because learning is so far beyond that. We do a pretty good job of looking at grades, but it's still tied to how we can

improve for next time, writing down goals, and focused around practices and behaviors, such as thinking creatively, trying different approaches, integrating what you know. Yeah, we have our common denominators in math, but we still talk about goals around those practices. The ultimate *what* of learning is self-esteem, confidence, a good sense of who they are, their academic self, as well as their personhood. They don't always know that they are a person, in school.

Krystal's story of learning is a chilling indictment of ways that learning can be used by educators and schools to dehumanize students of color. She knows firsthand the courage it takes to regain a sense of personhood, when at one time she wanted to be white instead of brown skinned because whiteness was considered normal in her school. As her closing observation indicates, some elements of her learning experience are shared by her students of color. She works to convey to them that the *what* of learning is that they have a personhood whether the school sees this or not.

And it should be noted, although not stated so by Krystal, that her experience of dehumanizing pedagogy likely had a negative outcome on many of her white teachers and colleagues. Their false perceptions that only white students can achieve academically limited their perceptions of what is possible and skewed their sense of power and privilege. In his 1963 address to a group of school teachers, James Baldwin pointed to a similar theme of how the misleading negative perceptions of Black achievement by white citizens distorts the humanity of both groups: "If I am not what I've been told I am, then it means that you're not what you thought you were either! And that is the crisis" (p. 3). In a perverse and traumatic fashion, there is a deep sense of strength that is learned in the presence of dehumanization and the realization that both the oppressed and the oppressor are living a false story of self. As del Carmen Salazar and Lerner (2019) noted, "While I experienced trauma that I wish I could change, it has made me a who I am. I am resilient, strong, and brave" (p. 30). Surely, educators can find better ways to teach strength, courage, and the humanization of the self.

Throughout the history of education, other competing notions of what students should learn have informed the day-to-day context of classrooms. Jacobs (2016), in *Teaching Truly: A Curriculum to Indigenize Mainstream Education*, argued that Indigenous ways of knowing are thousands of years old and as such they are "natural and thus best for most children" (p. 183). The *what* of his curriculum for learners includes "courage and fearlessness, not fear, is the ultimate mandate in most Indigenous cosmologies, with great generosity being the highest expression of courage" (p. 3). Nel Noddings (2015) asserted that the liberal arts curriculum is too narrow and inadequate to address the contemporary needs and demands of society. She believes that students need to learn the value and virtue of care before learning to master content or other skills deemed essential for formal schooling. For Noddings, *what* we learn has deep moral and ethical implications for how we treat self, others, ideas, and the world, as so clearly exemplified by the stories of Paula and Krystal.

In addition to content knowledge, learners often learn interesting unintended lessons. For example, students often develop the ability to read an educator and to know how to adjust their learning to the preferences of the teacher. This is a valuable skill as students move throughout the day, from one classroom to the next. Knowing what an educator expects, knowing their temperament, and knowing their instructional moves can reduce conflicts and improve chances for a good grade in a transactional model of learning. Athletes learn to read a coach and often adjust according to the coaching style; without it, they might not be selected to participate on game day. In a small way, learning to read others and to act in accordance with their expectations is to set aside aspects of the self, to become slightly less human, inasmuch as humanness is defined as truly existing in one's skin.

One truth that is often hidden in plain sight is that at the end of the day it is not the educator who determines what has been learned. It does not matter how caring, creative, innovative, or disciplined an educator is; only the learner determines what is learned. This can help explain why students often learn different things within the same classroom or experience. The power and agency of learning lie fully in the hands, heart, and head of the learner—and while the educator can help create a learning environment that is open and inclusive, the overall power of learning is with the learner. The learner, not the educator or educational policymakers, determines the full extent of what is learned. Learning can be difficult, and navigating the hidden curriculum and determining *what* is to be learned can be challenging. We cannot force learning and have a positive learning outcome.

The examples in this chapter show us that while we often may believe that learners are all being taught the same information and content, the opposite may well be true, and the ways in which young people are prepared may be very different depending on their contexts. As is often said, "We're not in the same boat—we're in the same storm. Some have a yacht, some have a canoe, and some are barely holding onto a raft." When we consider *what* is taught, we must remember that not every learner is as prepared, has access to resources, or even has experienced a cultural perspective that values different outcomes. For many learners, attending class is an act of courage as they navigate competing interests and expectations even as they seek to improve their life circumstances through education.

Opportunity for Reflection

What were the intended and unintended learnings from your K–12 education?

How did you adapt to the style and expectations of educators to enhance your learning?

Whenever you engage in a new learning experience, what do you notice in the educational space? How do qualities (social, ethical, and norms) impact the content of the learning experience?

As you reflect on the hidden curriculum, what seems more apparent to you now? What do you believe about the world, and how do you know this to be trustworthy?

If you are currently engaged in a role of educating or facilitating in some manner, to what extent is your own educational style self-made? To what extent is it an artifact of how you were taught? How might you answer a learner who asks "What are we learning today?"

5

THE *HOW* OF LEARNING

Education is not the filling of a pail, but the lighting of a fire.

—*William Butler Yeats*

In the Rumi (2004) poem that anchors this book, we are reminded of the dual focus of education, which includes both its outer and inner dimensions. Specific to this chapter, Rumi noted that the *how* of learning for many learners is memorization of content delivered by the teacher, "one acquired, / as a child in school memorizes facts and concepts / from books and from what the teacher says" (p. 178). Although Rumi's description of learning predates the period known as the Enlightenment, or the Age of Reason, by roughly 500 years, he spoke to the same values of education: the proper development of the mind and intellect, or what is often considered by educators as a "traditional" institutional framing of curriculum and pedagogy. Often in this model, a teacher conveys subject matter, and a student is expected to absorb concepts, content, and understandings, like a dry sponge soaking up precious wisdom or an empty pail passively waiting to be filled. Traditionally, this model of learning and teaching is considered a "rigorous" education because to master it requires rational discipline, time, hard work, dedication, and commitment to facts and concepts.

The *how* of learning in the second half of Rumi's poem is less clear. He anchored it in the heart and simply described it as "the fountainhead from within you, moving out." Exactly how knowledge from the heart is sustained or flows into and through educational spaces is not obvious. The *how* of the heart, or inner knowing, according to Rumi, is already formed and waiting to be uncovered. Rumi, with telling insight, described the ways in which our learning conversation partners have described both the outer and inner *how* of learning. We begin this consideration of these two methods of education and learning, which can at times appear to conflict with one another, by reflecting on personal memories of the educational process.

When you think of education, what images or places come to mind? For many, this means a K–12 school; when you think of school, you might envision teachers, friends, extracurricular activities, and maybe something about the courses you took. But what is often not at the forefront of many descriptions of schooling is a detailed understanding of "learning." What is it? How does it work? What does it mean to be a learner? Instead, many of us think of the consequences of learning or of the paths we took during that learning. For example, when Catherine remembers her high school, she thinks of playing in the marching band and of her friends. She remembers where her locker was. She remembers the difficulty she had getting purple spray paint out of her hair on the fateful day she and her friends decided to use their high school colors to get ready for a pep rally. While all these memories are ones that she experienced at school and through the education process, they do not really focus on what she learned or what her teachers wanted to teach her. For Catherine, did significant learning occur in high school? Absolutely. Was it all formal learning? Absolutely not. How can we better consider the concept of education with a focus on what is learned and how that learning really happens, and how do we go about describing the complexity of learning?

Learning as a Process

The classic definitions of the *how* of learning involve broad descriptions of the process by which we acquire new knowledge or information (Dewey, 1938; Piaget, 1964; Vygotsky, 1978). Learning in the traditional sense is considered a physical action or a mental process, something that involves the learner doing something, even as sometimes the "doing" is being oriented to the process of learning. Learners build their knowledge as they interact with others or observe someone else doing something or modeling a behavior. Learning often involves making connections between existing ideas and adding new concepts to what has been learned. Learning almost always builds on something that the learner already knows.

P. A. Alexander (1996) argued that our existing knowledge allows for "a scaffold that supports the construction of all future learning" (p. 89). Throughout the learning process we are actively building as we go. Notice that much of what has been discussed so far in this chapter focuses on what the learner, rather than the educator, does. This is an essential point: Learning is an active process that cannot happen without the work of the learner. The teacher is often the person who may seem to be doing a great deal of the work (and teachers do work very hard to make sure that their students learn!), but learning does not happen without the learner actually engaging with the process in some way. It is interesting that in much of the research and theory of education, the scholarship focuses on teaching to facilitate learning. Oddly enough, the work of the learner is rarely a major focus, except perhaps when learners resist, or fail to understand what is being taught. Why is so much power invested in the teacher when learning is fully learner dependent?

In this chapter, we focus on the *how* of the work in which learning occurs and the ways in which an educator can involve the learner in the process so that significant and meaningful learning can transpire. When we consider learning, it can be a difficult concept to capture. We cannot actually "see" the learning happen within the brain or predict how learning will materialize in the future. It is often more ineffable, less concrete and, as such, difficult to fully understand or describe with language. It is sometimes rife with ambiguity and meanings that change with content, context, and the subjective condition of the learner (Dewey, 1938). Rumi captured this feature of learning by employing the metaphor of a "spring overflowing its springbox." Our learning conversation partners affirm this mysterious nature of learning, especially the ways it might be blocked in some formal settings, only to emerge much later in unexpected places.

Like water, learning always finds its way through any obstacle, but it might just take time. Jasmine's story of learning shows that, like a river flowing, learning often takes unexpected avenues and inspirations well beyond the classroom setting. Jasmine is respected as the director of a philanthropic organization that supports young people who are exceptionally dedicated to service. Organized, decisive, and outgoing, she is known for her hardworking, practical, and responsible work ethic.

> It's interesting, how I got into this field. Many years ago, I had a bachelor's degree and at that time, all my decisions were based on family choices. Basically, I found myself [in a particular city] and I said, OK, I'm staying here, so what am I going to do? Hey, it was an opportunity for me to escape my closed little town. But I landed in a place that placed tremendous emphasis on your pedigree—how many letters came after your name? I applied for an administrative assistant position, the only thing I seemed to be qualified for. I really needed the work, and honestly, the idea of being a secretary didn't thrill me—not that there is anything wrong with this kind of position—but I needed to do something.

Jasmine was hired as an administrative assistant in a program that focused on student career development. As a first-generation college student, she quickly found that she understood students' journeys. During her job interview, it really "clicked"—she formed a strong, immediate connection with the supervisor, who would become an incomparable mentor. After Jasmine was hired, she was forthright, saying that she had a degree and, much as the job was a terrific path for many, she did not want to be a secretary for the rest of her life. She told her supervisor she would do everything and anything, "but please, teach me: Tell me everything you know."

Incredibly, Jasmine says, her supervisor did help her acquire essential skills. Jasmine followed through on all her daily tasks and typed a plethora of letters, and her supervisor began to slip her other work: résumé critiquing, interview techniques, how to conduct workshops for students:

> I discovered that I had a natural propensity for humans. [My supervisor] allowed me to step outside my job duties and I perfected my craft through learning by doing. And then, she encouraged me to work on a graduate degree so I could do this work in an official capacity. I basically took courses that allowed me to legitimately engage. Ultimately, I took over her job as director of that career office. Her teaching method was effective! My soaking up the information was effective, too.

Now in her late career, Jasmine reflects on the *how* of her learning. She is concerned that the mentoring or apprenticeship model of being taught over time by a caring guide on the side might not be possible for this generation of young people. She believes that professionals have become too busy and with the added emphasis on credentialing and degrees; learning from someone who takes time to communicate the tricks of the trade, so to speak, might belong to a dying era:

> I don't think formal education is the only way that people learn and we have to be more open to opportunities for alternatives. We must understand that there are many ways for people to use their skills, it's not about the letters that follow their name—not to dumb down things yet understanding it's more than this. It's someone's attitude, their dedication. I worry that we are not open to valuing other ways of learning and knowing.

In fact, Jasmine is committed enough to this path of transformation that she has paid it forward:

> Following the model that my former director afforded me, I feel I did the same for my administrative assistant—encouraging her to go for her degree—but also allowing her to reach beyond her job description and work directly with students before she had the credentials. I recently was able to promote her to assistant director.

Whether through the guidance of a caring mentor or other unique paths to acquiring core knowledge in a field, there are many ways to gain mastery. As such, the *how* of learning is not always easily captured in a traditional lesson plan, workshop activity template, or curriculum standards. In this chapter, we articulate the technical dimensions of learning, the science, and concrete practices of learning. In addition, we uplift the deeper, indefinable elements of learning such as awe, wonder, and courage. We take solace in the writings of Abraham Heschel (1976), who named the ineffable as that which is known but not fully knowable. He defined the ineffable as "that aspect of reality which by its very nature lies beyond our comprehension and is acknowledged by our mind to be beyond the scope of the mind" (p. 104). Yet while the ineffable is beyond the mind to fully comprehend, it still exists within the realm of human understanding and behavior: "The ineffable, then, is a synonym for *hidden meaning* rather than for the absence of meaning" (p. 105, emphasis added). Learning can be as concrete as facts memorized and repeated and as mysterious and hard to pinpoint as the mentoring process Jasmine describes.

A Brief History of "Learning" Through the Lens of *How*

As a starting point for an expanded notion of the *how* of learning, one that reaches beyond memorization and mimicry of the educator, we turn to the early evidence of human learning. The archaeological record suggests that learning has a long partnership with human development and the formation of community norms. The earliest known records of human intelligence are the carved or painted images on sacred sites. They go back at least 40,000 to 60,000 years. These visual representations are widespread in their distribution, beginning with early humans in Africa and quickly becoming global in scope as humans migrated across the earth. Drawings, paintings, rock carvings, and other imagery are evident in Spain, Australia, South America, Italy, North America, Somaliland, and Bulgaria.

Karen Armstrong (2009) presented a compelling argument that these sacred sites and images represent early lessons and learnings on how to be in community. If she is correct, the *how* of learning can be traced far back in antiquity. Her work focuses on the cave walls of Lascaux, France, dating back approximately 20,000 years. She believes that the Lascaux Paleolithic art was used in elaborate rituals signaling the transition into adulthood and full membership into the community. For the people of the Lascaux region, the caves were an ancient classroom. The *how* of learning consisted of a willingness to be led into the caves, an intentional learning space designed to disorient the learner, and a willingness to experience mystery and transcendence as a gateway into the new identity of an adult. The paintings, flickering torch-light, and the confined space acted to both disassociate the learner from their previous frames of knowing and to offer new frames of meaning by which to understand the world outside the cave.

This is an important distinction with respect to many contemporary forms of education that are based on the layering or retraction of knowledge by an external authority. In some classrooms we see an additive layering of socially prescribed definitions of self as the main outcome of learning. Other times, what happens in education is subtractive (e.g., removing a student's language or cultural references). In an additive or subtractive education the *how* of learning is an external process of norming in which the teacher pours knowledge (that affirms or denies a learner's identity) into the mind of the learner, who typically passively receives the offering.

In contrast, the cave classrooms described by Armstrong (2009) require the learner to act courageously, activate internal resources to enter the cave, grapple with personal uncertainties and fears, and make meaning of the embodied experience. Learning in the caves of Lascaux was robust and took work. The learning journey was facilitated by a teacher, the ancient "animal master" who embodied the spiritual world and who acted as a conduit to transformation. They dressed in furs and wore an animal mask to signal their transitional human identity, which kept the power of learning focused on the young person as an emerging adult. Such was the form and function of Paleolithic learning. It took courage and a deep sense of personal agency to abandon the identity of child and accept, upon leaving the cave, the identity of adult and full acceptance into their clan. The *how* of learning was a syn-thesis of individual commitment, disorientation, skillful spiritual guidance, and reorientation to self in community.

Moving closer to contemporary times, in the 2nd and 3rd centuries AD, the divergent images in the Rumi poem of imparting and drawing out knowledge were personified by two types of educators. Just as in the caves of Lascaux, the *how* of learning was informed and influenced by the *how* of teaching. In Greek and Roman education, the first teacher a learner encountered, if they were privileged enough to be born into a family of means, was the *pedagogue*. The pedagogue's job was to teach the basic ele-ments of grammar, rhetoric, and logic, which persist today as the founda-tions of the liberal arts curriculum. Because their teaching techniques were characterized as harsh, didactic, and often physically abusive, they earned the nickname "ear benders" (McGuckin, 2017). The task of learning under the guidance of the pedagogue was a good match for *educare*: education as imposition from outside and into the head of the learner. The pedagogue aligns with the *how* of learning in Rumi's (2004) poem in which "a child in school memorizes facts and concepts / from books and from what the teacher says" (p. 178). In the 21st century, the pedagogue, although using less strenuous techniques, is still the normative model for teaching. Many lesson plans favor rote memorization and reproduction of knowledge as the primary form of learning.

In antiquity, if a student showed promise, and if the family was wealthy, the young scholar (typically, though not always, male) was placed under the intellectual care of the *mystagogue*. As previously noted, the first stage of a learner's education was focused on the natural sciences, mathematics, and arts, what are known today as the liberal arts. Although building on the foundation of the pedagogue, the mystagogue's approach to learning was to "mystify" the teachings of the pedagogue. The primary tools of the mystagogue were metaphor, analogy, and intentional falsehoods designed to complicate and add complexity to the knowledge of the learner. The mystagogue, as educator, was closer to the meaning of *educere* because learners were led out of their intellectual confinement into relationship with the robust truths of the world, truths that were stable but subject to interpretation as the learner's wisdom grew and matured. The *how* of learning for the mystagogue required attention to the inner life of the student (moral, ethical, and spiritual), and knowledge was viewed as a constructed endeavor among learner, teacher, and text. Learning theory in the 21st century calls this coconstruction of knowledge *constructivism*, and it relies heavily on centering the learner in the *how* of learning.

With this very brief historical glimpse of pedagogy and its implications for the *how* of learning completed, we now turn to addressing the question of *how* people learn. What tools or skills are necessary for learning to occur? One line of inquiry leads to the *social efficiency tradition*, which is often closely associated with a classical education in the liberal arts. Early examples of the social efficiency tradition can be found in the Platonic ideal that members of society are born with specific talents that, once identified, can be effectively applied to the needs and interests of society. Plato's (1969) "myth of the metals" (p. 415), which he defined in *The Republic*, suggests that people are born with either gold, silver, bronze, or iron mixed into their soul. Anyone possessing gold is destined to become part of the ruling class, and anyone born with bronze or silver is best suited for production and guarding the republic. Another noteworthy but discredited example of social efficiency is *phrenology*, the late–18th-century belief that the physical structure of a person's skull corresponded to their level of intelligence, providing a justification for social sorting and racism. What you were born with was essentially a "track" or a role within society and within education. The *how* of learning was less about a process and more about finding the right fit between learner abilities and societal needs and structure.

Aspects of the social efficiency tradition are present in many elementary classrooms. For example, students are put into reading level groups (perhaps the "bluebirds" or the "redbirds"), and this reading level group sets a frame for what they learn and how quickly they learn it. From the point of view of teaching, these groups are instructionally efficient. From a developmental point of view, leveled groups can be problematic. Because this tracking often begins in early elementary school, a pattern of learning can form whereby it becomes more and more difficult for learners to demonstrate the mastery of knowledge that would move them into a different (probably higher) reading group. The social efficiency tradition is also evident in the formulation of national, state, and district testing regimens designed to ensure learners are performing academically in accordance with standard measures of success, learning outcomes that are often understood as correlating with college preparation programs or workforce readiness. As such, students may be tracked into a selection of courses that are less of their choosing and more based on the perceptions of educators who are relying on external measures to inform what is developmentally best for the student.

Along one track, the *how* of learning (reading, writing, and thinking) presupposes the student's enrollment in the academic track and entry into higher education. In the second track, the *how* of learning is practical and experiential (internships, technical experiences, and field trips) and involves classes as vocational education in preparation for the trades. In both models, *how* the student learns is seen as an indicator of their future function and role in society. A proxy for the *how* of learning is the intelligence test, which historically sorted learners into categories of differing learning types. As a byproduct of the testing industry, students learned *how* to take tests and *how* to improve their test scores. Mastering these skills often carries longer term consequences related to academic tracks, access to higher education, and potentially higher income. Although efficient, the inherent subjectivity in student–educator relationships can introduce bias into academic decision-making that can affect learning for a young person's foreseeable future. While there may be reasons for the social efficiency tradition, such as determining which students need additional services to bridge the educational attainment gap, this potential use is sometimes, often inadvertently, used to "keep students in their place."

Learning as a Constructed Process

Think back to a time when you learned something new. Perhaps this was in elementary school or even later in life. When we learn something new, we must find ways to make what we are learning relevant and to fit in with what we already know. Sometimes, this new learning will change what we think we know (a process that Jean Piaget [1964] called *accommodation*). This process can be difficult since we need to rethink what we believed to be true. And yet, this process of constructing what we learn is one of the most important aspects of learning in which we engage. It takes courage to reconstruct what we know and to take into consideration new information or perspectives. Cranton (2016) recognized that *transformation*, the ability to set aside old ways of knowing and embracing new understandings, is the definitive definition of learning. For Cranton, learning is synonymous with a change in identity; becoming a new person is a true act of courage. When we engage in this type of learning, we need to make sure that we are taking the time to do this to allow the mind, in a way, to wrap itself around this new way of thinking. So often in education the focus is on efficiently attaining new content, and we often forget that whatever new thing we are learning must be reconciled and connected to what we already know.

Here is what a college student, Gwendolyn, has to say about this process:

> Generally during the semester at my university, I never feel okay about spending my time "unproductively." I hate returning to this mindset, like each second of allotted time must be devoted to accomplishing something, otherwise I'm getting behind or "wasting" time. And so the first time I went to sketch in the conservatory, I felt a bit guilty for spending an hour out of my day doing something that was not explicitly required of me or penciled into my planner. I was not really "accomplishing" anything, not checking anything off of the list of things I needed to do, so what was the point? But the enjoyment I found from this was so complete, once I relinquished my feelings of guilt and anxiety over this unprofitable use of my time, that I keep returning to waste time in such a perfect way. And of course it is not wasting time, because I am learning so much through this close observation of plants. It is only a waste of time when viewed through my university's achievement lens that values time based on productivity and results. It has meant I got a bit behind on my actual assignments/exercises for this week, because the sketches I've been doing aren't submittable, so next week I'll have to divide my time more evenly between allotting enough time for at-home practice on assignments and free observational study.

When we take time to contemplate the connections between what we are learning and what we have already learned, the *how* of learning changes and can become more potent. Returning to Gwendolyn's story, she shares:

> Through my time in the conservatory, I have felt this shift occur, where once-complicated leaf patterns and strange twists and folds intimidated my eye, I now revel in their complexity and the growing ease with which

I feel I am able to capture them. Where once looking at botanical intricacy overwhelmed me, I can now calmly and slowly appreciate it, noticing further details.

From the learner's perspective, taking the time to reflect can support and enhance learning new information. And from the educator's perspective, building in time allows learners to slow down and consider *how* new content or skills connect to what they already know from previous lessons. In this reflection space, powerful learning can occur as the learner is empowered to make the *how* of learning personally relevant and meaningful.

As noted in the previous discussion about social efficiency and schooling, creating a space for reflection and the construction of knowledge can be difficult since educators are often focused on the learning outcomes and tasks that need to be accomplished within a short time frame. However, research and practice show that not integrating this reflection time usually weakens the learning (Cranton, 2016). Educating with a focus on helping learners to construct their knowledge is incredibly influential and can be life changing for students. Since learners build new knowledge into their preexisting foundation of information, we can see how important that interplay is between what has been learned and what is being learned.

This makes the learning an active process, not just a passive one. This active learning is more engaging and meaningful, and simultaneously this also can make it seem more challenging. As students learn new information they are actively involved in "making meaning" (Vygotsky, 1978), and this involves not only the learner and the new content but also the community around that student. Imagine the power of a student going back into their home or community and talking about what has been learned that was personally meaningful and transformational. The resulting conversations reinforce the learning and will provide that student the space in which to listen to other perspectives and gain new insights into the learning connections they are making. As an educator, providing reflective practices with prompts to students that involve discussing the new learning with friends, family, and others can be a powerful tool to advance learning.

Significant Learning Experiences

While not all learning is significant and impactful, much of it is (or can be). When a student experiences significant learning, this is almost always an experience that will change how they think, provide another perspective on how to approach an issue, and may even result in knowledge that they remember for the rest of their lives. These types of learning experiences do not often occur by chance, and yet they can. Think back to the journey that Marcia shared in chapter 2. She had the experience of her brother coming in as a substitute teacher for her math class. Students were confused about some of the calculus principles that they were supposed to learn. They were not making the connections between what they were learning and how to use that new principle. But their new teacher asked them questions and showed other ways of thinking about what they were learning. He "demonstrated some things we'd never been taught. I vividly recall looking around the classroom and watching the light bulbs go off over a few students' heads" (p. 32). This type of "Ah-ha!" moment is powerful, and we have all likely had at least a few of these experiences. So, how do we make more of these important and significant learning experiences happen for ourselves and for students? The *how* of deep learning seems to include mystery and surprise.

According to Dee Fink (2013), if this is our intention then we need to create interactions that involve what students are interested in and care about; the actual foundational material learned; and specific information about the learner, including what they already know and how they learn. When students are actively engaged and experiencing their learning as interesting and meaningful, they tend to think more deeply about and internalize what they learn. This leads to very impactful learning that has the power to change perspectives and how learners think.

When Brooke was in sixth grade, she took a class in sign language. She learned many of the signs quickly and enjoyed the class. It was not until her teacher invited her to come with her to visit a school for the deaf that Brooke finally saw that what she had learned was more than just physically making words with her hands:

> When I went to the school and saw the students in the hallways signing to each other and to me, I suddenly realized that what I had learned was a way to communicate with them—and they could understand me and we could have a conversation together. They were the same as me, but they communicated with their hands and now I could be a part of them. It wasn't just learning words and vocabulary for me anymore. I saw a different way to know people. And, if you can't communicate with someone, you will never know them.

These types of experiential learning opportunities can take time. And yet, when students can deeply embed themselves in what they are learning and they find ways to connect that learning with what they already know, they will have learning experiences that can be transformational. Like Armstrong's (2009) description of learning in Paleolithic times, students can emerge from the metaphorical cave with new ways of knowing and a new identity as a learner. As we think about how we learn, finding ways to connect learning and experiences, along with the opportunity to care about what is learned, will generate these types of significant learning.

Learning as Problem-Solving

Another way to think about *how* we learn is to consider the role of problem-solving in the learning process. When we approach any problem, we must simultaneously consider several things. These include (a) information about the problem itself; (b) our past experiences with this type of problem; (c) possible solutions, as well as ways to consider which solutions might be best; and (d) deciding on a path forward with a solution. This constitutes a lot of learning that can be enacted when facing any type of problem. Barbara Duch, Susan Groh, and Deborah Allen (2001) of the University of Delaware have extensively studied and practiced the process of problem-based learning (PBL) to connect real-world problems with student interests and background knowledge. The *how* of learning becomes a rich interactive plane between the immediacy of practical problems, the expertise and interest of the learner, and new forms of knowledge that address the gap between existing knowledge and what a learner needs to know to adequately address the real life situation they are encountering.

In formal education, more times than not we think of "problems" as the purview of mathematics, in which students are given problems to solve in the classroom or as homework to demonstrate mastery, and it is often the case that there is only a single correct answer derived from a singular approach to solving the problem. While a student can and does learn how to solve math problems, the type of problem-solving discussed in this chapter on the *how* of learning is broader and addresses larger issues. In the real world, many problems are complex, multifaceted, and have a multitude of possible solutions. These types of problems are called "wicked problems" or "authentic" problems that engage students in the *how* of learning with the combination of content and application. Peter Johnston (2012) discussed why there is a need to "normalize struggles" as part of the learning process so that students learn that most problems they will face do not have an easy answer and it is expected that there will be work required to approach any problem as a part of the overall process.

Problem posing is an important teaching tool in every discipline. In PBL, teachers lead with an open-ended issue and a set of critical questions that help to focus the students on what is to be solved and the overall nature of the problem. When students get engaged with these types of real-world problems, they not only are learning the material, but they also are engaging with others in ways to ask questions, evaluate solutions, and use a variety of sources to think differently (Duckworth, 2016).

There are many examples of teachers using PBL at every level of education. For example, University of Delaware faculty, through research and practice, show the level of complexity and engagement that can be achieved a problem at the center of the learning experience. In the handout developed by Deborah Allen (2001), "Who Owns the Geritol Solution?" a PBL exploration of iron applications to ocean waters to address global warming, students are asked to challenge assumptions and consider concepts related to the difficulties of addressing climate alleviation, several concepts and theories in biology, overall ways to evaluate and test solutions in real time, and whether they would fund such endeavors. When students experience PBL they are sometimes shocked at the amount of work involved in the learning process. The *how* of approaching problems is an active and participatory way of learning!

Consider the experience of Susan, a 10th-grade student. When Susan realized she would have to take an American history course, she was not overly excited. She said that learning a bunch of dry and old facts about things that had already happened was a waste of time. Her teacher set up the learning environment by offering up a critical question:

> You are a teen-aged revolutionary living in Boston in 1773. Several laws have recently been passed by your king in Britain, and there is a lot of unrest around town. A proclamation is read in your community that says "Hear ye, hear ye! You are called to a town meeting to discuss the incoming tea shipments. Don't let your rights be dismissed! Attend this town meeting and let your voice be heard!" What do you do? What information do you need to have?

When students discussed this issue, the teacher asked further questions focusing on what laws were in place, how decisions about revolution and fighting back were made, and how leadership worked. Susan became very engaged and went to the library to find books on the Boston Tea Party and was amazed to find out that many of those who had been involved were her age or even younger. She learned more about the Boston Tea Party, the resulting conflicts, and even some information about different forms of government. Years after the class was over, Susan still brings up facts and ideas that she gained from this school assignment.

Certainly PBL is not limited to the classroom setting. Solving real life problems is at the heart of every community, municipality, district— anywhere in which real life issues are paramount. How we collaborate to solve them is vital.

Cooperative Learning With Others

Learning is sometimes approached as an individual, solitary process. That can be true, but learning also can be a collaborative process that allows for powerful learning experiences beyond what an individual can typically achieve. In fact, collaborative learning is considered one of the 10 most impactful strategies for effective instruction (Millis, 2010). Drawing learners into conversations about content, problems, and community needs is critical for learning success because it bolsters a sense of engagement. Key to cooperative learning is a readiness to learn on the part of all who are engaged.

When the *how* of students' learning is collaborative, they often take ownership of the process and are often more engaged in the interactions, which can lead to impactful and deeper learning. "Collaborative learning is based on the idea that learning is a naturally social act in which the participants talk among themselves" (Gerlach, 1994, p. 8). There are many ways to incorporate collaborative learning, including informally; when students seek one another out, and ask questions of each other, they may find they are more engaged in what they learn. Whenever a learner discusses what they are learning with another person, they can better understand the material, put it in their own words, and do more than memorize facts. In these informal spaces, the space between the *how* and the *what* of learning is narrowed and expanded at the same time. Collaboration narrows the learning space to the relational dynamics between peers, and it broadens the outcomes to include content, process, and social–emotional elements.

In addition to the informal process of finding other students, many educators work to create cooperative and collaborative learning opportunities within the classroom structure; this takes work in the context of thoughtful preparation, not assuming cooperation and collaboration will simply happen. In her book on collaborative learning, Millis (2010) weaved back and forth between the theory and practice of collaboration. Through the articulation of learning theory and concrete stories of educators' practicing collaboration, Millis demonstrated the positive impact of collaboration, including student responsibility, constructive interdependent relationships, the importance of mixed teams, effective communication, and leadership that builds community.

In the classroom setting anchored in collaboration, students are often challenged as they listen to different student perspectives that may not always align with their own. In these cases, students must articulate clearly, and sometimes defend, their perspectives and ideas. Through this engagement and inquiry, students create their own conceptual framework, helping to make learning more powerful and personal. This type of learning is courageous because what has been learned and internalized may diverge from what the student knew before. Restating what an expert said or what was in the textbook is no longer a true representation of learning. The learning is now owned by the student, shaped by their prior experiences, and becomes a part of their identity.

A case in point is Dajah's experience with collaborative learning. She learned new concepts and facts, and she began to think about her life in different ways. As a university student, Dajah was taking a class on a topic that was not that interesting to her. Because of the collaborative nature of the course and the performance narrative that was required, she became more engaged with other students, with the wider community, and with the course content. This combination of collaborative, community responsibility and ownership of learning changed the ways in which she thought about climate change and her role in making a difference:

> You know, it was funny because when I enrolled in this course I thought it was going to be about social justice. I didn't know it was going to focus on climate change and when I found out, I almost dropped the class. At the time I thought, "I don't really want to learn about this, I don't think I can do anything about it anyway, it's just too much! Nothing's going to change unless we go back to hunting and gathering. What, you think we're going to go back to not relying on electricity? How are we going to go back on our technological advancement?"

Dajah was smiling as she shared this story of learning. She had just completed a course with so many layers that it is difficult to articulate all of them. The class was indeed focused on social change, as she hoped, but in ways she did not expect. An important aspect of her learning was the performance assignment, "Climates of Change," a collaborative production involving the commitment of university students, faculty, and community members. Dajah learned that the assignment was an experiment by the instructor to move away from a lecture-heavy course format that favored the presentation of theory and social change frameworks. Instead, the collaborative assignment offered a more engaging and practical theater-in-action approach to learning that was more student centered. In his book *Teaching as the Art of Staging*, Anthony Weston (2018) argued that staging learning simulations and situations offers instructors a middle ground between teacher-centered and student-centered learning. In the "Impresario With a Scenario" model of teaching the instructor sets the staging and framing and the students take their learning forward, at times with additional guidance and at times fully independent of the instructor.

Dajah decided to stay in the course because she found the framework intriguing. The first 7 weeks of the course were designed as a learning period, delving into both the scientific foundations of what is known to date about climate change as well as the application of that learning to theater. Students were immersed in a living-newspaper approach that became common in Russia during the Bolshevik revolution, which presents accurate information on current events in a compelling manner. Guest presenters offered information about climate change to build a foundation of knowing to inform the final performance. To craft the performance narrative, students participated in afternoon meals and story circles with community members and organizations, including a local neighborhood community center and historical agency. When it came to interviewing people to draw upon their stories, Dajah was hooked:

> I discovered that I appreciated learning about climate change in this way, rather than something dry and hard core. I wanted to know about real people and their lives. The last seven weeks, we developed the play, coming up with the characters and the big questions based on the stories we heard. Although I began by thinking we couldn't do anything at all about climate change, I had to sit back, accept the facts to the best of my ability and try to be positive. I wanted to give justice to all the stories we told, and I discovered that performing is fundamentally about effectively providing a meaningful message to people.

The performance spoke to the known effects of climate change, through a narrator, main characters, projected images of environmental research, and a focus on farm life. The audience members did indeed learn about climate change—and yet in a way that brought it back to their own lives instead of the more remote, critical-analyses strategy characteristic of many teacher-centered educational settings.

As a result of an immersion in this unusual learning format, Dajah's perspective has changed. No longer blindsided by the huge and overwhelming issues about which she may have very little influence, she adds:

> If I do a little bit every day and be conscious, such as reducing the plastics that I purchase, looking at my food choices, composting, recycling, not buying processed foods, these are little changes which can snowball into

bigger changes. Because there are so many different people in the world, it's going to be hard to come to a unified place of lasting change—but I've learned that what you can do is to focus on yourself. Surprisingly, people were really affected by this performance. They were inspired! In our story circles, people said out loud toxic things going on and how they worked with it—it was a big realization to find out that there were small things, things they did, they had real life experiences that made a difference, and that made this performance meaningful. The facts are scary and make me sad but what touched our hearts were the stories of everyday people working hard. Now I'm saying, "So what can I do?"

Cooperative and collaborative learning is a powerful way to engage with the material and use the content of what is learned to do more than merely memorize information. The *how* of cooperative learning can be difficult and challenging, and many students may avoid doing this because of the level of work that must happen with this type of engaged learning. Often, students must show the courage to be vulnerable and enter a cooperative learning experience without knowing exactly what will happen or how successful they will be at the end. It takes courage, both for an educator or facilitator creating these learning experiences and for the participants who engage with them. But this courage can be rewarded with greater enjoyment of the learning process and new perspectives from which to view the world. Because of its nature, collaborative learning allows a growth in how to question, consider, and learn with others. Learning in this collaborative manner takes courage and persistence, but the result can be a vibrant community of learners in which there are growth and joy in the learning process.

The Important Role of Prior Learning

Earlier in this chapter, we addressed the idea of *how* learning is constructed. As we learn new information, we usually connect that new learning to what we already know or have seen. The connections that are made between what is new and what we already know are an important part of understanding why learning can be so difficult. The information that we already have (often labeled "prior learning") can help or hinder the construction of new knowledge. In the 17th century, the philosopher John Locke suggested that at birth, humans have a *tabula rasa* ("blank slate"). He speculated that the infant's mind is clean, with nothing in it until experience and learning provide something to add to this blank space. We know that this is not the way infant minds are at birth; there are many aspects to infant memory that have been well documented. The idea that any new learning for us goes on a "blank slate" is simply not true. Whenever we are exposed to a new idea or see something for the first time, we compare it to what we already know. In some cases, this can be helpful in organizing our thoughts and gaining more knowledge; sometimes our prior learning can actually hinder new learning.

We all learn things that are incorrect. Sometimes these misconceptions can be easily remedied by gaining new insight or recognizing our error, and yet this is not always the case; prior learning can also lead to bias that prevents us from accepting new information that challenges our established view. There are many times when we will not (or cannot) change the misconception that we hold. This may be because we are embarrassed by our misunderstandings, or because to embrace new knowledge means re-forming our identity, or we just do not have the time to deeply reflect and understand why change is necessary. In a classic example of misunderstandings, in 1987, the Harvard–Smithsonian Center for Astrophysics filmed a short documentary that demonstrated that many people (even Harvard graduates) could not correctly explain why it is colder in the winter and warmer in the summer (you can see the full documentary here: https://www.learner.org/series/a-private-universe/1-a-private-universe/).

Why is it that many of the students in this documentary could not seem to let go of their incorrect misconception that summer heat is caused by being closer to the sun? The students' informal learning was clear: When you bring your hand closer to a heat or light source, it gets hotter. Therefore, this must work to explain summer heat. This is, of course, incorrect. But the strength of the misconception is so powerful that many students could not let go of the misconception even when faced with facts and demonstrations. We all experience this, and for educators who are working to change these previously learned misconceptions it is an ongoing challenge. In this context, the *how* of learning is a form of unlearning; mistakes and false starts can be an important element of *how*.

Overcoming these misconceptions takes several steps. The first is that the prior learning must be recognized and identified by both the instructor and the learner. Rather than jumping in to teach new material, educators often find that they will be more successful in the long run by asking open-ended questions to find out what students already know (or think that they know). Asking questions that start with "Why . . ." or "How come . . . " can be very useful to better understand where there are misconceptions already. Then, both the teacher and the learner can discuss the misconception and find ways to debunk it. Using experiential and more hands-on learning at this point can be helpful since this will better engage the learner with the learning process. Then, teaching the new learning and comparing it with the previous misconception can help to construct new learning that is accurate and lasting.

The Importance of Grit and Hardiness

In this book, we center courage as an important aspect of learning. Psychologist Angela Duckworth (2013) noted that "Grit is living life like a marathon, not a sprint." When learners have a passion for something and they persevere through challenges to learn or be successful, we often label that as "grit." Learners with higher levels of grit and persistence are more likely to show perseverance as they work toward long-term goals that are important to them (Wotters & Hussain, 2015). Developing this grit and hardiness is an important part of successful learning. But how do we develop this? And how do we keep working even when learning something new is difficult and frustrating?

When Margaret was in middle school, she wanted to learn how to play the French horn. She signed up for beginning band in sixth grade and was so excited. The first thing that the class taught was how to read music. Since Margaret had already taken piano for several years, this was a skill she already had—it was easy for her. However, when the band director brought out a French horn and tried to teach her how to blow into the instrument to produce a sound, she found it difficult. After several tries and many corrections, she was able to make a sound on the instrument. She was thrilled and thought that playing the horn was going to be easy. It wasn't. As she tried to make the sound of the correct note, she was off more times than on. Because there are only three keys on a French horn, the same fingering can produce several different notes. To be successful, a French horn player must "hear" the note in their head and pair that with the right breath support and embouchure.

But Margaret could not hear the note in her head—she did not have a good sense of pitch. Once she got the right note, she could move on to other notes more easily, but making the first note in any piece of music was difficult. When she played with the other musicians in the band, she would often miss the note. This was embarrassing and frustrating. And yet Margaret loved to play. She took her French horn home every day to practice. She would play the note on the piano so that she could truly hear the note and find the way to hit the right note on her horn. This took years of work and training. Margaret was eventually successful and was able to play in several orchestras and bands over the years. She wasn't going to give up; she wanted to play, and she knew that nothing would stop her.

While there is no easy way to develop grit, Duckworth (2016) suggested that we do the following:

- Know that mistakes happen, but they are temporary, and we can use mistakes to learn and grow.
- Develop problem-solving abilities by breaking the problem down into smaller, more manageable parts and find ways that we have control over the problem situation.
- Never underestimate the importance and usefulness of timely, relevant, detailed feedback.
- Keep asking questions that encourage self-reflection about what you are learning.
- Find ways to develop goals that are just outside of your current abilities—create aspirational goals that you truly care about.
- Keep practicing the skills that you want to gain and improve—never give up!

Persistence in Learning

We know that learning can be challenging, and it can be even more difficult for learners who experience learning in a nontraditional fashion. Eric's story is one of persistence and dedication to his goal in the face of some learning disabilities that added additional layers of difficulty to the ways that he approaches learning. Here is a look at his story.

It is early in the morning, and a boy is getting ready to leave for the day. Bedroll and pillow, check. All his meals, including breakfast, lunch, and dinner, check. Comfy clothing, check. Snacks and beverages, check, check. A camping trip or school outing? Sports tournament? No, not at all. Eric is getting ready to take two exams. He has learning disabilities and is about to use a modification, extended testing time, to ensure his success. He has two 3-hour exams in one day, and he is ready for the long haul.

He tells the proctor, "I hope you don't have anything to do for the next 12 hours, because I'm using every minute. I want to do really well." And he did. Eric took every minute of the 12 hours. He did well.

Now, as an adult and educator, Eric is beloved as a high school technology teacher, soccer coach, Carolina Tar Heels fan, and warm and caring presence in his family. By those who know him well he is known affectionately as "E." Always up for activities with family and friends, he is the kind of educator who lights up a room when he walks in:

> I was diagnosed in first grade—that's when I remember a big change. The change involved going to a specialist with a group of us removed from the classroom. At an early age I was identified as having issues with processing and reading. I went to a reading specialist and that helped, since reading was a huge struggle from first grade all the way through college. And throughout that entire time I've worked with it. I can remember early on what a difference it was in first grade, three or four of us getting pulled out into a separate classroom.
>
> I'm telling you, I had a lot of anger, a lot of issues because of this growing up.
>
> About fifth grade things started clicking for me. It was the first time I had a male teacher and he helped me start recognizing learning disabilities, what I had to do about it, how to cope with it, and basically just accepting it. This was the age I went through a period of deep acceptance. Up to that point I was butting heads with it and tried to fight it like it wasn't there. From fifth grade on, I started moving past the idea that this was the only thing to define me and getting to that next level. Getting the concept in my mind that this was something that was going to be with me, this is a real thing. And I said, alright well, I really need to deal with it, accept that sometimes it's going to take forever to do reading assignments. Know that everyone around me might take 15 minutes on something that's going to take me an hour and a half. Everything is going to take me a lot longer.

Eric credits his parents and top-notch resources in high school for helping him understand those vital accommodations that were available to him. For example, he talks about a program that scanned his books and would read them back to him. He recorded everything and listened to assignments in his room at the end of a school day, walking from one place to another, snatching bits of time any place he could get them. As he notes, "I used my testing modifications to the max. Extended test time was double time, so during high school and college, I always had to prepare to camp out there for a full day."

Eric discovered that the *how* of his learning is a highly visual, pictorial learner and that excessively lengthy written instructions "shut him down." He was fortunate to have a talented high school learning specialist to teach him to advocate for himself, which became critical in college. Eric chokes up as he recalls what he had to do in each course:

> Every semester I approached every single professor at the beginning of each class. I needed to say who I was and what I needed to be successful. I'm telling you, it's a tough thing to walk up to the front of a classroom with

300 students and say, "I'm Eric, I have a learning disability, and here's what it's gonna be. I need to come in for extra time. I'll need to sit up front. I need to use all of my accommodations." I'd say what I needed to pass at the start of every single class. I also took a lot of my general education classes in the summer at community colleges so that I wasn't overloaded during the actual year. Every semester, I took the bare minimum, 12 credits each semester, only four classes during the semester, and then two summer classes.

According to a state requirement, Eric needed a master's degree to teach, and he soldiered through a program to attain his graduate degree. Along the way, he made a powerful discovery that if he can re-create something or mimic it, it adds significantly to his learning. In fact, this has been the most important aspect of his success as a teacher:

> The creation of YouTube has helped me excel as an educator. I teach a lot of graphic design professional programs that are highly detailed. To get ready to teach, I've got to take a deep dive myself. First I get curious. I'll look for videos and use a tutorial with lots of screenshots and follow along. Give me lengthy step-by-step instructions and I'll give up on it. Textbooks: No way. My learning these days begins with experience. Before any assignments, I'll go through that process first and then do something myself, struggling through, making mistakes. For example, woodworking—if someone needs to know how to do something, I'll try it first, make the mistakes so I know what they might encounter. There is so much new stuff to know, always something a student is trying that I haven't done myself. They'll come to me and I won't squelch any ideas, I'll say this is possible, I don't know how, but I'm glad to learn, let's mock something up.

One of the biggest challenges for Eric is knowing his own struggles and then seeing young people with the same issues who are not ready to face the challenges:

> It drives me nuts. I don't think they realize that it isn't just now they're having the trouble; it's forever. They haven't accepted it's long term, that when you leave these walls it isn't over, and some of them don't seem to be making the strides to learn the strategies to help themselves along for the future.

Eric often opens up and shares his own trials with particular students to help them understand how to work with every person around them to maximize their resources and advocate for themselves. He willingly tells students that:

> It's going to take you a lot longer and you're going to out-work everybody because this isn't just today, it's tomorrow and the day after. It's not going to get any easier. Start understanding your strategies now and start using them.

As Eric reflects on the key things that led to his successful persisting, he credits all the people along the way:

> It wasn't one person, it was 16 years of people, not one particular moment, it was having great, great leaders that would give anything to help. I didn't want to let my parents down. I wanted to follow the footsteps of my brother. Always just wanted to do the very best, not wanting to settle. In my life I have been surrounded by so many successful people. Not wanting to keep up, but just to do well.
>
> Whether it comes easy or not, you have to work for it. I haven't ever thought about why I've done it. I just know you can accomplish the same thing using a different tool. I might know one way, learn a different way, and find it's a whole lot easier doing this or that.
>
> There is more than one way to get home.

Eric's persistence took courage. His family, friends, and teachers who supported and encouraged him showed courage. It isn't easy to learn—and yet we are surrounded by wonderful examples of so many people who can help to show us how to be persistent.

As this chapter closes, it is important to recognize that learning at its best is complicated and difficult, even when we are not trying to focus on what we are learning. Learning takes chutzpah, and if we are going to keep learning throughout our lifetime we must access that form of bravery to keep learning. Aisha's story can help guide us through this process.

Aisha has found the answers to her most important questions outside the classroom. She talks about more difficult types of ethical questions about whether she is doing what she thinks she should be doing. She cannot step-march her way through these questions, and she might think about them for a very long time without having it all worked out, yet she can reach a point of satisfaction. To Aisha's way of thinking, these efforts are less conscious and deliberate, different from finding out the kind of answer she can look up. She notes the thrilling experience of learning purely on a whim, because it is really fun and fascinating, even though she will not necessarily gain anything from it—the process of learning and exposing herself to new ideas and ways of thinking is the exciting part. Digging into a research wormhole might reveal some fascinating learning that will not show up on an exam, and at the same time Aisha acknowledges the difference between pursuing a passion and drowning in data:

> Failures are easy because you see them coming. Especially in an academic setting, you often know that you'll fail at something and eventually you may need to go back and relearn to make sure you understand it. It requires identifying what kind of problem it was—a decimal point being off, or truly

a lack of understanding. You might have to figure out why you learned it the way you did and then, discover a different way. That is not always easy, yet it's not so difficult as to be a tedious endeavor to learn again. If you've been exposed to it, it's easier to figure out new avenues and illuminate your understanding about why it didn't work out the way it should have . . . To me failure isn't a problem with the learning or learning process. It's a human thing that just happens sometimes.

Aisha laughs as she says, "Everything is going to be OK, it's been proven to me that just like in our Bollywood movies and real life as well, everything is OK in the end, and if it isn't OK it isn't the end."

Opportunity for Reflection

Which aspects of the *how* of learning stood out for you, based on your own learning experiences? Does your *how* vary by context and setting, formal or informal?

As you consider your experiences, what is a situation in which you believe you learned really well? Perhaps you learned a lot, or you learned something that was completely different from what you expected. What was it, specifically, about this learning situation that made it work well for you?

When has the form of *how* to learn shut you down? What was it like when the way you wanted to learn something did not match the educator's measure and expectations of mastery?

If you are an educator, when have you fostered learning that felt significant and transformative? When have you, upon reflection, set up a situation that could have been improved for all learners by expanding the range of *how* to learn?

How do you like to learn? How does that impact the choices that you make about learning? About educating students?

How often do you assume that everyone learns the same ways that you do? How does reflecting on this chapter shift your perspective?

6

THE *WHY* OF LEARNING

I would like to learn.
Can you tell me how to grow?
Or is it something, unconveyed,
Like melody, or witchcraft?

—Emily Dickinson

Earlier in this book we introduced the metaphor of a Mobius strip as a physical representation of the paradoxical relationship between the outer and inner dimensions of life and learning as well to frame the distinctions between Rumi's (2004) learning through the "memorization of facts and concepts" for the purpose of becoming "ranked ahead or behind others / with regard to your competence in retaining / information." We spoke to his description of a second intelligence that "does not turn yellow or stagnate. It's fluid, / and it doesn't move from outside to inside / through conduits of plumbing-learning. / This second knowing is a fountainhead / from within you, moving out" (p. 178).

The Mobius strip is a visualization of the outer and inner dimensions of learning as separate, yet connected, entities. In chapters 4 and 5 we described the outer elements of learning through the questions "*What* is learned?" and "*How* is it learned?" The next two chapters, 6 and 7, mark the point of turning on the Mobius from the outer to inner dimensions of learning. In chapter 6, we examine "*Why* learn?," and in chapter 7 we plunge into the rarely examined question of "*Who* is the self that learns?"

For some readers, the next two chapters may feel less familiar than the previous two, in which we examined the more concrete phenomena associated with the *what* and *how* of learning. As Palmer (2017) noted in *The Courage to Teach: Exploring the Inner Landscape of a Teacher's Life*, the *what* and *how* of teaching and learning are more commonplace and accepted. *Why* and *who* questions in teaching and learning are less conventional as starting places for conversation around what it means to be well educated in the world today. Answering Emily Dickinson's questions in the epigraph at the opening of this chapter about "how to grow" when addressing the *why* and *who* is more mysterious and less subject to standardized assessments. After all, how often do you see a question on a final exam that asks, "Why did you learn?" At best, the *why* question might surface when students are asked to reflect on their learning, which is more subjective and, as Dickinson noted, "like melody, or witchcraft."

> Look well to the growing edge! All around us worlds are dying and new worlds are being born; all around us life is dying and life is being born. The fruit ripens on the tree, the roots are silently at work in the darkness of the earth against a time when there shall be new leaves, fresh blossoms, green fruit. Such is the growing edge! It is the extra breath from the exhausted lung, the one more thing to try when all else has failed, the upward reach of life when weariness closes in upon all endeavor. This is the basis of hope in moments of despair, the incentive to carry on when times are out of joint and men have lost their reason, the source of confidence when worlds crash and dreams whiten into ash. The birth of the child—life's most dramatic answer to death—this is the growing edge incarnate. Look well to the growing edge! (Thurman, 1956, p. 134)

In its most basic form, the answer to the *why* question is straightforward when a second question is asked: Is it humanly possible to not learn? Even before the moment of birth and entry into the world, a child is learning. Recent studies, for example, have shown that a fetus is learning how to respond to stress from the hormone transfer from mother to child (Menakem, 2017). Food scientists have noted that babies exposed to the smell of a food preferred by their mother show a distinct interest in that food scent as well as disinterest in smells of food their mothers did not regularly eat. Popular literature is full of books on the ways in which mothers, parents, and caregivers can teach a child important life lessons before they are born. From childhood through old age, Howard Thurman implored his readers to "look well to the growing edge," the place in which there is opportunity to experience newness about self and the world is uncovered.

The disciplines of philosophy and theology are the historic academic homes for most *why* questions. Answers to *why* questions provide a rationale or justification for actions and thoughts beyond the technical and procedural; they are particularly good at providing answers to the bigger questions, such as "What does it mean to live intelligently in the world today?" Sometimes the answer to *why* questions falls along the dimensions of Rumi's strategic and instrumental forms of intelligence. In other contexts, *why* takes on less concrete and more elusive qualities that can be described only in metaphor, nodded to in Dickinson's "witchcraft." Our *why* may involve something that arises out of us, or through the power of engaging with others. Jasmine, to whom readers were introduced in chapter 5, articulates the *why* that many of us can relate to—the incredible gift of an inspiring mentor:

> Having someone who believed in me—and frankly who believed that I was more intelligent than who I thought I was—was my biggest motivation. I was so smart when I was in the room with her! I loved having a champion, having the opportunity to knock around ideas with somebody who was equally jazzed, who was right there with me.

There are several themes related to the *why* of learning that the Thurman quote presented earlier raises. The most obvious is growth, and for Thurman this often meant a deeper and more complex spiritual relationship with that which is greater than self and self-knowing. To learn is to grow in relationship to self, texts, and knowledge.

The American philosopher and educator Dewey (1938) wrote, "Every experience is a moving force. Its value can be judged only on the ground of what it moves toward and into" (p. 38). But Dewey was quick to point out that the maxim of "every experience is a moving force," when applied to learning, should be attended to with care. Some experiences lead to growth while others do not, even though they have a forward trajectory. For example, Dewey asked, if a burglar who is learning to be increasingly effective in the practice of breaking into homes and places of business, does that equate to growth? The *why* of learning and all its complexity are worth consideration in any discussion about learning.

Complexities of *Why* and the Meandering Path

Consider the challenges and intricacies of learning presented by Shaun, a college student in his mid-30s. Shaun has experienced many twists and turns, and at the time of this conversation he was within about a month of completing an undergraduate degree. He was deeply reflective at this point in his life, during which he had been wrestling with the questions that motivated him and the bigger *why* of his learning journey:

> I didn't even think of myself as a learner; early on, I was not even aware that I was capable of learning. That didn't happen until I was a physiological adult, well beyond high school. Learning in high school wasn't even a thing. It wasn't relevant. Want to tell me about trigonometry? Then we should have built a treehouse together; you could've taught me that way,

but the setting, the approach, it was all wrong. I thought it wasn't something for me. I realized in high school that something was different. I wasn't able to keep up with the others, and since I couldn't keep up, I just assumed I didn't have the capacity.

I've been homeless and in prison. I was in the military and went from there to diving, to starting a clothing company. The clothing company netted half a million in six months. Two years before that I was a borderline street person. I experienced all these social stations in life, just going from one thing to the next. It was a roller coaster ride and it plummeted. So it wasn't until later in life that I began a kind of awakening around the questions of what have I been doing, who am I, what do I want to do, what is important? I went through a time of deep reflection, which before, I suppose I had done, but nobody told me it was important, and I didn't know it was a thing.

In a conversation with Shaun that was also something of a roller coaster ride, he talked about the wildly divergent points along his eclectic path. After he left the military and wondered what would come next in his life, as a competitive swimmer, Shaun was a natural for commercial diving and, as such, he perceived it as the next step on his path.

This is hard hat diving, building, and working with concrete and steel, all under water. You have to go to a year-long trade school to prove yourself and with this certification for top-side welding, that is, above-ground welding, you can get a job anywhere. This was the first step and then I could go to diving school to become an underwater welder.

Shaun ended up living on a boat 8 months of the year, working for 12 hours and sleeping for 12 hours.

You make a lot of money, have no time to spend it, and when you do get a couple of days of vacation, you go to Vegas with a bunch of guys and spend all of it in a matter of days. We're talking tens of thousands of dollars. Then you go back and do it all over again. It could be a decent living, but it's not healthy or safe as a young man.

Not surprisingly, this did not feel sustainable as a way of life:

After about five years I began thinking about a way out, wondering about what I was working on, who I was working for. Could I make this a career—and did I want this to be a career? I wasn't really ever home and I lived in hotels instead of a boat. Sometimes I worked with good guys, sometimes with guys who spent all their money in Vegas. I started looking into things like, what does messing up our waterways do and who does it affect? I didn't feel great about that. I finally realized I didn't want to work for these companies.

Shaun went from commercial diving to, on something of a lark with a group of friends, starting a clothing company that made hooded jacket tuxedos with embedded electro-luminescent lights in them. They began to sell for $300 to $500. The company quickly began to make serious money, and Shaun and his friends did well financially. However, the *why* questions continued to pursue him:

> Again, I was left wondering. I didn't feel good about selling a product that had no guarantee. Our factory where people were doing the sewing was OK—but if you trace back to who makes the thread, who does the fabric dyeing, who drives the truck, you start seeing all those moving pieces and the way in which the people involved lived. It felt delusional and crazy. Just like with hydroelectronic dams, there's something not right here.
>
> I started realizing that I was so excited to sell people an article of clothing they might wear 10 times before it goes in a landfill, all so I could turn a profit. That's the way I understood the dream. Get rich, be famous, and be my own boss. It's cheap, it's manipulative, and it isn't a good business. It isn't good for the soul. From the military to diving to clothing.
>
> What on earth was I supposed to be doing? I seemed to only do things that solved the problem of feeling good.
>
> After the clothing company, I was 30 and I stopped. I didn't have a next thing. I didn't know what was next, and I felt exhausted and tired. Reflection was on me. I had to be with myself and sit with myself. I was 30 years old and back with my mother, wondering what was going to be next.

Shaun did not know at that time that eventually he would discover a passion for the earth and farming; he knew only that his "Why am I doing what I'm doing?" was not working for him, and that he wanted to try living differently. "Are there people living harmoniously with the planet? Are there people living in a healthy way in their communities? Are they eating a good diet? And if there are, is there a name for them?"

After graduating from college, Shaun, his partner, and their baby eventually headed abroad to a permaculture research institute, to pursue certificates and deepen their connection to the harmony that Shaun had been seeking all along. He is still engaged in farming; this bigger *why* (along with *what, how,* and *with whom*) finally had sticking power.

Shaun helps us to plainly see that aligning our deeper motivations with what we eventually choose to do is vital for our very humanity. As we move deeper into a description of the *why* of learning, we offer an additional caution in support of Dewey's (1938) observation that the intention or direction of learning is hard to determine ahead of time or even anticipate. In this sense, the question of "why learn" can change from the initial experience as reflection occurs. As our conversations with our learning conversation partners such as Shaun demonstrate, the *why* of learning can take on multiple answers across time and space. In his description of the kinds and reason behind the relationships high school students form with adults, Jay Gillen (2014) called into question attempts to limit learning as knowledge:

> If school were only about learning and knowledge, then accurate observation of schools could settle for literal descriptions of reality, as The Wire is taken to be. . . . No literal description could possibly represent this purpose, because the young people's acts or purpose cannot be "observed" or "depicted": you literally cannot see what young people are doing in schools; you can only interpret what they are doing from the surface that you see, and then re-act from your own purposes. (pp. 155–156)

Situating *Why* Stories of Learners

In the stories of learning that follow, we offer reflections on the *why* of learning that is informed by the words of our learning conversation partners and by our professional, personal, intellectual, and intuitive experiences. We offer our understanding with a necessary element of uncertainty, an awareness that any description of learning, by its fluid nature, is always subject to revision on the part of the learner as they grow and experience the world anew.

We invite all educators to resist the temptation to base their pedagogy on hard determinations that might be accurate in the immediate sense but false when viewed in the long term or from a different interpretative lens. As Gillen (2014) pointed out, this is particularly important when attempting to make sense of student resistance or behavior that suggests disinterest in the topic, teacher, or assignment. He noted that the pedagogical literalists "see reluctance as reluctance and a challenge to authority as a challenge to authority" (p. 149). An educator taking a wider social–contextual lens is open to alternative understanding, creating spaces that invite a better understanding of those behaviors of reluctance and challenge by leaning in to discern what might be underneath the surface. These openings move toward what Gillen calls a deeper instructional relationship of "gestures, tokens, songs, dances, words. Courtship is made up of a to-ing and fro-ing between beings that are in many ways alike and in some important ways different" (Gillen, 2014, pp. 150–151).

Thurman's (1956) charge to "look well to the growing edge" applies to both learner and educator. We hope that through exploring these stories of learning, educators will remain open to the possibility that what they think students are learning at any given time must be held lightly. The *why* of learning can be as simple as acquiring a good grade and simultaneously as complex as carrying a lifetime of trauma, an outward signaling of disinterest, and an inward wondering about just how serious a teacher is about their subject matter.

A Conventional Learner

In high school, Sophia was a high-performing A student, considered successful by the standards of grades. She describes herself as a conventional learner, someone who was comfortable doing what she was told to do. Her strategy for learning was memorization of the assigned material. Here is how Sophia described learning and its limitations prior to attending college:

> I have to wean myself off of this form of learning. I look at it now like I can learn what I want to learn. It's easy to fall into the trap of learning this to get that credential, but what's the use of all that learning if you can't navigate with it? Now I want to learn just for the sake of learning.
>
> I failed a couple of classes. Coming from [being] an A student to failing, I really had to reevaluate my self-worth. I cried for days. But then, you look at people who don't have this opportunity to cry over a test, a failed grade, even though I do care about the classes. My needs are met regardless. Grades don't mean anything unless you actually learn something. Yes, they do help you get a better this, a better that—but if you can't think for yourself, you haven't learned. Grades are just a way to easily identify what someone knows. You sure shouldn't rely on that for your self-worth.
>
> You can't just read about the problem. You've got to do it—through tons of questions and practice. I think learning is coming to a certain point of understanding and applying it.

Given her robust grade point average, Sophia showed a high degree of competency in Rumi's first form of intelligence, which values technical expertise, like memorization and recitation. By her own admission, she placed her class ranking, relative to other students, above her own interest and the intrinsic value of learning.

Dewey (1938) might have asked, to what end is Sophia's learning serving? Or why go to school if, like the burglar in his example, growth as transference and personal change seems questionable? We will have more to say later in this chapter about Sophia's story because learning is rarely unidimensional. For now, the primary *why* of learning for Sophia would appear to be transactional. In an apt and colorful description, Rohr (2011) referred to this approach to managing life as *merit badge thinking*, in which the goal is to accumulate markers of success that are determined by authority figures. She does the required work, memorizes what is expected, and she is accomplished at meeting the assessment criteria for the class. In exchange for her compliance with external sources of authority she expects high grades. Knowledge, for Sophia, has the feel of a commodity with little or no reciprocity, relationship development, or responsibility toward knowing and its impact on the world (Kimmerer, 2013).

Sophia's strategy is a common one employed by many learners in K–12 schools and is coupled to an overreliance on standardized forms of assessment and teacher-driven curriculum. Henry Giroux (2013) described the process by which students and teachers are lulled into a sense of complacency relative to their own agency and self-determination as the *disimagination machine*. Giroux is a scholar in the radical tradition of education that emerges from the Marxist critique of unequal power distribution in Western capitalist societies.

In classrooms, this means a focus on conventional or institutional forms of teaching, which, according to this way of knowing, are concerned with assimilation and culturalization to accepted social norms in contrast to, for example, social justice and equity. A reframing becomes necessary, away from social reproduction and toward the enactment of radical pedagogy dedicated to the liberation of the student; to learn is to gain agency and autonomy. According to the radical tradition, contemporary models and delivery of curriculum encourage and value the formation of students like Sophia, who might be less inclined to resist the loss of agency and self-determination. This is an age-old and cross-cultural phenomenon, as evidenced by Rumi's observations on the kind of intelligence emanating from formal education settings, a form of thinking and learning that can "turn yellow and stagnate."

While Sophia's story takes place in the formal context of high school, learning as a transactional process can be a central feature of informal learning spaces as well. Lave and Wenger (1991), in their book *Situated Learning: Legitimate Peripheral Participation*, argued that learning is essentially a social process taking form in human-to-human interactions. As such, some social settings involving more and less experienced practitioners are open and allow for the free flow of knowledge and expertise from experts to novices. Other settings, such as professional or trade networks, are closed, and novices are denied access to key understandings. Only after demonstrating narrow bands of expertise or after enduring years of stagnation are novices allowed to move to the next level of professional development. In this way, commitment and compliance are exchanged for upward mobility and increased status.

Sophia, in Greek, means "wisdom." The Sophia in this example is wise to the ways of acting like a student. She learned and mastered the strategy of turning compliance into grades and turning grades into status. Whether or not her form of wisdom can be considered growth is an open question. Her own observations and reflections suggest that her disempowerment by the disimagination machine of education left her wanting more:

> Grades don't mean anything unless you actually learn something. Yes, they do help you get a better this, a better that—but if you can't think for yourself, you haven't learned. Grades are just a way to easily identify what someone knows. You sure shouldn't rely on that for your self-worth.

What might thinking for ourselves and developing a more expansive sense of self-worth look like in the form of learning? How can the "conduits of plumbing" that result in knowledge that can "help you get a better this, a better that" be reconceptualized into growth that expands outward? How might the *why* of commodity knowledge be transformed into a relationship among self, text, and others that is reciprocal and generative?

Building Community Through Learning

Aisha's story of learning provides some sense of the challenges and opportunities associated with empowered learning. She grew up in the Northeast, the daughter of parents who immigrated from Pakistan. Aisha shared that her views on learning and what it means to be fully human in the world were influenced by the South Asian and Muslim communities in which she grew up. Through study of the Quran, religious practice, and training to think critically about life choices, she developed a stance that learning is something she does for herself:

> There was already that huge component of learning implicit in religious practice. You were supposed to study this language, you learned polite manners according to the Islamic tradition, and you were always steeped in the perspectives of how ethics, morality and values are viewed. . . . Bringing that effort, critical thinking and processes to different platforms, including school and the classroom, is a natural extension.

Like Sophia's story, compliance, submission to an outside authority, informs Aisha's process of learning. However, unlike Sophia's narrative, Aisha's experience with structured learning leads to "critical thinking" and the ability to transfer that skill to "different platforms, including school and the classroom." Her story points to the value of learning that goes beyond learning for the sake of learning, learning that stops at the individual. The *why* of learning for Aisha is to build community:

> Especially for people coming from Eastern cultures, coming to the U.S. is difficult, because Western cultures emphasize individualism so much more. I was raised with an emphasis on the tightly knit family unit. Building a strong community and a sense of inclusivity was important.

Yet despite the influence of family, community, and a personal commitment to the "deep learning [she] should be doing," Aisha finds the pull toward Rumi's "plumbing learning" and strategic short-term thinking hard to combat. Conceptually, and by cultural norms, she knows she should be learning for the pure joy of learning or learning in support of wider community needs. Yet even a strong and personally committed learner like Aisha finds her rationale, her *why* of learning, getting foggy because of the emphasis on performance and grades associated with school learning. Aisha's struggle with framing learning that is generative seems rooted, in part, in historic power differentials between educators and learners as well as a compliance relationship. Her attempts to make learning meaningful echo Gillen's (2014) claim that "The essential difficulty here is that we enter into the dramatic relations of the school or classroom encumbered by the frozen, unhelpful social categories that pit the young people's wildness against adult control" (p. 142). As such, at times Aisha is closer to Sophia's *why* of learning to perform well on a test:

> I find myself stretched for time and it gets hard to approach all of my subjects with the kind of deep learning I should be doing, as opposed to the strategic learning just to get through this exam. With strategic learning you forget most of it, despite putting so much time in the course. It's terrible not to be able to remember. Because of that desire to remember, it favors the more deliberate or purposeful style of learning even though it's a lot more time consuming—learning that is often associated with leaps, linkages and associations to other aspects of learning.

An important attribute of Aisha's approach to learning is that, for her, learning with intention began before she started school and, as such, learning extends beyond the enclosed space of a classroom. As she noted:

> Religion had a significant influence on my thought process in general, which has shaped the way I learn anything. It takes a lot of reminding myself of why I want to do this or what I aim to get from this, and trying to work my way through, to find the logic in something, and to conclude what ultimately makes sense.

Aisha's expansive views on learning are likely a product of her commitment to community over individualism and the ways in which she constantly pushes back against the transactional model of learning that defines her formal schooling experience. But the struggle between outer demands toward compliance and her internal freedom to learn is an ongoing process for Aisha. Her *why* of learning regularly switches back and forth, depending on context and her ability to foster the courage to learn.

Because of her expansive understanding of learning, Aisha views failure as a necessary *why* of learning. She cannot step-march her way through the tough questions just for the purpose of arriving at an answer that will give her a form of intelligence in which she can "get ranked ahead or behind others / in regard to [her] competence in retaining / information" (Rumi, 2004, p. 178). Failure for Aisha is a luscious gift of fully engaging the process of deep learning she longs for. She likes to think about questions and live into them.

She seems to follow Rilke et al.'s (2000) advice to a young poet:

> I want to beg you, as much as I can, dear sir, to be patient toward all that is unsolved in your heart and to try to love the questions themselves like locked rooms and like books that are written in a very foreign tongue. Do not now seek the answers, which cannot be given you because you would not be able to live them. And the point is, to live everything. Live the questions now. Perhaps you will then gradually, without noticing it, live along some distant day into the answer. (p. 35)

For Rilke, the *why* of learning is to live the questions, and for Aisha, living the questions that intrigue her means embracing failure as the next step forward in learning. She speaks of failure with the ease and comfort of someone who no longer judges her sense of self-worth through the deficit language of failure. Instead, she flips the script, and failure is now an asset, a valuable walking companion on the journey of learning:

> Failures are easy because you see them coming. Especially in an academic setting, you often know that you'll fail at something and eventually you may need to go back and relearn to make sure you understand it. It requires identifying what kind of problem it was—a decimal point being off, or truly a lack of understanding. You might have to figure out why you learned it the way you did and then, discover a different way. That is not always easy, yet it's not so difficult as to be a tedious endeavor to learn again. If you've been exposed to it, it's easier to figure out new avenues and illuminate your understanding about why it didn't work out the way it should have. . . . To me failure isn't a problem with the learning or learning process. It's a human thing that just happens sometimes.

Returning for a moment to Thurman's (1956) charge to learners to "look well to the growing edge," we can lift up an additional element of the *why* of Aisha's learning, which is to look well as an invitation or perhaps command to pay attention, to understand that the ways in which one learns or does not learn, because of the numbing effects of the "disimagination machine," can dramatically impact notions of self and the world. The *why* of Aisha's deep learning is to better see and respond to the complex problems that mark out the classroom, living in community, and following one's natural interests.

For Sophia and Aisha, *why* has a strong personal connection: to learn is to see the world differently as a person and therefore to engage meaning making with new eyes. The next two stories of learning, by Jamila and Holly, reach beyond the individual as the center of learning to include notions of a wider community of others, human and nonhuman. We will offer their stories in greater detail in chapter 7, "*Who* Is the Self that Learns?," yet, given the ways in which the *why* and *who* of learning are often intertwined, it seems important to address the *why* of their learning in this chapter.

Radical Mothering

Jamila sees herself, and is known by her local community, as an activist, and she has been instrumental in, among numerous other activities, the Black Lives Matter movement for social justice. She has a role in youth development statewide through a Cooperative Extension system, focusing on innovation in youth programs, and she is a well-respected organizer on behalf of the needs and interests of area youth, serving as a role model, inspiration, and powerful advocate for young people of color. As she learned the ins and outs of creating spaces for the voices of young people she reframed the end goal, the *why* of her work. She moved from a strategic stance of getting something done to the metaphor of *radical mothering*:

> I'm working on an article on radical mothering and the biggest piece is around relationships, even more so, the ways in which mothers shape relationships with young people, with their partners, families, in their communities, how mothering shapes our lives . . . I'm thinking, though, of the ways in which eloquent writers and activists talk about how we can know our own rich history, our connection to land liberation, by building meaningful relationships. I'm inspired by someone named Tanya—she is known in food justice circles as "Mama Tanya"—who is a mother in real life and also in the way she builds coalitions and intergenerational spaces.

We hear in Jamila's description of radical mothering the importance of community and relationships. The connections she forms through her mothering with young people she serves are the bedrock for her activism, and she is supported by others who provide it, too. She is deeply inspired, energized, and "fed" by Mama Tanya, who is a mother in real life as well as in the way in which she builds coalitions and intergenerational spaces. For Jamila, the *why* of learning is bigger than self and self-knowing; it is relational in the ways that Kimmerer (2013) described the value of a gift: "The essence of the gift is that it creates a set of relationships. The currency of a gift economy is, at its root, reciprocity" (p. 28).

Jamila links the *why* of learning to a reciprocal relationship with her wider community. In her early years as an activist, she entertained the notion of legacy as an answer to the question of why she does the work she does on behalf of others. It seems, rather consciously or not, as if she may have been confined in Rumi's rationale for learning as the ability to rank oneself ahead or behind others based on accomplishments. As Jamila grew in her learning, she realized the limitations in legacy learning:

> I found myself listening to this beautiful piece with an Indigenous farmer, talking about growing white corn—she offered a metaphor about giving seeds freely to people as an insurance policy. I began thinking about what if we thought about our work not as legacy but as insurance policy? If something happened, since invariably something happens, if we've shared our seeds, then we are rooted in all these other communities. Our acts are not just of kindness but as preservation—our acts are insurance policies, reminding us of our goals. We've always been in spaces where we've had our hands in the soil, dreaming deeply of the long history of land-based pursuits and this long tradition of not just farming, but of being able to see these different iterations of liberation. That's really our legacy. I'm going to start to remove "legacy" from my vocabulary and use the metaphor of the insurance policy. Those are the same policies we see as we work with comrades such as Soul Fire Farm, who remind us that our ancestors braided seeds into cornrows [in our hair]. I'm leaning into the question of where are the other spaces in which we see insurance policies—and I don't mean State Farm or MetLife—that produce beautiful dividends we never dreamed of?

The contrast between a *why* of legacy as goal setting and the *why* of seed planting for a future she will likely never see is striking. For Jamila, "Why learn?" becomes almost mystical and bound up in a mothering relationship that exists far off in the future. As an activist who is often outward leaning and engaged in constant struggle for equity, Jamila seems to be attending to Thurman's (1956) affirmation and instructions for living fully offered in the passage on the growing edge earlier in this chapter. Birthing, mothering new beginnings and new relationships, and reflecting on legacy through a unique lens are reasons enough for *why* Jamila continues to lean into the role and identity of an activist.

Listening to the Earth

Like Jamila, Holly is involved in fostering community through her work, as the executive director of a small not-for-profit that connects individuals and organizations, convenes experiential learning opportunities, and facilitates reflective practices. Holly's learning and engagement are motivated by a profound commitment and connection to the earth. Her deep identification with nature leaves little doubt of her earth teacher's impact on her knowing:

> I feel like I am a different learner. I've felt that for many years. I'm an earth learner; I learn most from the earth. I come to learning through my relation with earth, that's primary. Figuring out how human beings fit into learning can be my kerfuffley challenge.

As she notes, one motivation for her *why* of learning is to decipher the ways in which human beings fit into learning that emerges from, alongside, with, and through nature. Holly views the earth as a rich catalogue of knowing, in contrast to institutional forms of schooling, which are limited and more narrowly focused; what she really longs for in her education is developing an more-than-human language and understanding:

> I was just outside during a conference call, listening to people talk and talk. I stood in front of this old tree—oh, this tree had something to say! I learn about the aging process through the trees. They are so wise; they have so many ways of teaching and being, of cracking and shedding. Reaching, touching the sky, their roots and their branches, and sap moving inside them. The natural world is so diverse, complex and multidimensional. What we think of as education, as human education—it's so limited. I remember being in a group of people talking about the earth, talking about the authors they were learning from, and above us there were two red-tailed hawks, and all around us were maple samaras coming down. What might we learn from the samaras, from the circling of the hawks? I can read about them, I can read about trees, but that's an interpretation.

We hear in Holly's question and wondering an openness that mirrors Gillen's (2014) description of attempts of formalized schooling to assign intent to students' learning. "You literally cannot see what young people are doing in schools; you can only interpret what they are doing from the surface that you see" (pp. 155–156). Holly's questions to nature have the palpable texture of someone leaning deliciously in to *know* meaning in nature, to decipher the ineffable in the real presence of the living world. At the same time, she is aware that the patterns of circling hawks and falling samaras do not fit neatly into the little boxes of concrete answers.

Holly embodies the sense of patient watching and learning that the poet Rainier Maria Rilke (2000) nods to, encouraging patience in all that is unresolved in the heart and to try to love the questions themselves. Her attentive listening is partly motivated by her longing to pierce the human and more-than-human interface, and it forms her foundation. As such, Holly's life work, the driver of her learning is, not surprisingly, not a definite goal but a series of rich questions:

> I've lived near a brook for 36 years and hear the brook poem, which shifts its melody each day. As human beings we focus on publishing and citations, as if this is the definitive piece, the definitive poem. Is there a definitive sound of the brook? There isn't, actually. Sometimes there is a bass note under the ice; sometimes a little hole emerges that has a whisper. Other times it's a gurgle or a thump.
>
> My learning is informed by a longing for the lack of separation between the human and natural world. We're out of integrity and it's devastating, really. The separation gives us permission to dominate and discard. When we see ourselves as part of nature and what we do to nature we do to ourselves, then there we can take ownership of the harm that's being done. We get into trouble assuming we understand words as stationary objects. Other ways of knowing are the way in for me.
>
> What if we didn't consume a poem, but were to be with it? To give time to taste it, know it, to listen to its way in? We overconsume poems. Could we just chew on them? Let them digest us? I don't think we know how to be in relationship. If a book is alive, then what is it saying to you and where does it land in you?

For many years, the physics community puzzled over the question "Is light a wave or particle phenomenon?" The conversation and evidence went back and forth for more than 100 years, starting with experimentation in the 1800s. It was eventually decided that light is both things: wave and particle. The manifestation of light is informed by the experimental questions and mathematical formulae. When scientists ask wave questions of light, it appears as a wave and, conversely, when they ask particle questions, it behaves like a particle.

We offer this abbreviated and highly simplified story of physics as a way of describing the *why* of learning for the people with whom we sat in conversation. If an educator asks concrete, assessable questions to a learner, the *why* often becomes a static and standardized answer, what Rumi (2004) described as the "memorization of facts and concepts" for the purpose of becoming "ranked ahead or behind others / in regard to your competence in retaining / information" (p. 178)

And when a teacher asks open-ended questions or questions with ineffable roots, learning can, as Rumi (2004) noted, become "fluid, / and it doesn't move from outside to inside / through conduits of plumbing-learning. / This second knowing is a fountainhead / from within you, moving out" (p. 178).

Opportunity for Reflection

Why do you choose to learn something new? Does your motivation for learning come largely from inner or outer forces?

Consider writing your personal vignettes of learning. What energized your learning in each situation? Have the layers of motivation changed, perhaps with an initial one, and others that surfaced then, or surface now in reflection? What was your *why* at each stage of transition?

Looking back across the history of your learning, what surprises you now about your reasons for learning?

If you provide significant learning experiences for others, what do you perceive as your *why* behind the learning? What do you think learners might believe is your primary motivation for their engagement? How might you find out if there is a gap between your intent and learner perceptions of intent?

What was unexpected as you read this chapter?

Is there anything you might do differently when considering the why of learning after exploring this chapter? If so, what might that be?

7

THE *WHO* OF LEARNING

*Getting grown means learning how to work that current: learning when
to hold fast, when to drop anchor, when to let it sweep you up.*

—*Jesmyn Ward*

In chapter 1, we centered learning, and to usher you in we invited you
to recall learning how to listen, an essential tool involved in human
communication. The *what*, or content of your learning, was vast, likely
bringing joy, challenge, discovery, inquisitiveness, and, at times, pain.
Although the *how* of this learning probably involved using your ears, you
might have required a device to assist in this process, and you may have
additionally learned pictorially, through gestures, and/or in other ways.
With time, perhaps you became adept at listening with your eyes and your
heart, more skillful in the subtle ways of reading the body language of others. The *why* of learning to read other humans ranged from absolute necessity to keep you from danger, to the desire to connect with someone you
loved, the hunger driven by your fascination with the world around you,
and the excitement of listening to the different ways in which your earliest
friends were unique, using language in such interesting ways that you had
never heard expressed, whether through their words or their bodies. You
likely leapt up to make great strides and failed, too, making assumptions
that were incorrect, saying things that were inappropriate or hurtful, and at
times you surely experienced the pain of wishing you could retract something you communicated because of your assumptions. As Ward says at the
beginning of this chapter, getting grown meant learning how to work the
current, and while you may have been taught some elements of communication through your formal education, most of your learning took place in
the river of life, with all its attendant delights and sorrows. It took courage
to pick yourself up when you had messed it all up, and this formation was
foundational in the *who* that you are today.

At times, deeper, more intrinsic, and open-ended notions of learning break through the barrier to reveal learning for self-knowing. In this chapter, we explore the *who* of learning, including the ways in which the learning process can form and de-form learners. Of the four lenses—*what, how, why,* and *who*—*who* is perhaps the most abstract and yet personal at the same time. It speaks to the question of what becomes of a person during the learning process.

Most educators hope, or at least plan, for a shift in the learner because of the education they offer. What other reason is there for teaching? The depth of *who* the learner is becoming is measured in changed behavior; sometimes this change is toward uniformity. This is the essence of the educational philosophy of behaviorism, which theorizes that, with the proper stimulation and rewards, a student can learn to behave in predictable ways, such as learning to act in ways consistent with the norms of a classroom or school or learning to mimic content when prompted by the educator. The *who* of learning in these cases is set by an external authority; the student becomes a predictable quantity.

Other educators take a more radical stance on the question of the *who* of learning, seeking to move away from structure and form and toward openness and freedom. The goal is transformation of the learner toward liberation and confirmation of inner ways of knowing. Paolo Freire, the Brazilian educator, famous for his contrasting of the *banking model* of education with the *problem posing* model of education, argued that the goal of education is humanization. He spoke of this process as a lifelong endeavor, or vocation, of learning to be free from elements of social and educational oppression (Freire, 1968/2013).

It seems that Freire and Rumi (2004) would share a basic understanding that one type of learning is "acquired, / as a child in school memorizes facts and concepts / from books and from what the teacher says, / . . . With such intelligence you rise in the world" (p. 178). In other words, the outcome of this type of learning is the quantification of the learner for the purpose of measuring one person against the other. The learner, metaphorically, becomes a cog in a bigger machine designed to sort, compare, and contrast students. Freire and Rumi would seem to agree that there is a second way of knowing that is less bounded and not subject to external sources of authority, "a spring overflowing its springbox." In this framing, the *who* of learning is less predictable and implies a relationship among the learner, their context, and their emerging sense of self. Cranton (2016) referred to this form of learning as *emancipatory knowledge* because it centers power and agency on the learner and away from the "sovereign power" of educators when they exercise external power to control the learner and learning outcomes. We can find an example of this less predictable learning in a student who is surprised at her self-discovery regarding her need to speak often in class and how reflection is informing a new way of being for her:

> Much like I tend to speak up in class, I tend to respond quickly, sharing the first thought that pops into my head, especially if I hold a contrasting view from what has been shared by another student. I have come to realize that this means I don't leave space for wonder in my thought process, rather I quickly form conclusions and opinions with the information I have access to. Turning to wonder requires facing the unknown and acknowledging that there may be more to the picture than there seems at first. One of the biggest lessons I will take away from this semester is the need to make room for wonder in my mind.

Instructional "Moreness" and the Integration of Selfhood

We discussed in an earlier chapter about how contemporary scholars of language contend that the word *education* is composed of two Latin words: *educare* and *educere*. *Educare* means to "train or mold," and *educere* means to "lead out." We explore this theme of education as dual identities in this chapter. As a way of illustrating this tension around the *who* of learning, Paul offers an excerpt from an article he wrote of the ways in which the contexts of teaching, at any given moment, call forth a different sense of *who* is the professor as learner. Although his story draws from his experience, the themes are universal to anyone (parent, teacher, leader, caregiver, grocery clerk, factory worker, etc.) who finds themselves in a learner stance through their educational endeavors. As we have emphasized throughout this book, it is perhaps more helpful to center learning over teaching, even when the story is told from the educator's point of view.

> Frederick Buechner (1993) famously defined a professional calling as "the place where your deep gladness and the world's deep hunger meet." As much as idealism and joy are powerful forces, what happens when the flames of idealism flickers out and an educator succumbs to external markers of success, the constraints of benchmark assessments, data sets, instructional rubrics, disinterested learners, and standardized assessments? What happens to self when my deep gladness is stifled or boxed in by institutional imperatives? Do I become a different person?
>
> In these darker times, when my passions rage, the centering and reassuring influence of my calling can seem far away and elusive. Joy is replaced with frustration and a sense of vocational amnesia. In the medical world, amnesia often results from trauma. In education a form of trauma, the

loss of true identity, often emerges from the normalizing power of form and structure. My teaching amnesia can take the form of a lack of classroom presence and the realization that I no longer know why I'm teaching. The self-affirmation "I'm a teacher" is replaced with "Who am I?" Or even worse, "Why am I here?" These are dangerous questions for a professor to ask. They can introduce doubt when a fierce commitment to student liberation should dominate. When I lose touch of my sense of "deep gladness" I am less effective at meeting the "deep hunger" of my students, and the educational endeavor can falter.

Luckily, there is another sense of self that I can lean into, a sense of who that draws from a different source of energy beyond fear, frustration and anger. When I teach toward a classroom as sacred space there is often an emergence of instructional "moreness," where my students and I "go beyond what we were and are and become something different, somehow new" (Huebner et al., 2012, p. 344). Huebner et al. (2012) names this human desire for transcendence as "moreness:" "The moreness in the world, spirit, is a moreness that infuses each human being. Not only do we know more than we say, we "are" more than we "currently are." That is, the human being dwells in the transcendent, or more appropriately, the transcendent dwells in the human being" (Michalec, 2018, p. 404).

The *who* of learning, for both learners and for those who facilitate learning experiences for others, speaks to a sense of identity and presence that can include, but goes beyond, static definitions and metrics. With respect to the *who* of learning, the "moreness" of human awakening has a spiritual sense of being connected to something larger than self, a largeness that both names the uniqueness of the learner and integrates that distinctness into the integrated whole of existence.

The Western framing of learning values separation and classification, that is, the *who* of learning as a measurable outcome to be tested and sorted. Kimmerer (2013), in *Braiding Sweetgrass: Indigenous Wisdom, Scientific Knowledge, and the Teachings of Plants*, told the story of the contrasting ways in which Indigenous and Western peoples know and are known by the world and its implications for what constitutes science. One of Kimmerer's graduate students, Laurie, designed a study to determine the impact of harvesting methods on sweetgrass production. Key to her study was finding a way to have "a conversation with plants" (p. 154), a tough problem for a Western-trained scientist. Indigenous and traditional ways of knowing offered a way into this relationship between researcher and plant. Kimmerer reported that, during Laurie's proposal hearing, one committee member pushed [the proposal papers] aside dismissively. "I don't see anything new here for science," he said. "There's not even a theoretical framework" (p. 155). In Kimmerer's reflection on the dissertation hearing, she noted that the most difficult challenge she and Laurie faced was "getting scientists to consider the validity of Indigenous knowledge," which felt like "swimming upstream in cold, cold water" (p. 156).

Alongside these external manifestations of learning (in this case, science) there are other ways of knowing that flow in nonlinear, weblike patterns that pull toward integration and wholeness, a form of authenticity that allows for deep self-reflection and critical thinking, resulting in an integrated notion of self (Cranton, 2016). In chapter 6, Aisha drew a similar contrast between Western individualism and Eastern communitarianism, two different ways of knowing the world and being known by it in a manner that fosters very different notions of *who* one is as a learner and an emergent being in the world. She pointed to this distinction when she commented on the experience of transitioning from her Pakistani immigrant home to the culture of American schooling:

> Especially for people coming from Eastern cultures, coming to the U.S. is difficult, because Western cultures emphasize individualism so much more. I was raised with an emphasis on the tightly knit family unit, building a strong community and a sense of inclusivity was important.

In this chapter, we explore this sense of moving past metaphors of the individual as an isolated learner, to metaphors of community, which carries with it multiple meanings. On the surface, it means connecting the emerging self, an outcome of learning, to the needs and interests of a wider community. And on a deeper psychological, emotional, and spiritual level, it means integration of self across these elements and in cooperation with energies and frames of knowing that are larger than self (Cranton, 2016). *Who*, in this sense, becomes a metaphysical and mystical form of consciousness that extends beyond the concrete labels of Western fixed categories. Again, Aisha points to this extension of self beyond the confines of reason—Descartes's "I think; therefore I am"—to the inclusion of her heart and body:

> Prayer is hugely emphasized with Islam—there are the five pillars and it is said that you can leave everything else but don't leave your prayers, it's the last thing you should stop doing. From the very early years, we saw our parents doing it. At some point, a child learns it. At first, it is purely ritualistic—you think you're supposed to do it, so you have to. It's spotty, you might miss some, but then at a certain point, you would not even consider not doing it, it is incorporated into your day such that you couldn't imagine skipping it.

It's never something that you miss since it becomes something you rely on heavily. It becomes so innate that if something runs late, you almost panic a tiny bit. It's essentially a form of meditation, so at five times each day, even in the midst of a hectic day at school, I find a way to stand still and clear my mind. It serves as a reminder that there are bigger things than the small things that are freaking you out at that point. It gives a sense of tranquility and serenity. There are things I can't control and things I can.

For Aisha, religion and prayer are the gateways to integration of self and the formation of a more interconnected relationship with the largeness of life, and the process of stepping outside the Western ranking of self-worth through intellectual achievement was facilitated by her strong cultural and family structure. The process involved some level of challenge and questioning:

> There was already that huge component of learning implicit in religious practice. You were supposed to study this language, you learned polite manners according to the Islamic tradition, and you were always steeped in the perspectives of how ethics, morality and values are viewed. . . . Bringing that effort, critical thinking and processes to different platforms, including school and the classroom, is a natural extension. Religion had a significant influence on my thought process in general, which has shaped the way I learn anything.

Kinesthetic Learning, Flow, and Presence

Aisha's story beautifully captures the transient nature of *who* as a learner, the movement between fixed and open notions of self. Whereas her cultural and religious upbringing frames the development of her *who*-ness as a learner, another conversation partner, Joe, comes to a similar understanding through a more physical embodiment, through activities such as skateboarding. His path to understanding the deep wholeness of the *who* of learning was a painful journey with many moments of suffering. Joe is an active learner who crackles with energy, an avid enthusiast for the vibrant and varied currents of life who has followed a nontraditional path in his education and his approach to learning and the *how* and *why* of previous chapters, and he discovered early in life that his *who* rarely matched the expectations of public schooling; he often felt like a round peg trying to fit into a square hole:

> It was an irony: I didn't do well in school because I learned easily, absorbing the information in one sitting, but I was restless, bored, and it wasn't enough, so I would fill the gaps by performing elaborate jokes to entertain my classmates, drawing funny pictures while the teacher was talking, and

getting into mischief. It's a little embarrassing to admit, but I viewed the teachers as not being as sharp as I was. Frankly, I found school boring. It's not how I wanted to spend my time. That's not how my body is meant to spend time. I sat squirming because I was meant to be mobile. Growing up, I was misunderstood because I thought they were doing a bad job teaching and I suffered for that.

As a learner, I am self-taught. Even when I take a class, when someone teaches me something, I have to pick it apart and understand why. I am kinesthetic, learning best through the use of all of me. I learn best when I've got the power to drop something and say screw this if I don't like it. One hundred percent of my education stems from my own interest; if I'm not interested, you can forget it, there isn't any way I'll learn anything about it. I learn in an atypical way, it's been evident from early life. To call it learning disabilities—sometimes it frustrates me to say that, since I see it as learning in a different way. Anything where I'm using my body and the tool for learning the skill is muscle memory then I'm going to thrive.

Growing up, I was told I couldn't pay attention and focus—had I just hopped on a skateboard, in the afternoon I could have focused on algebra no problem. Millions of people have a different learning style, and the public school fails them. If we look at the current public education system, it hasn't innovated, it hasn't changed, it could be a canvas on which young people find out what they love, to prepare them to be adults, voters. When it comes to the *who*—a part of my identity is as someone who doesn't learn in the normal way but loves to learn.

The *who* of Joe's learning self was rarely validated and affirmed, causing high levels of social–emotional stress and uncertainty. He eventually left the public school system and his parents enrolled him in a private school setting to find a better fit between his love of learning and the pedagogy of the school. After graduation, he continued the search for places that enabled his expansive sense of learning as an embodied experience. Only later in life was he able to put words to his understanding of self as a learner. For years he knew more about what did not work than how to name what felt, in his bones, like a genuine and authentic linkage between the *who* of his learning self and the *how* of pedagogy. In his post–high school wanderings, Joe worked at an outdoor school, took a semester abroad to learn rock climbing, recorded a sizable number of music albums, and lived in three states before serving for 3 years as a health-care worker for a home health agency. He eventually enrolled in college and is thriving in a renowned business program at an Ivy League institution.

Joe's story of becoming a learner, although painful, offers several important clues into Rumi's (2004) vision of a second kind of intelligence that "does not turn yellow or stagnate. It's fluid, / and it doesn't move from out-side to inside / through conduits of plumbing-learning" (p. 178). This image of knowing self as a fluid process has been identified by numerous philosophers and educational theorists, most prominently by psychologist Mihaly Csikszentmihalyi (1990) and his articulation of flow theory.

Csikszentmihalyi's research proposes that *flow* is the ideal state of learning for humans, during which the distinctions between the outer and inner notions of selfhood dissolve and the person is one with the activity they are doing. In a state of flow the learner is at ease and "in the zone." They experience a sense of all-encompassing connection to self, task, and the wider world. It is important to note that the state of flow is often described by athletes who articulate a sense of oneness with the activity; one action flows naturally from the previous action in perfect response to the immediate physical circumstances, culminating in a sense of complete harmony among body, task, and the external features of the world.

Yet, states of flow can occur in other settings, for example, such as Aisha's description of prayer as dropping into a more inclusive reality. In his teaching, Paul experiences flow when in class discussion a student makes a comment or observation that dissolves the walls of the classroom and everyone present seems to integrate into a wider and more inclusive sense of the world. His subsequent instructional moves are fluid and seem to come from an external source of knowing and wisdom. Marcia and her students experience flow when, during arts-based activities in which they are so deeply involved they are startled to look at the clock to discover that class is nearly over.

For Joe, engaging flow is physical; learning is embodied and requires the fullness of his being. It involves a sense of integration he never experienced in his formalized education:

> With snowboarding and skateboarding, for example, there's a quality of moving the experience of life out of your head and into your body, natural strengthening and physical training that goes along with having a pursuit that requires you to be in good shape. And that goes into every other corner of your life, from walking up the stairs to getting out of bed.

Snowboarding, skateboarding, and song writing are examples of Joe's preferred venues for experiencing flow, activities in which the external and internal qualities of self and the world dissolve and reform into an integrated whole. Joe is quick to note that what he experiences as embodied learning is personal to him, and he advocates that there are many ways to achieve integrated wholeness, or a flow state. In fact, he is hesitant to speak of his form of learning out of the fear that it will seem as if it could be packaged up and marketed to the general public:

> When I think about learning I sometimes refrain from talking about how I learn, this sort of thing, because I don't want to dip too quickly into a Hallmark motivational speaker thing—just "having a good attitude" sounds like a cop-out. It is about the belief in yourself and also having whatever hobby or activity is very accessible to you, not crazy expensive, not hard to get to—the closer the hobby is to you, the more likely you can do it. Skateboarding is nearby. Art, like painting and sculpting, might have the same effect with another person. Whatever tool you're using for consistent presencing it should be something that you don't have to force yourself to do. Life does take force, hard days that you have to go back and do the same thing; it takes will. It's easier if you love to do it. I believe everybody has something like that and it's tragic that not everybody discovers it.

Rumi's first form of intelligence has a strategic and transactional quality to it. In most contemporary classrooms this means students master knowledge through memorization and didactic forms of instruction, nodded to in the description of Freire's (1968/2013) banking model of education. The result is a sense of *who* that can be measured and ranked ahead or behind the capacity of other learners to demonstrate knowing based on external performance indicators. In this transactional model, students exchange a good grade for compliance with the instructional requirements of the teacher. Joe seemed to understand and resist this model of learning from an early age. He intuitively knew that he was more than what the school offered, although he initially saw this as his deficit rather than the inability of the school to address his learning style. Yet the *who* of learning is so much more expansive than instrumental and transactional outcomes:

> It's so important to have something separate that we do, aside from the drive for things such as money or relationships, something to turn to where the world falls away and we can focus on what we're doing—not for the sake of improving or any kind of goal—just aimless enjoyment that can be systematically scheduled in the week.
>   It's taken me 23 years to like learning. This is the first time I've said, I like learning and it isn't a problem with me.

It seems that humans—including educators and learners—are hardwired to seek the transcendent in ourselves, others, and nature. At times, the *who* of self as learner can be constrained, pinched, and less than what it means to be fully human. The *who* of learning seems to fluctuate among a variety of forms, from structure to free, depending on experiences, contexts, or dispositions. Joe names this human drive for the "moreness" of life that exists beyond formal school as presence—presence to the moment, the body, to our very bones:

> It's all about presence, being entirely present in the moment. People spend a lot of time forgetting that their bodies are not only incredibly sensitive to the activities and environments we put ourselves around and in—but they can be maintained in a way that increases the quality of life. We have so much focus on thinking! And when it comes to our bodies, it can be very superficial, on lookin' good, having a beach body—we forget what's on the inside. There is a level of functioning in our bones and brain that have a huge impact on well-being.

Investigation and Curiosity

Mason would agree with Joe about the innate nature of learning. Mason is a science guy. Beloved as a professor in the life sciences, he began with a strong research program, and over the years this has shifted as he has furthered his passion for learning and teaching. Currently a director of undergraduate studies, his journey has taken on a freewheeling expansion well beyond his discipline into such explorations as leadership development; creativity in the context of learning; and involvement in the preservation of a delicate ecosystem in his hometown, about which he has recently coauthored a book.

Mason's relationship to deep learning is something he has always known, even as a child. He begins his description of self-as-a-learner from the position of learning as just who he is, who he has always been:

> There are some people that are naturally more curious than others; I suspect there might be a curiosity scale, with people falling along on different points. As far back as I remember, I have been curious about why things are the way they are.

Curiosity is central to Mason's *who*-ness; to be fully human for Mason is to live a curious life. It is innate to his being to such an extent that in his early teens he spent all his time out in the woods of rural Pennsylvania, collecting and identifying plants, tracking animals, trying to figure out why things were the way they were. To separate curiosity from Mason's identity is to separate him from his humanness. As an educator, the "fire of curiosity" becomes a central tenet of his teaching. Mason shows how the *who* of learning for a learner can become the *who* of teaching for an educator.

> Somewhere along the way we stifle curiosity so innate to being human; instead of instinctively encouraging exploration, we want students to memorize the steps of what is already known. Sadly this quenches the fire

of curiosity. I think it's why I enjoy teaching a hands-on course so much; I don't make assumptions about what they already know and I'm thoroughly invested in conveying it in a way that is engaging and intriguing to stimulate their own inquisitiveness. I generally try to teach concepts in terms of "Let's try to figure out what's going on here." I might show a pattern, offer some data, generate some questions—I want students to ask probing questions and use that as a launching point to go more in depth into what's happening, and to go on to look for patterns to explain things for themselves.

Mason's identity as a curious learner suggests the fluid nature of a fully engaged *who* in learning that naturally flows into the *who* of educator. He seems to embody the way in which, as a curious person at his core, he naturally wants to become an educator to share his curiosity and knowledge. Interestingly, his first attempts at teaching were a failure as he realized that not everyone learns the ways in which he learned, a lesson that became vivid to him when he first began to help a family member whose learning style was radically different from his own. This understanding fostered another change or transformation in the *who* of Mason emerging from his process of learning to teach.

As a scientist informed by his inherent bent toward curiosity, Mason began a systematic reflection on his process for learning. He eventually landed on the central question "How can you be a teacher of things other people don't know anything about?" Not surprisingly, he found himself back on the familiar ground of a sense of self as curious and wondering how to ignite that in others in ways that were meaningful to them as learners. And as someone considered a renowned expert in his discipline, it was refreshing to discover that Mason centers himself as a learner, naming as a part of his *who*-ness the importance of integration over expertise:

> I don't really consider myself an expert—I know about a lot of things, but not any one thing in depth. I'm not one of the most knowledgeable in the world. What I'm really good at is being able to integrate within a system, to figure out what's going on by drawing on many fields of science and pulling it together horizontally instead of vertically. I'm not a detail person—I'm integrative across fields, from the sciences into human dimensions.

Joe's story illustrates the importance of considering the forms of learning that exist beyond the confines of the intellect. Mason's story speaks to the inherent quality of learning that, when tapped, can fuel a life and career with equal enthusiasm.

From Compliance to Reintegration

Andy's story offers another perspective on the self that learns. Andy was the kind of teacher in whom students like Joe might find affirmation for his energetic and kinesthetic learning style. But unlike Mason's story of learning that teaching can be a form of curiosity that is life giving, Andy's stint in teaching ended in pain, suffering, and a near-total loss of direction. For Mason, the learning associated with teaching was consistent with his inner core. For Andy, the learning associated with teaching moved from consistency with self to compliance with external sources of authority and assessment and, finally, to a reintegration of self as part of a wider community of others, primarily his family.

Andy seemed to connect with every student; whether the student was struggling or a superstar, Andy was warm, motivating, and appropriately challenging. He inspired young people to reach for greatness. He was popular among students and peers alike. In many respects, he seemed perfectly matched for the work of helping students transform their lives, to liberate them while learning the required elements of the curriculum. And key to learning, for Andy, was developing connections with students at the level of their heart, before bringing the intellect into the mix:

> Basically what happened, I got into teaching because I liked kids and I wanted to teach them in a way that would interest them in learning. I had wonderful methods teachers and my first teaching job was in a Waldorf school, which was all about connecting to children's hearts, making things hands on, and then the intellect happened through that.

But as time went on the years flowed by, and Andy found that the shining potential of transformative learning began to dim; the freedom to teach in ways that fueled his spirit and that was trustworthy was slowly derailed by institutional imperatives and external performance criteria.

> At first, I was given a long leash to make things creative, with lots of support, resources, just basically trust all the way around. As years went on, things got thicker, with expectations from the state. The time it took to teach a normal day started to bleed into my home life. Even if I said I was done and tried to put work to the side, there was an incessant barrage of "I need this from you now." The expectations changed and became fear-based education that I found myself being a conduit of—an agenda I could no longer get behind. Not only that, it was affecting my family life. I found myself spending inordinate times on minutiae. I wasn't into the

data collecting and it also affected the quality of my home life. I started losing sleep, and I tried to cope with the stress by buying into the philosophy that by keeping up with that pace, I'd stay on top of it.

As noted in chapter 6, Giroux (2013) called the diminishment of human flourishing at the hands of an educational system bent on efficiency, commodification, and accountability the *disimagination machine*. Under the influence of the disimagination machine the principal educational goal becomes the substitution of "critical thinking and critical pedagogy for paralyzing pedagogies of memorization and rote learning tied to high-stakes testing in the service of creating a neoliberal, dumb downed work force" (p. 264). The openness of learning can become captive to static and predictive educational practices in the classroom. As such, a primary purpose of contemporary schooling becomes the lulling of educators and students into a state of complacency to self-will and compliance with external authority. Educators and students alike learn that the *who* of self does not have the freedom to explore and imagine the fullness of human potential; instead, the *who* of learning becomes a cog in the wider machine of industrial knowledge.

Andy realized that he was beginning to fall asleep, to lose track of the bigger world and things that brought him alive:

> Over a handful of years, I began to feel like I was on auto-pilot. I wasn't a full participant in my own life. I went along with things, hopped in the car, drove to work, did the daily things, played my part and I was a bystander— what do the kids need, how do we want to raise them, all those logistics, I had missed them by giving everything to teaching.

The watershed moment came without warning, a reminder of what life is like outside the system in which he had nearly fallen asleep. Andy took the day off to celebrate the birthday of his son. Later that day, he began thinking about his family and what he was missing. That same afternoon, after speaking privately with his supervisor, he resigned his teaching position. Centering integrity as an inner compass for how to navigate this spur-of-the-moment and yet long-years-in-coming move, he sent thoughtful letters to family, his colleagues, and building leadership explaining his decision. He eventually posted an open letter on Facebook to alleviate the now-common challenge of people rapidly hearing and interpreting this type of news from others, explaining what was in his heart; the core of this communication was reconnection to self, family, and others and that by leaving he was saving himself. In an apt metaphor of the transformation of *who* through learning, Andy explained that he wanted to "put compost back into the soil before the

Dust Bowl laid it to waste," reclaiming his place in his family as his deepest priority: "I wanted to offer the metaphor of trying to slow down the crazy train so that I could nourish the things that nourished me."

Of course, Andy still had a family to care for and bills to pay. In an interesting twist, he remained in education, close to the young hearts that originally fueled his passion for teaching, only now he drove the big yellow school bus that picked kids up and dropped them off every day. He had the same benefits as teaching and none of the structures that reigned him in. He was free to imagine a more robust and connected sense of self.

> As a bus driver I don't need to buy into the latest state request, who has come up with the latest acronym or read the latest book—I just drive the bus. I see bus driving as being like teaching, only on wheels, and instead using a mirror to discuss things—making eye contact and talking to the kids. And then when I come home, I can coach baseball, I can take a walk with my dog and my wife, I can be a part of my daughter's volleyball tournament, my son's baseball, unlike teaching, when I didn't have time to truly exhale.

Currently, Andy has greater independence and greater responsibility to be true to the fullness of self and his relationships with others. He says that he has a long way to go, seeking opportunities to practice and make mistakes. In ways like Rumi's contrast of external and internal forms of knowing, Andy notes:

> In public school you get a test, you pass a test and move on but I see little focus on mastery, unless you play an instrument or engage in a sport. I'm intrigued now with day-to-day life—how a refrigerator works, how to paint a wall or fix a vacuum cleaner. I'm drawn to learning how things function, which requires that I have some persistence. I'm more patient with the process, rather than giving up.

Balancing a sense of profound humility with a nearly wry challenge to the system that nearly destroyed his sense of self and his relationship with this family, Andy states, "And so now I'm just the bus driver, and I'm OK with that."

Book Group: The Book and the Group

Andy, Mason, and Joe tell the story of learning to be comfortable with more authentic notions of self, the *who* of learning. The next three stories of learning shift the focus with respect to gender and the scale of learning. In the story that follows, we focus on a collective experience, in this case of people engaged in an ongoing book group and the ways in which change occurs in and with community. One of the conversation partners here is Marcia, a coauthor of this book; some book group conversation partners were able to convene for a conversation about what it is to meet monthly to talk about books. When reflecting on learning as a community endeavor, Marcia notes:

> It's kind of like the group is this lovely container. You know what to expect, in terms of who will show up and how, with each of us knowing we can take something away that's unique, and you can trust that. But the contents in that bowl—the book, the subjects, and what we each throw in—that changes each month, as everyone contributes and learns in her own way.

The *who* of learning is both about individual growth and change, but only as it is facilitated by the group, which itself changes in response to the individual learning of each group member. There is a strong mutual and reciprocal emergence of *who* as a learner in the relational bounds between self and the members of the group who participated in this conversation.

The five women—Marcia, Judy, Sandra, Karen, and Laura—wander in and drop their belongings onto the mudroom floor with the kind of familiarity that nods to the simple comfort of having spent so much time together. Each month, they gather in someone's home to catch up and talk about their learnings for that month's book. Neither stridently intellectual nor the type of social club that uses a book as an excuse to entertain and gossip, these women seem to take their books (though not themselves) seriously. Three of them are former librarians, and several members are retired; they come from all walks of life, which makes for a dynamic mix.

This morning, there is an initial sense of awkwardness as they sip coffee and eye one another, anticipating who will start the conversation flowing. During the book group meetings, someone always starts, and then the conversation flows like Rumi's springbox, free but focused on learning about self and others. Judy begins by articulating how learning in the context of this book club invites a deeper sense of understanding of both text and self. She enters the conversation as one person, an individual who read the book, and she slowly morphs into a new person through communal dialogue:

> It's interesting how the book is the catalyst for our collective conversation and learning. There is our own reading of course, but when we come together, we seem to enter into our own, deeper understandings in the company of others. It depends a lot on the book, but really, the book is just a focal point—a forum—for talking about ourselves. We end up

talking about how it makes us feel. In this group, I think more deeply about something I just read, seeing a character through another's eyes, perhaps picking up on this theme or that one.

Literature, even stories that are less well written or are outside the typical genre of the reader, can invite the reader into unexpected places of self-examination and growth. There were many such books that landed flat or were a complete dud that no one liked. And yet these disasters, when read solo, become memorable conversations and moments of learning in the context of the group. What seemed flat and uneventful becomes fodder for a provocative conversation of multilayered themes with penetrating characters and plots.

The poet Emily Dickinson (1976) wrote, "Tell all the truth but tell it slant" (pp. 506–507). In a similar way of sideways talking about the value of art, literature, and music in opening new passageways of knowing self, the poet Valzhyna Mort noted, "When we listen to a great poem, we cannot really paraphrase it. It seems like nothing was said to us really, yet everything was said to us" (as heard on National Public Radio, *Morning Edition*, November 9, 2020).

Dickinson and Mort, both poets, are pointing to a truth about poetry and literature in general, that the women in the book group encountered as they learned to listen to the text and listen to each other responding to the text. In ways that only art can do, the women shared their insights and confusions with one another, as the books also brought their conversation alive, and in this dialectic of speaking and listening new notions of selfhood emerged.

Sandra captures the importance of tangential learning when she notes, "It's often not even related to the book. We might go veering off on a side tangent because there is everyone's personal and emotional connection to something in the book." Something in Sandra's observation touches Marcia, and she begins to speak but stops, almost as if she cannot quite grasp the essence of what she is coming to understand in the moment of this conversation. She fumbles for words, hesitates, and Judy gestures with her hands, warmly encouraging her. Marcia gathers up her thoughts and plunges on:

> Initially I found myself—how do I say it?—well, having a strong internal response to the ways in which some presented their points of view. Maybe someone might come with extensive notes or offer a heavy intellectual perspective. Over time, I've noticed a couple of things. If I'm honest with myself, what's happening is that a negative reaction is a reflection of something in ME that's really going on, maybe not having read very closely or worrying that I'm lacking depth. So, there are two lessons here.

One is to lean in instead of back, if I notice that, and be curious: What does my response say about my own judgment? And next, how wonderful to have the staying power here, to deepen into what it is to be in a community over time.

Karen echoes Marcia's observation that her initial fear was the book club was going to be too formal and academic, that she was going to be "ranked ahead or behind others / in regard to [her] competence in retaining / information." (Rumi, 2004, p. 178) But over time she felt comfortable showing up as herself and talking about the passages or ideas in the book that she connected with:

Yeah, at first, I was a little resentful of folks who showed up with notes and sticky tabs. I thought, oh no, this is going to be like homework, I don't want to be part of this, if that's what's going to be expected of me. Every once in awhile, I might mark a passage—but mostly I like to just read and talk about it. I realize now that there aren't any expectations for how we all show up or what anyone's experience is going to be. We are all unique, we each bring something different, and that's OK.

Both Karen and Marcia are pointing to an element of learning about themselves that, if not challenged, can impede the formation of who they are learning to become through communal conversation. They both harbor an embedded distrust of learning that feels like school in that it is overly structured and performance oriented. They seem to embody a natural form of learning that flows from the center of their unique experience of the world and, by implication, the more everyone brings their stance to the text and the conversation, the more opportunities emerge for others to change in response to the formation of communal knowing.

It is Laura, the newest member of the group, who summarizes the complex way in which text, self, and community interact in ways to foster new learnings of the text, self, and the community. She notes that this process feels "spiritual" and transcends the realm of everyday experience:

The book group—the book AND group—are so important to me, I can almost cry, I'm so happy. I love to learn from life, and good literature is a reflection of real life—if that's combined with actual, real relationships in a trustworthy setting—that is literally a spiritual experience for me. I'm interested in learning to be in the world and considering things such as how do we reflect on our own growth areas, how do we learn forgiveness, and all the themes that are in literature, the ones we want to grow into. I don't tend to get much out of serial relationships—and so to be actually sitting with the book with other people, that learning is so much greater for me. Instead of just, "Oh well, that was interesting."

Laura notes, "I love to learn from life . . . it is literally a spiritual experience for me." Holly, whom we introduced in an earlier chapter, echoes Laura's assertion and offers a rich description of what learning through an inclusive spiritual lens looks like. Belden Lane (2019), in *The Great Conversation: Nature and the Care of the Soul,* noted that "The planet longs for a body of wild souls who will love it intensely, acting boldly on its behalf" (p. 4). Holly is one of those "wild souls" who is not afraid to speak out on behalf of the earth and all its more-than-human forms. Her fierceness for caring for the earth derives in fundamental ways from her relationship with nature as a teacher and mentor.

Building Meaningful Relationships

Holly leaves no doubt about the center and source of her learning:

> I feel like I am a different learner. I've felt that for many years. I'm an earth learner, I learn most from the earth, from the wind—today I was out on the snow and it's been so blustery and frozen—today it was soft. I learn through my cells and bones, how my feet are on the earth, from the wind, stars and moon. I think it's about echolocating myself on land, first with the shape of the trees or the sound of the brook, for example.

To remove Holly from the natural world is to severely trim her sense of self that is deeply rooted in her cells and bones. For Holly, the boundary between self and nature is fluid and less rigid than is often the case in more formal learning in which objectivism and a stance of distancing self from object is valued:

> We talk about our inner life. But what layer of the inner life are we talking about? There's a whole spiral. There's what's beneath the skin, but that's not the inner life. In my innermost layers, is the essence. And that's where I'm most connected to earth, not my book knowledge, but my bone and my breath knowledge.

There is an element of deep relationality in her sense of self as a learner. She speaks of living next to a brook for 36 years and "hearing what the poem is for each day." Holly is more than a casual listener; she immerses herself in a learner–educator relationship with nature. She has formed such a deep mentoring relationship with nature that she is constantly learning, even when interacting with other humans.

Martin Buber (1923) spoke of two contrasting ways humans interact with the world: *I–It* and *I–Thou.* The I–It relationship is premised on a separation between self and the world. This way of knowing values distance and objectivity. Buber called into question the long-term value of I–It relationships as an avenue to human flourishing; it is inherently limited because an "It" as an object can provide only so much knowledge about the world. He argued instead for the formation of an I–thou relationship, in which the other has standing both as an autonomous agent and as something that can be entered into a learning relationship with. In the I–Thou relationship the "I" of self is not fully isolated from the other but rather is consciously willing to be changed by the interaction.

To engage in an I–It relationship is to name boundaries and draw distinctions between self and the world. This form of knowing the world is therefore self-limiting. In the I–Thou relationship this limitation no longer exists because the It of knowing has been transcended by the focus on the relationship with Thou. Holly explains a similar I–Thou relationship when she notes:

> To me, everything is a teacher, and the less you know the better off you are. Learning is about following clues and noticing. We're not taught [in schools] to notice; we're taught to make sense of things. I've been wanting to become fluent in nonhuman languages—the currents of the wind, you know there are waves of wind.

For Holly, learning is not an abstraction of facts by which she can organize and rank experiences; learning is a verb, as nodded to by Kimmerer (2013). To be successful as a learner takes the courage to break free from Western, formalized, and scripted interactions with nature.

In describing the importance of the "Great Conversation" between human and more-than-human beings, Lane (2019) stated that "The Earth yearns to Teach us language we didn't even know exists" (p. 4). The language of the Earth is speech that Holly also yearns to understand and speak from her mentor, nature:

> Milkweed has been a big teacher for me. What is the language of milkweed? I could write a doctoral thesis on the language of milkweed and the lessons it teaches me—on letting go, the way they open up like prayers, how milkweed floats on the air with its own propeller that takes its seed and it isn't in control of where it lands and takes root. I don't know how it ties into book learning, I'm not a good book learner, I can't recite authors, I'm not good at facts and figures, but I can tell you about the milkweed. Right now I'm learning from the grapevine. I'm interested in nonlinear learning—grapevine is nonlinear. I'm wondering what hieroglyphics there are, what are the forgotten languages, the ones we've snuffed out, the languages of

people who lived more closely to the land that honored that relationship. My learning is informed by a longing for the lack of separation between the human and natural world. Our education system—to be educated—is in book and head learning, in human-centric learning.

Learning for Holly is more than a discrete set of descriptions of the natural world that can be put to use. She has learned, as Kimmerer (2013) described, that "science and traditional [Indigenous] knowledge may ask different questions and speak different languages, but they may converge when both truly listen to the plants" (p. 161). It is essential to Holly's emerging sense of self as informed by the Great Conversation and relationship with nature. And because of the reciprocal quality of the relationship between herself as learner and nature as teacher, there is an element of responsibility and activism on behalf of the Earth.

This theme of responsibility and activism is evident in our last story of "Who is the self that learns?" It speaks to the way in which learning can lead to unexpected notions of self that seemed impossible and unrealistic when the learning journey was in its emerging stages. Like the dynamic nature of Rumi's springbox, this learning does not have a determined, predictable endpoint, even within the life span of the learner.

We featured Jamila in chapter 6. She identifies as an activist and has had a rich career as a youth development specialist. Her sense of commitment and responsibility to her work fosters participation in numerous aspects of her community. As she learns new ways to practice her activism in service of area youth, Jamila is developing a sense of self she calls *radical mothering* even though she is not a mother and is often reminded of this fact by others. "I was struggling with [radical mothering] since in a lot of spaces, people remind me that I'm not a mother." But as Jamila understands her role and the role of other writers and activists, at its core, mothering is about building meaningful relationships. This is something one can learn to do, whether they have raised a child or not. Learning to embody the identity of radical mothering was unexpected for Jamila. It occurred seemingly without warning. She realized she was working hard to form meaningful relationships with others, but it never occurred to her to form a meaningful relationship with her self. Jamila frames self-care as a form of love that is the precursor to supporting others: "To open a love letter to ourselves, to connect with our hearts and others is vital." Self-love and other love are mutually connected in relationship, similar to Holly's I–Thou relationship with nature.

Jamila's story speaks to the courage it takes to recognize the socially learned limitations on identity and to learn how to embrace the role of radical mothering for a person who is not biologically a mother. And Jamila's story of learning has another important lesson regarding "Who is the self that learns." Cornel West (1989), the social activist and critic of capitalism and its power to distort equity, invited individuals fighting for social change to consider the philosophical stance of *prophetic pragmatism*. For West, a *pragmatist* is a person who knows how to bend and flex while remaining true to the goal of confronting injustice and advocating for individuals who have been marginalized by society, and a *prophet* is a person who realizes that the act of speaking truth to power is never ending. Prophets are courageous learners because they are planting the seeds of change that they will never see emerge and grow to maturity.

Jamila's understanding of a "love letter to self" mirrors many of the attributes of West's articulation of prophetic pragmatism. Both are committed to making the world a better place for historically disempowered individuals, and both recognize that the struggle is never ending. Through the course of her work as an activist, Jamila learned that grounding her *who*-ness, her emerging identity, in the Western social construct of legacy was problematic. It externalized her sense of self-worth and kept it captive within a social context that favors power over rather than power with others. She came to realize that instead of forming her identity and work around legacy, she could form better relationships through the metaphor of an insurance policy. The process of learning her true and full identity involves two courageous steps. The first is rejection of notions of self that are imposed from outside her internal sense of self and embracing the love of self. The second step involves letting go of images of self that are caught up in metrics of success defined by the social world. There is a paradoxical effect between the act of coming to know oneself more fully through the act of unlearning self as something that can be measured through the qualities of legacy:

> I'm leaning into the question of where are the other spaces in which we see insurance policies that produce beautiful dividends we never dreamed of? Life teaches us [that] it's in those moments, we can't predict the trajectory, life really happens and it's where all the action is. I'm thinking about goal setting and what is going to happen next—thinking of legacy and milestones—when I was young, what was my 50-year plan? It's not for me to worry about anymore.

For Jamila, writing love letters to self is something she learned to do through the identity and actions of a person concerned about the well-being of others, especially youth who are historically marginalized. Her love of others led to a love of self and the formation of relationships based not on legacy but a future she dreams of, and she no longer measures her sense of worth by whether elements of those dreams are realized.

In this chapter, we have contrasted ways of knowing that are intellectual, structured, individual, and objective with other ways of knowing that are embodied, natural, open framed, and communal. Paying attention to the formation of "Who is the learning self?" is of great importance if the goal in learning is to create a context in which the fullness of human understanding can emerge. In our current world of pandemics related to health, environmental degradation, economic disparity, and social inequalities, humans need the fullness of our hearts, minds, and bodies to attend to these challenges.

Opportunity for Reflection

Throughout this book, we have centered Rumi's two intelligences. When you consider "Who is the self that learns?," how have you been impacted by the inner forms of learning that Rumi helps us to better understand?

As you read the vignettes of the learners in this chapter (and in the three previous chapters), with whom do you closely relate? Which story elevated your personal sense of *who* you are as a learner?

What are you discovering about who you are as a learner? In our foreword, Rendón offers that she views herself as "a learner whose heart and mind are open to learning." Who are you?

If you are someone with learners in your care, how can you build a sense of rapport that welcomes the richly diverse *who*-ness of learners in your setting?

What do you anticipate as the opportunities and challenges of inviting a richer array of *who*-ness into the settings with which you engage with others who are learners in your care?

8

FROM REFLECTION TO ACTION

Expanding the Conversation

When Someone Deeply Listens to You

*When someone deeply listens to you
it is like holding out a dented cup
you've had since childhood
and watching it fill up with
cold, fresh water.
When it balances on top of the brim,
you are understood.
When it overflows and touches your skin,
You are loved.
When someone deeply listens to you,
the room where you stay
starts a new life
and the place where you wrote
your first poem
begins to glow in your mind's eye.
It is as if gold has been discovered!
When someone deeply listens to you,
your bare feet are on the earth
and a beloved land that seemed distant
is now at home within you.*

—Fox, 1995, p. 58.

In this book, we have invited you to reflect—to pause and consider your learning journey; its influences; insights you have discovered; how you have come to know them; why they have mattered; and who you are now, as a learner, because of it. We introduced the Mobius strip as a tool for understanding the elements of interior exploration and outer action—the way in which we turn inward to reflect and then, more wisely informed by that reflection, we turn a corner and move outward again to offer our influence and to act, in an enduring, intertwined process. Courageous learning always invites us to move from that reflective stance of solitude, to go back into the world, to offer the strengths, gifts, and perspectives we have to offer that are so badly needed "out there"—before we again return to reflection "in here."

We close the book with an invitation to enter into conversations with others as a potential next step on this reflective path. Who are the people in your life who would benefit from engaging in a process of exploration into a learning stance alongside you, and what might you (and they) hope to gain from the conversation? We anticipate that students and colleagues might be natural starting points, benefiting from collective reflection on the kinds of questions contained in this text.

Numerous voices of learners have brought the subject of learning to life in this book. Since there are as many learners as there are grains of sand, there are many stories we did not include. As authors, we also recognize that we bring our own perspectives and the limitations that any outlook provides, and while we tried to include as many voices and their stories of learning that we could, we know that there are some that are absent from this book. What voices do you believe are missing? Who are the learners whose perspectives you would benefit from better understanding? As you reflect on the possibility of convening learning conversations, you may want to consider including the perspectives of others who may offer stories with which you may not be familiar. This type of conversation can offer a foundation for discovering more authentic aspects of others' lives—those with whom you may cross paths every day but do not know well—while cultivating the listening skills necessary to invite them forth. And, depending on the various roles you play in your professional and personal life, while you may begin with colleagues and students, perhaps you may be called to invite members of your community into a learning conversation as well.

Reaching Out Takes Courage

Throughout this book, we have drawn a link between courage and learning. We have argued that one cannot exist without the other and that this is especially true in situations in which transformative learning takes place. It takes courage to see past the limitations of formal learning, which often tends to narrow in on a few essential indicators of content mastery rather than see the larger picture in a more complex and beautiful world. Maxine Greene (1988), in her examination of the constraints and possibilities of human freedom in education, reflected on causes for why it can be difficult for educators to connect students to the fullness of their human potential. She lamented that "The world may not be problematized [in schools]; no one aches to break through a horizon, aches in the presence of the question itself. So there are no tensions, no desires to reach beyond" (p. 124). We hope that through the stories we have shared, we have shown the many ways in which learners are aching to break through the constraints of their formalized learning into a new horizon, a courageous place of learning that integrates self, text, and the complex world.

In addition, it takes courage to model a stance that may be different from the norms in many of our places of work. This stance may ask for your vulnerability—a willingness to begin by offering some of the longings, challenges, insights, and confusions set loose by your own exploration. For learners to engage in emancipatory and humanizing learning, it can be helpful to be inspired by someone who sees past the standardized forms of performance to learning that is waiting to be unstopped and set free within the heart of the learner—and you might be that someone! To model what might be possible in the field of learning, and to lean into those new beginnings and trust that they will lead toward flourishing and more holistic notions of the self in the world, may ask something new of you. It is, after all, the purpose of learning to enrich the experience of being human.

Our ongoing challenge is to imagine a possible world of learning that has yet to be fully named and recognized in those professions that engage learners. The act of imagination is an act of courage; it is a leaning into the unknown. In her search for models of imaginative thinking for the purpose of freedom, Greene (1988) referenced John Dewey, who was articulating an educational response to the anaesthetizing influences of schooling in the early 1900s. Both Greene and Dewey argued that "imaginative thinking" (Greene, 1988, p. 125) has to be a conscious process because it is risky. "Conscious thinking always involves a risk, a 'venture into the unknown' and it occurs against a background of funded or sedimented meanings that must themselves be tapped and articulated" (Greene, 1988, p. 125). The voices we feature this book exemplify both the expansion of new horizons for learning and the capacity to tap into each person's "funded and sedimented" forms of learning as seed sources for growing into fuller notions of self as learner. This capacity to imagine and tap into previously unexplored avenues of learning require particular forms of courage, and we hope that we have shown a light on this path.

In the book, *The Courage Way: Leading and Living with Integrity*, Shelly L. Francis and The Center for Courage & Renewal (2018) discussed four kinds of courage that are needed when fortifying one's self and others for hard times. These include the ability to live into our hearts and to cultivate the disposition that is required to help us regain our strength and composure. She noted that the most common form of courage is a physical act, which can involve putting oneself in harm's way in support of others. Yet, as she argued, and as the stories of our learning conversation partners indicate, there are other forms of courageous learning. In addition to moral and social courage, Francis focused on creative courage—perhaps the least recognized form of courage—and suggested that it may be the most important form to nurture. Creative courage generates new solutions, fosters community, forms meaning from difficulty, makes new symbols and meanings that others can rally around, and inspires the kind of change that moves us forward in our humanity. It means claiming our place at the table, saying what is necessary for our voices to be heard and to speak out and claim agency.

Holding a *Courage to Learn* conversation is a way to discover the stories of others—and to model the openness necessary to start a meaningful conversation that inspires fruitful change. We know that we cannot hate those whose stories we have come to respect and better understand. As such, this is a powerful way to bring people together, which is vital in today's world. As Rachel Naomi Remen (2006) stated, "When you listen generously to people they can hear the truth in themselves, often for the first time" (p. 159). Inviting stories evokes a generosity of spirit from which we all may ultimately benefit. As our society continues to face difficult conversations and histories around justice, equity, respect, and freedom, we need to focus on the power of listening and learning about ourselves and about others. Through this process, we can be always learning and can become a guide for others who want to do the same.

How to Listen to Learners

Throughout this book, we have emphasized the stance of the learner. If you are an educator, teacher, facilitator, clergy member, health-care professional, parent, or in another of the myriad roles in which learners are in one's care, you may have occasionally found yourself in the role of one who tells and talks. Shifting your stance to listening can empower learners and strengthen the bonds of relationship and growth. It can be additionally exciting since it naturally shifts you into the perspective of uncovering something new. The poem by John Fox (1995) in the epigraph that opens this chapter speaks to the power of listening in the process of learning to be fully connected to self, others, and the world:

> When someone deeply listens to you, / the room where you stay / starts a new life / . . . When someone deeply listens to you, / your bare feet are on the earth / and a beloved land that seemed distant / is now at home within you. (p. 58)

Whatever your path may be, the practice of active listening and of asking powerful, open, and honest questions will be a bedrock as you work to make a trustworthy space into which you invite the voices of others. It is vital to learn how to listen and hold space while also welcoming the stories of others more skillfully. This takes practice, and it takes a more expansive understanding of the purpose of listening. In educational spaces informed by the Western logical tradition, listening is frequently taught as a form of analytic aggression. In this tradition, the goal is often to listen for the logical missteps or misunderstandings of your opponent and to use this information to confront, challenge, and diminish the other, to put them in their intellectual place. Formal education sometimes teaches that being critical of others' thoughts or theories is a form of intellect, but this tradition can get in the way of active listening and empowering others by hearing their stories.

The form of listening we advocate emerges from traditions that value community, connection, and shared meaning making. Listening is an act of connecting, not disconnecting, from others. Lane (2019) considered deep listening as a prerequisite for entering into the "Great Conversation" of human and more-than-human communication and interaction: "The Great Conversation stretches us at every turn, yet it leaves us with the knowledge that we're in this together. We're part of a shared community with a growing respect for the whole" (p. 253). Perhaps even more fundamental to the task of courageous listening is the willingness to be changed by the conversation, and for educators to emerge as different people because they have listened and learned. This, as Belden noted, requires flexibility in thinking and acting; it requires the capacity to be stretched: "We need to develop our receptivity to other voices, resisting the impulse to connect exclusively on our own terms . . . to make ourselves open to what's already coming to us in ways we've not yet learned to receive" (p. 259).

The act of vulnerable listening is courageous because it opens the possibility of being wounded, shocked, or feeling guilt as the experiences of someone else are shared. Valarie Kaur (2020), in her memoir *See No*

Stranger: A Memoir and Manifesto of Revolutionary Love, noted that "Listening is a strategic choice: the more I listen, the more I understand" (p. 140). And she pointed out that it is not possible, or even warranted, to be a good listener all the time. With the strategic choice to be a good listener, there are times to not listen. Listening requires preparation and intention, so

> the question therefore is not *whether* or not to listen to our opponents. The questions are: *When* is it *my* role to listen? When am I emotionally and physically safe? When can I take on the labor of listening when others are not safe to do so? (p. 140)

Kaur values listening as a tool for confronting hate and violence in the world, so it is little wonder she emphasized the need to be "safe" when engaging in listening as an act of love.

We also believe that listening requires intention and the creation of a safer space in which being listened to is "like holding out a dented cup / you've had since childhood / and watching it fill up with / cold, fresh water" and knowing that feeling of being loved "when it overflows and touches your skin," as noted by Fox (1995, p. 58) in the poem at the beginning of this chapter.

Even if you are an educator with learners in your care, you are also part of this learning community. Educators have a dual role of teacher and learner. As a learner, how do you consider your own learning and listen to your own learner's voice? Reflecting on our own learning journey and gaining insight into what we learn and what we still need to discover positions us as wide eyed, open, and interested—always welcoming a beginner's mind. Actively listening to your own learning voice and giving yourself the permission to question, consider, and make mistakes can help you become a more courageous learner. Here, we offer suggestions for creating and sustaining a space in which listening is safe and inviting and where people can courageously share their stories.

The Practice of Asking Questions as a Tool for Deep Listening

Often, we think of questions as a way to get information from someone else and as part of an overall conversation that leads to solving an issue or problem. As such, our questions to ourselves and to others are often laden with advice or problem-solving, and we are listening for the purpose of creating our own response rather than to truly hear what is being said. Sometimes the listening process meets our needs to help others rather than focusing on what the others are saying or that the learner might consider.

The practice of asking open and honest questions shifts the dial to invite a more spacious, authentic conversation, thus enabling us to step away from our tendency to make assumptions and jump to conclusions. We can move away from leading the conversation with a specific goal in mind, problem-solving, or responding in a formal teaching fashion so that our listening goal is to learn and to empower. This kind of inquiry invites a person to call upon their own wisdom and knowledge of self, slowing the pace of a learning conversation while developing deeper mutual investment in being together as learners in a complex world. If we step in with advice and are too quick to interpret, we run the risk of narrowing or restricting the story instead of expanding and deepening an exploration. Stories often help us to explore important questions and complicated issues; asking powerful questions recognizes the value of listening without judgment. Our role as a learner who listens creates a safe and meaningful process for allowing stories to percolate up from the depths.

When framing questions within this tradition of listening it is best to keep them simple, brief, and to the point, not loaded with the content of your experience. Questions, such as "What surprised you?," "What was it you felt?," and "What was easy or difficult?" can help to continue the story that is being shared and open the door even wider for authentic and meaningful listening. Maintaining the presence to know when you are starting to slip into your own storytelling or speech making is important since these practices likely draw attention to yourself and away from the learner—making it about you rather than about them and their story.

Marcia found the practice of asking open and honest questions to be life changing. She was unaware of her inclination to problem-solve and, as such, it was a game changer to learn to listen and ask questions designed to take someone more deeply into their story and tap their own inner wisdom—not to give advice or help to "fix what needed fixing." Here, she describes her journey into this process and offers a way to reflect on it as a practice, adapted from an article formerly published in a Center for Courage & Renewal newsletter (Eames-Sheavly, 2018).

> When I first began participating in Circles of Trust®, the part that intrigued me most was the practice of asking honest and open questions. I began to witness just how many interactions were cut short by the offering of advice or a "helpful" suggestion, after which, the dialogue was over. So often it seemed that our hurried way of engaging with one another undergirded this phenomenon. If we are all too busy at work and a colleague describes something that's troubling her, why not help her out by telling her how to take care of the issue? Problem solved!

I went through a period of discomfort when I realized that sometimes, I was the one cutting off the dialogue. As someone who prided myself on being an empathetic ear, I couldn't help but be surprised at how often my inquiry was poorly veiled guidance-giving in the form of a friendly question.

So I dove in with gusto. As a righteous worker bee, I recall the effort aimed at asking just the right question. I was earnest as I sat listening with steam coming out of my ears, trying to come up with the supportive questions that would offer this good person just the clarity needed.

However, once in awhile, something would shift and I would find myself in a nearly altered state of quiet. The soundtrack would settle down and I was deeply listening for real. Occasionally this happened when I was out walking with someone. I experienced an intense realization that this practice was getting into my bones when someone close to me said, "Can we do that thing we've been doing lately, where we go for a walk, and you ask me questions so that I can figure out what I need to do next?"

So what made this different from the other approach—that of working so hard to be a virtuous listener? I have come to think of asking honest and open questions as a true contemplative practice. It asks the same of us. It begins with intention, presence, and a particular entering in. It takes discipline and courage. It is both a process and a transformed perspective that is different from our usual way of being (or perhaps doing) in the world. It takes practice.

Here are some approaches I have intentionally cultivated as I sit or walk with someone who is in a period of discernment—or someone whose story I want to know better without larding it with my own experience. I encourage you to engage in these as you invite others' stories of courageous learning and listen to take them more deeply into their learning journeys.

Approaches to Cultivate Deep Listening

Like any muscle development or practice, it can be helpful to have guidance for this process. In this case, the practice involved is more about being present as cultivating a skill set.

Settle In

Much as with meditation, begin deep listening by stilling your busy mind, quieting the river of observations, judgments, and endless planning-ahead thoughts that often unconsciously occupy our daily thinking. Take a few deep breaths and slow down. Sometimes that is easier said than done, and yet frequent practice with family members, friends, and colleagues makes this easier. You might pause to remind yourself of your role to hold space for this person—just to be there as a listener.

Behold

It can be astonishing to fully take in another human being with no agenda of your own. Something that can help to drop into noticing the "being" in the human being is to witness their eye color; it can be startling to see how often we miss that sparkling part of a person and its nuances. You may discover your own ways to settle and behold. Please hold them in a soft gaze—neither looking directly nor being detached—just taking in the whole of them; a friend uses the metaphor of a loving gaze, not a hard stare. As the other person is talking, you may need to again still the river of thoughts to tune into what they are saying, how they are saying it, and how their body moves with what they are saying, somehow capturing the whole picture at once.

Offer an Invitation

We all want to ask "good" questions. Instead of trying to *think* of them (which will change your focus from listening to preparing your questions), you might instead issue a deep invitation to your interior self to respond to this person sitting here and to offer a question from the depths—inviting it to bubble up from down inside. Every time you begin to overthink, simply return to the practice of sitting quietly, continuing to listen with all of you, trusting that the question will come without working at it, forcing it, or thinking too hard.

Stay With It

As the person continues to speak, it is often necessary to return to the practices previously described, intentionally holding that space without trying to get ourselves into it, quieting our thoughts, and continuing to issue the invitation from within. If they begin to cry, you might gently lower your eyes and imagine your heart opening wider.

Notice the Question That Bubbles Up, Instead of the One That "Thinks" Its Way In

When this happens, you might start to feel a question arising. It might be a simple question and may have an unexpected layer or two. It might be different from the kind you typically ask. Allow the question to simmer as you continue to listen.

Is It "True?"

Some questions are honest and open and yet arise from the intellect alone. A question that comes from your depths is different. It feels true. If it persists and continues to bubble up as you listen, you might quietly examine it and then, when the person pauses, ask if they would welcome a question.

You may have to continually remind yourself that it is not your job to ask the perfect question, nor is it to offer clarity or help the person discern the next part of their learning journey. Your role is to hold space without pushing into it, to listen deeply and well, to take in the being of the human being sitting before you.

Resources for Hosting a Courage to Learn Conversation

Hosting a *Courage to Learn* conversation, whether among your closest colleagues, students and other learners, or with people in your community, offers an opportunity to ask the kinds of questions that matter deeply to many people and can serve as a tool or way in to listen to one another's stories. Many people talk about the difficulties of living in isolation, feeling the frustration of the increase in divisiveness and discord and the challenge of reaching across the divide, whether that divide is political or along other lines of perceived differences. *Courage to Learn* conversations can serve as an avenue for understanding one another's perspectives through a unique lens— that of learning—since we are all learners.

There are many questions that point a finger in the direction of finding out one another's narratives. What is a learning journey? What most interests us? Why is it important to continue learning? How do we learn, and how do we best support the learning of others? Who are we—who are we *becoming*— who is this self that continues to grow wiser along the learning path? And again, the Opportunities for Reflection that follow each chapter can also offer a natural progression, structured to offer points of reflection that work well as a jumping-off point for engaging with others.

As you consider what piques your curiosity, you might reflect on whom you would most want to get to know, to welcome into a *Courage to Learn* conversation. It could take the form of a formal evening book group, a seminar, or more informal conversations over coffee or a meal. If you find yourself drawn to your community, there are limitless possibilities to meet in homes, schools, faith-based settings, or online—anywhere that people are curious and interested in one another. The discussions can also culminate in new "doings"—participating together in activities that arise naturally when we discover shared interests in learning a new skill, art, craft, sport, or other endeavor.

The *how* of engaging with others is important to consider. Allowing for time for individual reflection, small group discussion, and larger group sharing works well. Throughout this book, we have mentioned the Circle of Trust approach. This approach is distinguished by principles and practices intended to create a process of shared exploration in which people can cocreate the trustworthy space necessary to nurture personal and professional integrity and the courage to act on it. These principles and practices are grounded in the Center for Courage & Renewal's core values, which spell out the foundational beliefs and intended purposes for this work with individuals, groups, and organizations.

The center takes great care to prepare facilitators who have the knowledge and skill required to hold and guide Circles of Trust using these principles and practices. These core elements, in the hands of a skilled facilitator, give this approach structure and intentionality and create its transformative power. To learn more about the work of the Center for Courage & Renewal, please visit https://www.couragerenewal.org.

Whether or not you are a facilitator, you can still find the principles and practices of these circles to be helpful in forming the trustworthy foundation to host a conversation in your community. For more about the principles and practices of the Circle of Trust approach in theory and in practice, please see Palmer (2004).

Organizational Resources for Fostering Conversation in Community

There are other wise approaches to engaging in the necessary groundwork for community conversations. The following are some models about which you can discover more online.

The People's Supper

The People's Supper (https://thepeoplessupper.org/) is an ideal approach for situating your *Courage to Learn* conversation in the context of race, equity, and inclusion. A guidebook is offered for

> any multiracial community that is actively reckoning with how to build a more equitable future, and is particularly interested in the interplay between what it means to be in right relationship with one another, and how that translates into structural change. The practices and tips

in this guidebook reflect our learnings over the last several years working with civic leaders operating within the same city or town, managers and employees looking to have an honest conversation about race and to chart a better path forward within their workplace, and schools and faith communities.

The Dinner Party

If your *Courage to Learn* conversation involves those who are drawn to share one another's stories from a place of shared grief, The Dinner Party (https://www.thedinnerparty.org/) is one to consider. Their mission is:

> to transform life after loss from an isolating experience into one marked by community support, candid conversation, and forward movement using the age-old practice of breaking bread. We foresee a day in which people find amidst their deepest struggle the source of their deepest strength by connecting with others who've been there too, in an environment that's accessible and familiar, and marked by deep connections over time; a day in which grief is free of stigma and silence; and in which those who've lived through loss or hardship, whatever its form, are recognized not as objects of pity, but as better listeners and better leaders, characterized by profound empathy, resilience, agency, and a commitment to living a life of meaning.

StoryCorps

The mission of StoryCorps (https://storycorps.org/) is:

> to preserve and share humanity's stories in order to build connections between people and create a more just and compassionate world. We do this to remind one another of our shared humanity, to strengthen and build the connections between people, to teach the value of listening, and to weave into the fabric of our culture the understanding that everyone's story matters. At the same time, we are creating an invaluable archive for future generations.

The Practice Space

The Practice Space (https://www.practice-space.org/storytelling-guide/) is a nonprofit organization that provides communication strategies, concrete techniques, and coaching for people of all ages in a safe, supportive practice space. Of particular interest is their storytelling guide, which centers making storytelling inclusive and equitable.

Living Into and Reintegrating Learning in the Journey Ahead

Dorothy Day (1957) was quoted as saying that "People say, 'What is the sense of our small effort?' They cannot see that we must lay one brick at a time, take one step at a time" (p. 6). What small step will you take in the direction of learning that is more life giving, exciting, honoring, and ultimately makes a difference in the world that greatly needs your contribution? If learners are in your care, how can you listen to them, to begin to build spaces that welcome all learners—and all facets of all learners—for a more enlivening and engaging experience?

Throughout this book, we have grappled with the tension between Western analytic approaches to understanding the world and integrated ways of knowing (Indigenous, Eastern, and holistic) that value wholeness. The tension manifests itself in various dialectical relationships, including outer/inner, objective/subjective, structure/imagination, and parts/whole. We have tried, whenever possible, to assert the importance of both perspectives when talking about learning and the courage it takes to change. We are an advocate of both–and thinking, not either–or ways of knowing.

In her closing address as president of the Association for the Study of Higher Education, Rendón (2000) called for a unified approach to the study of higher education. She called for a new framing she termed "Academics of the Heart." She began her discussion in a place similar to the place in which we started our conversation about the limitations of conceptualizing learning as something that teachers do and students receive. "We have failed to acknowledge the limitations of our Western intellectualism. We have perpetuated dualistic, either/or thinking. We have privileged individual research over collective scholarship" (p. 4). As Rendón noted, this model of learning has a long Western history and is often critiqued as mechanistic and deterministic. Education, as Rohr (2020) argued, becomes the noun of structure, in contrast to its potential as the verb of transformation. Our goal in this book is to revitalize the heart and soul of learning.

In Rendón's (2000) insightful critique of Western analytic approaches to scholarship, she touched on a point central to this book, which is the overemphasis on Rumi's (2004) first form of learning, which values mimicry and ranking. Like Rendón, we call not for a removal of outer ways of knowing but rather for the inclusion and expansion of inner wisdom as a valid framing of learning. Rumi poetically described this form of learning as "a spring overflowing its springbox" (p. 178). Rendón (2000) described this form of being in the world as spiritual and humanizing:

> There is a deep imbalance in higher education that stems from a disconnected, fragmented view of teaching, learning, and research. We need a new framework that reconnects the intellect with the spirit, that allows

us to bridge our inner and outer knowing, and that honors our humanity while incorporating high standards in our work. We need a marriage between precise inquiry and poetic intuition. (p. 5)

In chapters 4 through 7, we aimed for an integrative, community-based approach that acknowledges the contributions of researchers and knowledgeable specialists in the field while centering the wise voices of conversation partners and their life experiences as authorities on the subject of learning. At the same time, we (the three authors) are still educated in a Western tradition, and it frames our thinking, and so we hold this as a both–and. We felt it would be helpful to the reader to see the unique elements of learning through the themes of *what, how, why*, and *who*. At key moments in these chapters we have pointed to the integrated nature of the themes. For example, the *what* of learning can directly impact the extent to which the *who* of learning is formed or de-formed. If the focus on learning is exclusively content, the learner becomes an expert in the knowledge of the discipline, yet they will likely know little about to whom they related and why they have a passion for the subject matter in the first place.

As we near the end of this book, we want to offer one last story of learning that blends the four elements into a unified courageous whole. Keith Basso (1996), a professor of anthropology at the University of New Mexico, studied the ways that Western Apache use landscapes as a primary teaching tool. His book, *Wisdom Sits in Places: Landscapes and Language Among the Western Apache*, is aptly named as it speaks to ways that landforms become teaching stories that are constant visual reminders of Western Apache wisdom.

When a young person does something that bumps into cultural and ecological norms that have allowed the Western Apache to survive for centuries, elders characteristically point to a landform. It is instantly understood, given the cultural stories associated with the landform, regarding what went wrong and what the young person needs to do to move back into "right relationship" with self, land, and Western Apache ways of thriving in the landscape. This approach to the wholeness of the self and the ongoing courage to be ever learning is crucial to understand and to practice.

Language, landscape, and learning are synonymous and integrated. In the language of this text, *what, how, why*, and *who* are often inseparable. The *what* of cultural knowledge is conveyed in the *how* of stories for the *why* of survival. In this dynamic dance, the *who* becomes a combination of language and landscape. Cognition, identity, and spiritual elements of self are intimately tied to content, process, and outcome—a unified whole that undergirds Western Apache culture and their capacity to live and flourish in relationship with the landscape.

We recognize that each of us holds several different perspectives; we may be partner, sibling, parent, or grandparent. We may consider ourselves as coming from a particular geographic region or as holding certain faith-based or historical traditions. We each hold multiple identities, and this intersectionality allows for a unique perspective for each person. And it necessitates continuous learning about ourselves and others that is strengthened when we listen, grow, and learn.

This image of integration and wholeness is one we invite you to consider when approaching the many possibilities and limitations of learning. We recognize that the cornerstones of learning (content, process, and outcome) are equally shared by many. Yet what matters, and we hope has been demonstrated in this book, is whether the educator approaches these elements as separate parts that can be moved around to achieve specific goals or as an integrated palette of possibility for the learner.

In the foreword, Rendón considered this text to be *"una ofrenda,"* an offering, to educators and learners who seek a more spacious way to reflect and engage in the learning process. How might you serve as a conduit, extending *una invitación*, an invitation, to consider how, why, and with whom your colleagues, students, family, and community members experienced their most powerful learning experiences? How might you invite those vivid lessons learned from both the painful and joyous moments in their lives? We know that learning is not easy. It takes courage to be a learner and to be part of a learning community. But this courageous act can provide us with an infinitely exciting and memorable way to be a part of the world as we engage with others on their learning path.

AFTERWORD

What's Next? A Wise Glance Ahead to the Next Steps Toward a More Inclusive and Equitable "Courageous Learning"

Estrus Tucker

To think incisively and to think for one's self is very difficult. We are prone to let our mental life become invaded by legions of half-truths, prejudices, and propaganda. A great majority of the so-called educated people do not think logically and scientifically. Even the press, the classroom, the platform, and the pulpit in many instances do not give us objective and unbiased truths. To save man from the morass of propaganda, in my opinion, is one of the chief aims of education. Education must enable one to sift and weigh evidence, to discern the true from the false, the real from the unreal, and the facts from the fiction.

—*Martin Luther King, Jr., as an 18-year-old Morehouse College student.*

To be a learner is the most powerful posture for a human being. Our courage to learn is how we thrive and survive as a species. Learning starts in the womb and is ripening with every breath we take. Learning drives adaptation, innovation, and evolution. Learning must always be in proximity to living because learning at its best serves life. To learn is to live and living takes courage.

The Ties That Bind Us: Clarity, Civility, and Truth

The wise words of a young Martin Luther King, Jr. call out a chief and perennial aim of education, and that is "to save us from the morass of propaganda." It is precisely this morass of propaganda that is the crux of our impediments to advancing the courage to learn in the spaces in which we live, lead, and learn. Concepts and tactics such as misinformation, disinformation, indoctrination, and propaganda are not new to any democratic struggle for integrity and equity. However, the increasingly covert and overt institutional deployment of such concepts and tactics fueled by the rapid advancement of technologies, including social media, virtual platforms, and so forth, is dramatically impacting our culture in ways known and unknown.

Can we listen to stories that expand and challenge our stories? Can we talk with people with whom we disagree? Can we work together for sustainable systemic change? These and other familiar yet changing questions to leaders, professions, and communities are too often superficially addressed or avoided to the detriment of our integrity. What are you learning? Where is our courage? How can I strengthen my courage to learn in service of the challenges I see?

Political censorship and the suppression of certain media, books, authors, theories and concepts deemed political threats are increasingly advocated for by trusted institutions and passed into law by many of our state legislatures. The hype of fake news and the spin of alternative facts combined with questionable consumption of news and reckless devotion raises the bar for a more resilient courage to learn.

Championing Our Humanity

In our increasingly diverse nation, systemic inequities continue to diminish our inherent human dignity by devaluing particular identities. Our identities designated by gender, race, ethnicity, class, age, gender identity, sexual orientation, immigration status, census tract residency, religious affiliation, and political labels are devalued, exploited, and manipulated to the detriment of human dignity and equity. At the core of these inequities, in systems and in personal attitudes and behavior, are our collective failures to champion human being-ness beyond any other identity. Beyond the growing chaos of our socially constructed identity labels, our capacities to honor the wonderful diversity of all our people and respect divergent viewpoints is being systematically delayed, deformed, and undermined.

To be human is to be deserving of inclusion, justice, and equity in all our systems and our collective culture. How might we envision and design structures and processes as if every human being mattered? This is the challenge and persistent invitation to every leader, within and without the institution. In a capitalist culture the conflict between profitability and human well-being is a perennial tension. Our economic, democratic, and moral choice is between unfettered capitalism and liberated humanity. The liberation of our humanity requires transformative learning, which is both a catalyst and an outcome of the courage to learn aspirations.

The Courage to Learn as a Path to Healing

The most critical application of our insights and inspiration from the courage to learn is in our healing, individually and collectively. As revealed in many of the learning stories, our formal and informal learning spaces are layered with wounds and heartbreak that can serve as stepping stones or stumbling blocks, rites of passages or patterns of decline, all depending on the quality of our courage and depth of our learning. Complacency and performance anxiety are chief among self-imposed impediments.

The growth edge of the courage to learn begins and ends with the audacity to be whole and the wisdom of self-love. Ultimately, we must reconcile our advocacy and our activism with equally rigorous, life-affirming self-care and regard for the well-being of others. Dare we listen to our brokenness and allow our wounds to teach us how to create safe spaces for others in proximity? To do so requires a more interior approach to agency and the discipline to resist the temptation to glamorize overwork and self-sacrifice. The quality of our courage and the impact of our learning grows in new dimensions when self-care and healing are valued and embodied.

Intersectionality of Identity and Inequity

To be a learner helps us explore, define, redefine, and claim our identities in ways that respect our human dignity. This journey of identity grounds our learning in the reality of our lived experiences.

Intersectionality is a powerful lens to see the whole of our humanity and is a provocatively human approach to adequately assessing equity. The concept of intersectionality sheds light on the interconnected nature of our faulty social constructs including race, class, and gender, socially applied to specific populations and manifested in overlapping and interdependent systems of discrimination or disadvantage.

Best Practices and Best Fit

To resource and support the courage to learn in spaces that welcome and engage the full depth and breadth of people living in our nation requires something more personalized than best practices, the courage to learn requires best fit, like a tailored garment for a person's life. It is in this "fitting" that courage is evoked, in a culture that defaults to a one size fits all. The courage to learn recognizes one's innate and unique gifted-ness and the essential role of key relationships that reinforce this life-changing way of seeing self. This way of seeing self facilitates the transformation in response to lived experiences, events, and relationships.

The Courage to Learn and the Love of Learning

The courage to learn is profoundly related to a love of learning. The root of the word *courage* is "cor"—the Latin word for heart. Courage, like love, is a matter of the heart. Both courage and love compel an inner journey of vulnerability, trust, and truth telling and an outer expression of agency and attention to relationships.

Our relationships are our learning laboratories from birth to death. At every age certain teachers are cherished and remembered by learners because of their relationship. Maya Angelou reminds us that "people will forget what you said, people will forget what you did, but people will never forget how you made them feel."

The journey of courageous learning increasingly recognizes the teaching relationships with everyday people, often small in scale but significant in insight. Honoring the presence of people with your attention shapes your appetite for learning and deepens your discernment in applying courage.

A New Old American Dream: A Nation of Learners

Now more than ever the American dream lies precariously on the grounds of an accessible, equitable, and quality education. Many of us from all walks of life grew up with the mantra that education was the way up, out, and over. Yet our systems plagued with inequity and designed disparities render such cherished notions questionable to many and mere fantasy to those denied access. Our bureaucratic systems laden with vested interests increasingly benefit many economically. On the other hand, working-class and middle-class children, particularly but not exclusively children of color, receive diminishing returns.

It is heartbreaking to witness children at increasingly younger ages become disillusioned with school and worse, disillusioned with their abilities to learn. As a nation we must demonstrate that we truly value education first and foremost to the learners. As we systemically advance machine learning in service of profitability, we must not financially, politically, and morally neglect human learning.

One day our nation and our planet will mature into the understanding that the opportunities, capacities, and nurturing of learning is an invaluable and irreplaceable human right worthy of ensuring and championing.

We must continue to respect the intentions of noble institutions but never relinquish the responsibility of our learning to any process, system, profession, or person, disrespectful of our identities or dishonoring of our integrity. The flourishing of our humanity is predicated on creating together more and better spaces where the courage to learn is alive and well.

We are not there yet. But equity is a horizon on the road we trod, and the courage to learn is democracy's faithful companion. The convictions and practices that undergird the courage to learn are in service of a democracy that is broadly and deeply experienced as a system of the people, by the people, and for the people. Such a system of equity cannot afford to be complicit with the shadows of partisan politics or the villainization of the other whose identities are deemed different from those we value. In truth, such a system of equity evokes the better angels of our nature in ways committed to honest dialogue, authentic relationships, and civil engagement capable of trumping the vested interests and narrow narratives that divide us.

Our courage to learn is at its best when we learn with those different from ourselves, exploring, engaging, and challenging our divergent perspectives in service of a truth greater than any one vantage point.

The future of our courage to learn is in our unfinished work of E Pluribus Unum—Out of Many, One. And that future is now.

REFERENCES

Alexander, M. (2012). *The new Jim Crow: Mass incarceration in the age of colorblindness.* The New Press.

Alexander, P. A. (1996). The past, the present and future of knowledge research: A reexamination of the role of knowledge in learning and instruction. *Educational Psychologist, 31*, 89–92.

Allen, D. (2001). *Who owns the Geritol solution?* [Handout]. CC BY-NC. https://docs.google.com/document/d/1RxIV7GQfdHwJBzTCipaIx__DIIAKLFY2Plg-Khl3fKyo/edit#heading=h.6vxku3f3k2ac

Ambrose, S. A., Bridges, M. W., DiPietro, M., Lovett, M. C., & Norman, M. K. (2010). *How learning works: Seven research-based principles for smart teaching.* Jossey-Bass.

Andreotti, V., Ahenakew, C., & Cooper, G. (2011). Introduction. (Towards) global citizenship education 'otherwise.' In V. O. Andreotti & L. M. Souza (Eds.), *Postcolonial perspectives on global citizenship education* (pp. 221–238). Routledge.

Anzaldúa, G. (2015). *Light in the dark/Luz en lo oscuro: Rewriting identity, spirituality, reality* (A. L. Keating, Ed.). Duke University Press.

Armstrong, K. (2009). *The case for God.* Random House Digital.

Baldwin, J. (1963). A talk to teachers. In R. Simonson & S. Walker (Eds.), *Multiculturalism literacy* (pp. 3–12). Graywolf Press.

Bass, R. V., & Good, J. W. (2004). *Educare* and *educere*: Is a balance possible in the educational system? *The Educational Forum, 68*(2), 161. https://du.idm.oclc.org/login?url=https://www-proquest-com.du.idm.oclc.org/scholarly-journals/educare-educere-is-balance-possible-educational/docview/220696155/se-2?accountid=14608

Basso, K. 1996. *Wisdom sits in places: Landscape and language among the Western Apache.* University of New Mexico Press.

Buber, M. (1923). *I and thou* (2nd ed., R. G. Smith, Trans.). SAGE.

Buechner, F. (1993). *Wishful thinking: A theological ABC.* HarperCollins.

Byrne, D. (2010). *Bicycle diaries.* Penguin.

Chung, L. C., & Rendón, L. I. (2018). Educating for wholeness in the intersections. *Diversity & Democracy, 21*(1), 8–12.

Cranton, P. (2016). *Understanding and promoting transformative learning: A guide to theory and practice.* Stylus.

Csikszentmihalyi, M. (1990). *Flow: The psychology of optimal experience.* Harper & Row.

Daloz, L. (1999). *Mentor: Guiding the journey of adult learners.* Jossey-Bass.

Daloz, L., & Parks, S. (2003). Mentoring big questions and worthy dreams for young adults. *Adult Learning, 14*(1), 20–22.

Day, D. (1957). Vocation to prison. *The Catholic Worker, XXIV*(2), 6. https://the catholicnewsarchive.org/?a=d&d=CW19570901-01.2.4&e=-------en-20--1--txt-txIN-------

del Carmen Salazar, M., & Lerner, J. (2019). *Teacher evaluation as cultural practice: A framework for equity and excellence.* Routledge.

Devi, S. (n.d.). *Shakuntala Devi quotes.* https://www.brainyquote.com/quotes/shakuntala_devi_598202

Dewey, J. (1938). *Experience and education: The Kappa Delta Pi lecture series.* Free Press.

Dickinson, E. (1976). *The complete poems* (T. H. Johnson, Ed.). Little Brown and Company.

Duch, B., Groh, H., & Allen, D. (2001). *The power of problem-based learning: A practical "how to" for teaching undergraduate courses in any discipline.* Stylus.

Duckworth, A. (2016). *Grit: The power of passion and perseverance.* Scribner's.

Duckworth, A. L. (2013, May). *Grit: The power of passion and perseverance* [Video]. TED Conferences. https://www.ted.com/talks/angela_lee_duckworth_grit_the_power_of_passion_and_perseverance/transcript?language=en

Eames-Sheavly, M. (2018). *Honest and open questions as a spiritual practice.* Center for Courage & Renewal Newsletter. https://couragerenewal.org/library/honest-and-open-questions-as-a-spiritual-practice/

Fink, D. (2013). *Creating significant learning experiences: An integrated approach to designing college courses.* Wiley.

Fox, J. (1995). *Finding what you didn't lose: Expressing your truth and creativity in poem-making.* TarcherPerigee.

Francis, S. L., & The Center for Courage and Renewal. (2018). *The courage way: Leading and living with integrity.* Berrett-Koehler.

Freire, P. (2013). *Pedagogy of the oppressed.* Routledge. (Original work published 1968)

Gerlach, J. M. (1994). "Is this collaboration?" In K. Bosworth & S. J. Hamilton (Eds.), *Collaborative Learning: Underlying Processes and Effective Techniques* (New Directions for Teaching and Learning, no. 59, pp. 5–14). Jossey-Bass.

Gillen, J. (2014). *Educating for insurgency: The roles of young people in schools of poverty.* AK Press.

Giroux, H. A. (2013). The disimagination machine and the pathologies of power. *symploke, 21*(1–2), 257–269.

Greene, M. (1988). *The dialectic of freedom.* Teachers College Press.

Hammond, Z. (2015). *Culturally responsive teaching and the brain: Promoting authentic engagement and rigor among culturally and linguistically diverse students.* Corwin Press.

Heschel, A. J. (1976). *God in search of man: A philosophy of Judaism.* Farrar, Straus and Giroux.

Huebner, D., Hillis, V., & Pinar, W. F. (2012). *The lure of the transcendent: Collected essays by Dwayne E. Huebner.* Routledge.

Jacobs, D. T. (2013). *Teaching truly: A curriculum to Indigenize mainstream education.* Peter Lang.

Johnston, P. H. (2012). *Opening minds: How classroom talk shapes children's minds and their lives.* Stenhouse.

Kaur, V. (2020). *See no stranger: A memoir and manifesto of revolutionary love.* One World.

Kimmerer, R. W. (2013). *Braiding sweetgrass: Indigenous wisdom, scientific knowledge and the teachings of plants.* Milkweed.

Kolb, D. A. (1984). *Experiential learning: Experience as the source of learning and development.* Prentice Hall.

Ladson-Billings, G. (1998). Just what is critical race theory and what's it doing in a nice field like education? *International Journal of Qualitative Studies in Education, 11*(1), 7–24.

Ladson-Billings, G. (2014). Culturally relevant pedagogy 2.0: A.K.A. the remix. *Harvard Educational Review, 84*(1), 74–84.

Lane, B. C. (2019). *The great conversation: Nature and the care of the soul.* Oxford University Press.

Lave, J., & Wenger, E. (1991). *Situated learning: Legitimate peripheral participation.* Cambridge University Press.

León Portilla, M. (1963). *Aztec thought and culture: A study of the ancient Nahuatl mind* (J. E. Davis, Trans.). University of Oklahoma Press.

Lopez, B. (2019). *Horizon.* Random House.

Lowery, L. (1998). How new science curriculums reflect brain research. *Educational Leadership, 56,* 26–30.

Margolis, E. (2001). *The hidden curriculum in higher education.* Routledge.

Marsick, V., & Watkins, K. (2015). *Informal and incidental learning in the workplace.* Routledge. (Original work published 1990)

McGuckin, J. A. (2017). *The path of Christianity: The first thousand years.* InterVarsity Press.

Menakem, R. (2017). *My grandmother's hands: Racialized trauma and the pathway to mending our hearts and bodies.* Central Recovery Press.

Merton, T. (n.d.). *Thomas Merton quotes.* Goodreads. https://www.goodreads.com/quotes/58620-the-solution-of-the-problem-of-life-is-life-itself

Mezirow, J. (1991). *Transformative dimensions of adult learning.* Jossey-Bass.

Michalec, P. (2018). *INSIGHT blog: Vocational Amnesia.* https://mcespeaks.wixsite.com/insight/post/in-sight-vocational-amnesia

Mignolo, W. (2018). Foreword: On pluriversality and multipolarity. In B. Reiter (Ed.), *Constructing the pluriverse: The geopolitics of knowledge* (pp. ix–xvi). Duke University Press. https://doi.org/10.1515/9781478002017-001

Millis, D. (2010). *Cooperative learning in higher education: Across the disciplines, across the academy.* Stylus.

Moroye, C. M. (2009). Complementary curriculum: The work of ecologically minded teachers. *Journal of Curriculum Studies, 41*(6), 789–811.

Noddings, N. (2015). *The challenge to care in schools* (2nd ed.). Teachers College Press.

Palmer, P. J. (1998). *The courage to teach: Exploring the inner landscape of a teacher's life*. Jossey-Bass.

Palmer, P. J. (2004). *A hidden wholeness: A journey toward an undivided life*. Jossey-Bass.

Palmer, P. J. (with Scribner, M.) (2017). *The courage to teach: Guide for reflection and renewal*. Wiley.

Parks, S. D. (2000). *Big questions, worthy dreams: Mentoring young adults in their search for meaning, purpose, and faith*. Jossey-Bass.

Piaget, J. (1964). Cognitive development in children: Development and learning. *Journal of Research in Science Teaching, 2*, 176–186.

Plato. (1969). Plato in twelve volumes. (Vols. 5 & 6, P. Shorey, Trans.). Harvard University Press.

Remen, R. N. (2006). *Kitchen table wisdom: Stories that heal* (10th anniversary ed.). Penguin.

Rendón, L. I. (2000). Academics of the heart: Reconnecting the scientific mind with the spirit's artistry. *Review of Higher Education, 24*(1), 1–13.

Rendón, L. I. (2009). *Sentipensante pedagogy: Educating for wholeness, social justice and liberation*. Stylus.

Rendón, L. I. (2020). A first-generation scholar's *camino de conocimiento*: *Una autohistoria*. In L. W. Perna (Ed.), *Higher education: Handbook of theory and research* (Vol. 35, pp. 1–47). Springer. https://doi.org/10.1007/978-3-030-11743-6_1-1

Rilke, R. M., Kappus, F. X., & Burnham, J. M. (2000). *Letters to a young poet*. New World Library.

Rohr, R. (2011). *Falling upward: A spirituality for the two halves of life*. Wiley.

Rohr, R. (2020). *The wisdom pattern: Order, disorder, reorder*. Franciscan Media.

Rumi, J. (2004). *The essential Rumi, new expanded edition*. (C. Barks & J. Moyne, Trans.). Harper.

Schneps, M. H. (1994). *A private universe: Misconceptions that block learning* [Video]. Harvard University & the Smithsonian Institution.

Schwartz, H. L. (2019). *Connected teaching: Relationship, power, and mattering in higher education*. Stylus.

Tatum, B. D. (2000). The complexity of identity: "Who am I?" In M. Adams, W. J. Blumenfeld, H. W. Hackman, X. Zuniga, & M. L. Peters (Eds.), *Readings for diversity and social justice: An anthology on racism, sexism, anti-Semitism, heterosexism, classism and ableism* (pp. 9–14). Routledge.

Tharp, R. G., Estrada, P., Dalton, S. S., & Yamauchi, L. (2000). *Teaching transformed: Achieving excellence, fairness, inclusion, and harmony*. Westview Press.

Thurman, H. (1953). *Meditations of the heart*. Harper.

Uhrmacher, P. B. (1997). The curriculum shadow. *Curriculum Inquiry, 27*(3), 317–329.

Uhrmacher, P. B., Moroye, C. M., & Flinders, D. J. (2017). *Using educational criticism and connoisseurship for qualitative research*. Routledge.

Vygotsky, L. S. (1978). Socio-cultural theory. *Mind in Society, 6*, 52–58.

Watkins, K. E., & Marsick, V. J. (2021). Informal and incidental learning in the time of COVID-19. *Advances in Developing Human Resources, 23*(1), 88–96. https://doi.org/10.1177/1523422320973656

Watt, S. (Ed.). (2015). *Designing transformative multicultural initiatives: Theoretical foundations, practical applications, and facilitator considerations.* Stylus.

West, C. (1989). *The American evasion of philosophy: A genealogy of pragmatism.* Springer.

Weston, A. (2018). *Teaching as the art of staging: A scenario-based college pedagogy in action.* Stylus.

Wiggins, G. P., & McTighe, J. (2005). *Understanding by design.* Association for Supervision and Curriculum Development.

Wotters, C., & Hussain, M. (2015). Investigating grit and its relations with college students' self-regulated learning and academic achievement. *Metacognition and Learning, 10*(3), 293–311.

Yousafzai, M. (July 12, 2013). *Excerpt from Malala Yousafzai's speech United Nations, July 12, 2013.* exploros. https://www.exploros.com/summary/grade-6-malala-yousafzais-speech-at-the-united-Nations

ABOUT THE AUTHORS

Marcia Eames-Sheavly believes that we have much to learn from plants: scientific concepts and principles, certainly, but also lessons about care, well-being, beauty, resilience, and relationship. An artist, earth tender, and senior lecturer emerita and senior extension associate emerita in horticulture at Cornell University, she has been a garden-based learning educator since 1984. She devotes much of her professional time to teaching and outreach, bringing people and plants together, whether they are students at Cornell, online students around the world, or members of communities from New York to Belize. As an International Coaching Federation certified integral professional coach and Courage & Renewal facilitator, Marcia facilitates meaningful conversations among her colleagues and in her communities, aiming to manifest the dispositions that she believes are central to personal growth and social welfare: reflective practice, inclusivity, creative collaboration, and deep listening. She leads retreats and other programs in which participants are invited to step aside from the busyness of their lives and reconnect with the heart of who they are. Marcia has been the recipient of two national writing awards as well as the American Horticultural Society's Great American Gardener Teaching Award, the highest teaching honor given by this society; the Innovative Teaching Award, offered by Cornell University's College of Agriculture and Life Sciences, for creativity in undergraduate teaching; the Kaplan Family Distinguished Faculty Fellowship, by the Cornell University Public Service Center for excellence in service learning; and, most recently, the Professor of Merit award, given by Cornell's College of Agriculture and Life Sciences in 2020, which is particularly distinguished as an award bestowed by the senior class.

Paul Michalec has more than 40 years of teaching experience in K–6, higher education, and alternative education. He brings to his teaching an affinity for ecological thinking, interdisciplinary knowledge, holistic models of teaching and learning, and transformative learning opportunities for his students. In 2005, Paul became a courage and renewal facilitator. He regularly leads courage-informed retreats and professional development for educators, clergy, community activists, and health-care providers. He is currently a clinical professor at the University of Denver and the Morgridge College of Education, teaching courses in the foundations and practice of educa-tion, including spirituality of education, history of education, philosophy of education, teacher identity formation, models of curriculum, curriculum theory into practice, teacher as researcher, and field supervision of teacher candidates. In 2015, Paul was honored for his teaching when he was named the University of Denver's Distinguished Teacher. In 2016, he partnered with University of Denver administration to redesign the professional devel-opment and professional formation opportunities for faculty. His ongoing work includes leading a monthly dialogue with faculty, staff, and admin-istrators called the "Heart of Higher Education" that explores the interface between calling and institutional roles/responsibilities. In 2020, Paul com-pleted a master of theological studies from the Iliff School of Theology. His thesis examined the formation of higher education in antiquity (2nd and 3rd centuries) and the founding vision of an educator as mystagogue, a teacher who mystified the curriculum, instead of a pedagogue, who mostly delivers content. In addition to conference presentations, refereed articles, and book chapters, Paul is an active blogger, exploring the interface between the deep calling to teach and institutional imperatives that often lean toward external measures of efficiency and effectiveness. His blog (IN:SIGHT) can be found at https://morgridge.du.edu/insight.

Catherine M. Wehlburg, PhD, is the provost and vice president for academic affairs and professor of psychology at Athens State University in Athens, Alabama. Prior to this appointment, she served as a senior fellow at AAC&U. Wehlburg has held many administrative and academic roles over the past 30 years as founding dean for the Department of Sciences, Mathematics, and Education at Marymount University; associate provost for institutional effec-tiveness at Texas Christian University; and department chair of psychology at Stephens College. In each of these roles she has focused on mission, student learning, and strategic decision-making, working collaboratively with others to improve and enhance the educational outcomes for all students. Wehlburg has published many articles, books, and chapters and has always had a focus on educating the whole student as the essential role in higher education. She has been recognized for her work in student learning outcomes assessment by being elected president of the Association for the Assessment of Learning in Higher Education; she also received their Outstanding Achievement Award. Her leadership has been called innovative and inclusive as she seeks to engage others in the ongoing discussions surrounding access and success for all. Wehlburg currently serves as the editor-in-chief for *New Directions for Teaching and Learning* and is a member of several advisory boards. She received her PhD in educational psychology from the University of Florida.

INDEX

Academics of the Heart, 146
accidental learning, 56. *See also* learning
accommodation, process of, 80
acquired knowledge, 3
active learning, 81. *See also* learning
activism, 131
activity theory, 51
Adams, Abigail, 39
ambition, 4
American dream, 152–153
arts, 3, 44–46, 57, 76, 77
assessment, 52
athletics, unintentional learning within, 70
attentive watching, 31

banking model of education, 120
behaviorism, 113
beholding, for deep listening, 142
Berends, Polly, 23
bias, of prior learning, 89
Black students, false perception regarding, 69
book group, 125–129

cave classrooms, 76, 77
censorship, 150
Center for Courage & Renewal, 144
Churchill, Winston, 12
Circle of Trust retreat, 35–36, 140–141, 144
civility, 149–150
clarity, 149–150
climate change, 86–87
code switching, 40
communication, 6, 82

community
  building through why of learning, 104–107
  learning endeavor within, 125–129
  organizational resources for, 144–145
  radical mothering metaphor within, 107–109
community college, learning process within, 53–54
competition, within learning, 26–27
complementary curriculum, 24. *See also* curriculum
compliance, to reintegration, within who of learning, 123–125
connections, learning, 13–14
conscious thinking, 136
conversation, organizational resources for, 144–145
cooperative learning, 85–88. *See also* learning
courage, 135–137, 138–139, 152
courage to learn, 2–3, 151, 152
Courage to Learn conversation, 143–145
courtship, 101
creative courage, 137. *See also* courage
criticism, 138
culturally relevant pedagogy, 17
culture, as norming behavior tool, 31
curiosity, 121–122
curriculum
  complementary, 24
  delivered, 18, 52
  development, teaching and learning within, 17–21
  hidden, 19, 56–60
  integrated, 62–63

intended, 18
received, 18–19, 52
scientific approach to, 19
shadow, 24
trends within, 19

deeper instructional relationships, 101
deep listening, 48, 139–143. *See also*
   listening
delivered curriculum, 18, 52. *See also*
   curriculum
demonstration, learning, 12
Dickinson, Emily, 2, 96, 97, 127
The Dinner Party, 145
disabilities, persistence through, 91–94
disimagination machine, 103, 107, 124
drawing, 44–46, 56

education
   creating space for learning within, 16
   focus on, 16
   humanization within, 113
   identity within, 114–115
   learning *versus,* 12
   limitations of, 109–110
   places of, 73
   power within, 17
   root meanings of, 48, 114
   trauma within, 114–115
   values of, 72
   who of learning and, 114–115
   See also learning
educators
   as arrogant, 24
   challenges of, 136
   deeper instructional relationships of,
      101
   defined, 2
   demonstrations of learning to, 3
   expectations on, 123–125
   as fearful, 24
   heart of, 41
   as hopeful, 24
   as learners, 20
   learning responsibilities of, 23–24

as lever of change, 17–18
limitations to, 123–125
listening by, 137–139
mindset of, 24
personal story by, 123–125
reading of, 40
student relationships with, 65–66
teaching characteristics of, 24
value-added measures regarding,
   19–20
Einstein, Albert, 2, 15
emancipatory knowledge, 113. *See also*
   knowledge
embodied learning, 119–121. *See also*
   learning
emotions, intelligence from, 41
Enneagram, 35
equity, 153
experiences
   within how of learning, 81–83
   learning process through, 12, 41,
      43, 53
   as moving forces, 53, 98
   See also school experience

failure, as why of learning, 106
farming, 108, 115–116
flow, theory of, 45–46, 119
formal assessment of learning, 52
friendship, 65
frogs, 30

gender, hidden curriculum regarding,
   56–57
gestures, meanings assigned to, 6
girls, education of, 10
Great Conversation, 130–131, 138
great cycle of social sorting, 17
Greek education, 77
grit, 90–91

hardiness, 90–91
Harvard-Smithsonian Center for
   Astrophysics, 89
healing, courage to learn as path to, 151

heart, intelligence from, 41
hidden curriculum, 19, 56–60. *See also*
    curriculum
history, problem-based learning (PBL)
    regarding, 84
homosexuality, 60–61
horticulture, 33–34
hospitality, 31–32
how of learning
    cooperative learning within,
        85–88
    grit and hardiness within, 90–91
    history of learning within, 76–79
    importance of, 36
    learning as constructed process
        within, 79–81
    learning as problem solving within,
        83–85
    learning as process within, 73–76
    overview of, 43–46, 72–73, 112
    personal story regarding, 30, 32,
        44–46, 80–81
    prior learning role within, 88–90
    proxy for, 79
    reflection regarding, 50
    significance learning experiences
        within, 81–83
humanity, championing, 150
humanization, as goal of education, 113

idealism, 114
identity
    championing, 150
    within education, 114–115
    inequity and, 151
    within learning, 7, 24–25, 37, 80
    limitations on, 131
    questioning of, 37–38
    reflection regarding, 37–38
I-It relationship, 129–130
imaginative thinking, 136
incarceration, 57–58
Indigenous people, 69, 115–116, 146
ineffable, defined, 76
inequity, 151

infants, 88–89, 97
inner journey of learning, 3, 18, 41, 96.
    See also learning
inspiration, from learners, 136
instructional arc, 18–19
instructional "moreness," 114–117,
    120–121
insurance, 58–60
insurance policy metaphor, 132
integrated curriculum, 62–63. *See also*
    curriculum
intelligence test, 79
intended curriculum, 18. *See also*
    curriculum
intention, for listening, 139
intention, learning with, 105
interactions, learning, 82
intersectionality, 151
investigation, learning as, 25–26,
    121–122
invitation, for listening, 142
Islam, 116–117
I-Thou relationship, 130

jug-and-mug theory of pedagogy, 4

kinesthetic learning, 117–121
King, Martin Luther, Jr., 149
knitting, 49
knowing, 4–5, 74, 116
knowledge
    acquired, 3
    constructivism of, 78
    emancipatory, 113
    existing, 73
    institutional forms of, 4
    layering of, 77
    organization of, 13–14
    prior to learning, 13
    reflection and, 81
    subtraction of, 77

landscapes, 147
languages, 40, 130–131
Lascaux Paleolithic art, 76, 77

learners
  active resistance of, 65
  behaviors of, 64, 113
  challenges of, 62
  within classroom experiences, 40
  cog metaphor of, 113
  composite of, 42–43
  as connected to learning, 10–11
  depth of, 113
  educator relationships with, 65–66
  as educators, 20
  engagement by, 73–74
  expectations of, 64
  as free thinkers, 61
  goals of, 47
  heart of, 41
  hidden curriculum impact on, 19
  inner wisdom of, 48
  journey of, 23–36
  knowledge building by, 73
  learning characteristics of, 12–13,
    15–16
  learning response of, 18–19
  listening to, 137–139
  misconceptions regarding, 66
  nation of, 152–153
  navigation by, 2, 7, 54
  power of, 149
  processing by, 4
  ranking of, 46
  reaching out by, 135–137
  as self-learners, 117–122
  theory of flow within, 119
  types of, 21
  See also who of learning
learning
  accidental, 56
  active, 81
  barriers to, 11
  challenges regarding, 9–10
  as community endeavor, 125–129
  complexities of, 53
  connecting learner to, 10–11
  connections within, 13–14
  as constructed process, 79–81

  cooperative, 85–88
  creating space for, 16
  defined, 11, 73
  as dehumanization, 66–70
  distrust of, 128
  by doing, 75
  embodied, 119–121
  as foundational, 1–2
  history of, 76–79
  identity within, 7, 24–25, 37, 80
  importance of, 16–17
  inner, 3, 18, 41, 96
  with intention, 105
  as intricate interplay, 36–37
  as investigation, 25–26
  as journey, 5
  legacy, 108, 132
  limitations of, 101
  locations for, 5
  love of, 152
  modeling of, 136
  motivation for, 14–16
  natural flow of, 128
  navigation through, 8–9
  necessity of, 2
  nonlinear tools for, 39
  outer, 3, 18, 40, 96
  as outside of structured school
    experience, 6–7, 65
  as painful, 20
  persistence in, 91–95
  personal story regarding, 6–7, 8–9,
    25–36, 66–68
  perspectives regarding, 148
  as physical, 119–121
  prior, 88–90
  as problem solving, 83–85
  process of, 2, 11–12, 15, 73–76
  purpose of, 63
  reintegration of, 146–148
  science of, 12–16, 19
  self-worth within, 104
  simulations for, 86–87
  as social process, 103
  as spiritual, 128–129

as spring, 4–5, 74, 146–147
stories of, 23–25
within structured school experience,
    8–9, 26
struggle within, 5, 83
teaching *versus,* 12
theory and practice regarding, 11–12
willingness within, 76–77
learning disabilities, 91–94
learning style, 117–118
legacy learning, 108, 132
legitimate peripheral participation,
    51–52
listening
    asking questions for deep, 139–141
    beholding within, 142
    changes from, 138
    courage for, 138–139
    cultivating deep, 141–143
    deep, 48, 139–143
    by educators, 137–139
    intention for, 139
    invitation offer for, 142
    to learners, 137–139
    for learning, 6
    questions within, 142
    settling in for, 141–142
    staying with, 142
    truth within, 143
literature, learning through, 125–129
living-newspaper approach, 87
love letter to self metaphor, 132–133
Luong, David, 10

marginalization, 67–69
mastery, 125
mathematics, 15–16, 26, 32–33,
    54–55, 57, 82, 83
measurement, 19
memorization, 10–11, 13, 14, 27, 40
memory, cluttering of, 13
mentoring, 75–76
merit badge thinking, 103
milkweed, 130
misconceptions, of learning, 89–90

Mobius strip metaphor, 3, 96, 135
modeling, of learning, 136
moral courage, 137
Mort, Valzhyna, 127
motivation, 14–16, 100–101, 109
multiplication tables, 10–11, 26
music, 3, 27–28, 90–91
mystagogue, 78
myth of the metals (Plato), 78

nature, 29–30, 109–111, 129
nonlinear learning, 130–131

openness for learning, 41
outer story of learning, 3, 18, 40, 96.
    See also learning

Pakistan, 10, 104, 116
participation, in learning, 51–52
particles, 110
passion, pursuit of, 94–95
Path of Freedom curriculum, 57
pedagogue, learning under, 77–78
The People's Supper, 144–145
persistence, in learning, 91–95
phrenology, 78
physical courage, 137. *See also* courage
physical learning, 119–121. *See also*
    learning
poetry, 2, 3, 53, 127. *See also Two
    Kinds of Intelligence* (Rumi); *When
    Someone Deeply Listens to You* (Fox)
power, social norming through, 31
Practice Space, 145
pragmatist, 132
prayer, 116–117, 119
preparation, for listening, 139
prior learning, 88–90. *See also* learning
prisons, 57–58
"A Private University," 13
privilege, social norming through, 31
privileged identity exploration model,
    9–10
problem-based learning (PBL), 83–85
problem solving, 83–85

professional calling, 114
prophet, 132
prophetic pragmatism, 132

questions/questioning
    for deep listening, 139–141
    of identity, 37–38
    learning through, 96–97, 110
    living/leaning into, 106
    open-ended, 111
    perspective regarding, 52
    process of, 28
    See also why of learning

racism, 57–58
radical mothering metaphor, 107–109,
    131
reaching out, courage for, 135–137
reading, 5, 70
reading level groups, 79
received curriculum, 18–19, 52. *See also*
    curriculum
reciprocity, 44
reflection, 36, 37–38, 80–81, 97, 114
reintegration, compliance to, within
    who of learning, 123–125
religion, 116–117
responsibility for learning, 131
Roman education, 77

school experience
    disimagination machine within, 103,
        107, 124
    forms of teaching within, 103
    learning within, 8–9, 26, 40
    limitations of, 109–110
    personal story regarding, 66–69,
        117–121
    power structure within, 17
    social efficiency tradition within, 79
    unintentional learning within, 70
    why of learning within, 102–104
seeing again metaphor, 56
self-discovery, 39, 119, 132
self-examination, 35

selfhood, 114–117
self-learning, 117–122
self-love, 151
self-worth, 104
settling in, for deep listening,
    141–142
shadow curriculum, 24. *See also*
    curriculum
shaming, 35–36
sign language, 82
simulations, learning, 86–87
social courage, 137
social efficiency tradition, 78–79
spring metaphor, 4–5, 74, 146–147
stories, of learning, 23–25
StoryCorps, 145
struggle, within learning, 5, 83
studying, 64
submission, within learning, 104
suppression, 150
sweetgrass metaphor, 115–116

tabula rosa, 88–89
tangential learning, 125–129. *See also*
    learning
teacher. *See* educators
teaching. *See* education
testing, 28–29, 79
theory of flow, 45–46
Thurman, Howard, 97, 102, 107, 109
transferability of learning, 55
transformation, 80
truth, 149–150
Two Kinds of Intelligence (Rumi), 1, 3,
    4, 61, 72, 77–78, 96, 111, 113,
    118–119
typing, 41–42

unintentional learning, 56, 63–64, 70.
    See also learning
University of Delaware, 83–84

value-added measures, for teacher
    performance, 19–20
vulnerability, 136

Ward, Jesmyn, 112
water metaphor, learning as, 74
Western Apache, teaching tools of, 147
Western ways of learning, 115–116,
    146
what of learning
    complexities of, 53, 60–66
    dehumanization within, 66–70
    hidden curriculum and, 56–60
    implications of, 69–70
    overview of, 40–41, 51–52, 112, 147
    personal story regarding, 26–27, 31,
        32, 34, 42
    power of, 42
    reflection regarding, 50
    ripple of, 55
    transferability of, 55
    as verb, 42–43
    why of learning and, 47
    worth within, 52–56
When Someone Deeply Listens to You
    (Fox), 134, 139
whiteness, 19, 31, 57–58, 69
who of learning
    behaviorism within, 113
    book group within, 125–129
    compliance to reintegration within,
        123–125
    curiosity within, 121–122
    educator within, 114–115
    fluctuation of, 120–121
    importance of, 36
    instructional "moreness" within,
        114–117, 120–121
    investigation within, 121–122
    kinesthetic learning, flow, and
        presence within, 117–121

love letter to self metaphor within,
    132–133
Marcia's journey regarding, 35
meaningful relationships within,
    129–133
as measurable outcome, 115
overview of, 48–49, 112–114, 147
Paul's journey regarding, 30, 31, 32
personal story regarding, 49
reflection regarding, 50
selfhood integration within, 114–117
See also learners
why of learning
    building community through,
        104–107
    complexities of, 98–101
    conventional learner within, 102–104
    debates regarding, 48
    failure within, 106
    growth within, 98
    importance of, 36
    listening to the earth metaphor
        within, 109–111
    meandering path of, 98–101
    motivations for, 109
    overview of, 46–48, 96–98, 112
    personal story regarding, 28–29, 30,
        31, 32, 36, 46–48, 98–111
    radical mothering within, 107–109,
        131
    reflection regarding, 50
    unease regarding, 47
wicked problems, 83
willingness, for learning, 76–77
words, meanings assigned to, 6

Yeats, William Butler, 72

CENTER *for*
COURAGE *&*
RENEWAL

The Center for Courage & Renewal is a nonprofit organization that exists to nurture deep integrity and relational trust, building the foundation for a more loving, equitable, and healthy world. Through Circle of Trust retreats and other programs rooted in the Courage & Renewal® approach, we nurture supportive communities of reflection and practice to help people come alive with a renewed sense of purpose, build trustworthy relationships, and cultivate the courage to rise to today's challenges, making a difference within themselves and their communities.

CCR was founded in 1997 by Parker J. Palmer alongside Marcy Jackson and Rick Jackson. First known as the Center for Teacher Formation, our Courage to Teach® program became the premier program helping teachers connect soul with role, rekindling their passion for educating the whole student. As our approach grew more popular within the teaching profession and other social sectors, the organization changed its name in 2003 to the Center for Courage & Renewal to create programs and immersive Circle of Trust retreats for people in education, healthcare, ministry, nonprofits, activism, business, and anyone yearning to become more authentic and whole.

For 25 years, we've helped people show up in their homes, relationships, workplaces, communities, and ecosystems rooted in their own integrity and with a deep bow to human dignity, inspiring hope in those around them and fostering the relational trust and stamina we all need to keep moving, step by step, toward the better world we know is possible.

You can learn more about the Center for Courage & Renewal, explore our program calendar, become a member, and engage with an extensive library of resources at www.couragerenewal.org.

Printed in the United States
by Baker & Taylor Publisher Services